Henry O Hildreth

Norfolk County Manual, and Year Book for 1876

Henry O Hildreth

Norfolk County Manual, and Year Book for 1876

ISBN/EAN: 9783744778176

Printed in Europe, USA, Canada, Australia, Japan

Cover: Foto ©ninafisch / pixelio.de

More available books at **www.hansebooks.com**

MANUAL,

AND

YEAR BOOK FOR 1876.

COMPILED, PREPARED AND PUBLISHED

BY

HENRY O. HILDRETH.

———•◆•———

DEDHAM, MASS.
1877.

Rockwell & Churchill, Printers and Stereotypers,
39 ARCH STREET, BOSTON.

PREFACE.

THE preparation of the statistical portion of this volume was commenced with the purpose of gathering up for future reference some details concerning the present financial and social condition of the several communities comprised within the limits of Norfolk County, to be deposited in the archives of the Dedham Historical Society. The historical portion — suggested by the resolution passed by Congress, recommending the preparation of county histories — was not commenced until late in the year, and was prosecuted under many disadvantages. Still later it occurred to the compiler that much of the matter he had accumulated in the progress of his work would be of value for present use as well as for future reference, and he finally decided to prepare it for publication. He has endeavored to make it a reliable compendium of facts and figures, obtaining his information from the best available sources, and spending much time and labor in the work of verification. The volume is offered to the citizens of Norfolk County not only as a convenient manual for use in the practical matters of every-day life, but as a contribution to the historical data of the county, most of which has never before been brought together. In the progress of the work much valuable material has been accumulated, which it was impossible to use in the present book, but which may appear in a subsequent volume.

The compiler desires to express his obligations to the many friends who have rendered assistance in furnishing statistical and historical information. The valuable papers to be found in successive volumes of the " New England Genealogical Register " have been of essential service in the preparation of the biographical portion of the work.

DEDHAM, March 22d, 1877.

CONTENTS.

STATISTICAL.

—o:◦:o—

NORFOLK COUNTY.

[Incorporated March 26, 1793.]

Shire Town, Dedham.

—◦—

COUNTY OFFICERS.

—

Judge of Probate and Insolvency.

GEORGE WHITE, ... Needham.

Register of Probate and Insolvency.		Assistant Register.	
JONATHAN H. COBB,	. Dedham.	JONATHAN COBB,	. Dedham.

Sheriff.		County Treasurer.	
JOHN W. THOMAS,	. Dedham.	CHAUNCEY C. CHURCHILL,	Dedham.

Clerk of Courts.		Register of Deeds.	
ERASTUS WORTHINGTON,	Dedham.	JOHN H. BURDAKIN,	. Dedham.

Assistant Clerk.		Assistant Register.	
EDGAR H. KINGSBURY, .	Dedham.	WILLIAM H. REED,	. Dedham.

County Commissioners.

NATHANIEL F. SAFFORD, Chairman.	. Milton.	GALEN ORR, .	. . Needham.
		JAMES HUMPHREY,	. Weymouth.

Special Commissioners.

JOHN Q. A. FIELD, . . Quincy. | GEORGE P. MOREY, Walpole.

District Attorney.

ASA FRENCH, ... Braintree.

Overseers of House of Correction.

CHAUNCEY C. CHURCHILL, HENRY O. HILDRETH, SANFORD CARROLL,
Dedham.

Chaplain of House of Correction.	Physician of House of Correction.
Rev. WILLIAM A. COTTLE, Dedham.	Dr. JOHN W. CHASE, . Dedham.

Jailer and Keeper of House of Correction.

JOHN W. THOMAS, ... Dedham.

With the following Assistants : — *Keepers* — Henry White, Willis J. Smart, William Worley. *Night Watchman* — Carlos Slafter, 2d.

Sessions of the Courts.

SUPREME JUDICIAL COURT, at Dedham, Third Tuesday of February.

SUPERIOR COURT, *Criminal terms*, at Dedham, First Monday of April, September and December.

SUPERIOR COURT, *Civil terms*, at Dedham, Fourth Monday of April, September and December.

The PROBATE COURT is held at Dedham on the First and Third; at Quincy on the Second; and at Hyde Park on the Fourth, WEDNESDAYS of every month — *except the month of August.*

District Court of East Norfolk, with jurisdiction in criminal matters in Braintree, Cohasset, Holbrook, Milton, Quincy, Randolph and Weymouth; established June 1, 1872. EVERETT C. BUMPUS, of Weymouth, *Justice;* JAMES A. TOWER, of Randolph, *First*, and SOLOMON J. BEAL, of Cohasset, *Second Special Justices;* J. WHITE BELCHER of Randolph, *Clerk*. A session of the Court is held daily at Quincy.

Trial Justices.

Thomas E. Barry, Emery Grover, Needham; J. Merrill Browne, Stoughton; Charles H. Deans, Medway; Charles H. Drew, Brookline; Frederick D. Ely, Dedham; Thomas E. Grover, Canton; Henry B. Terry, Hyde Park; Samuel Warner, Wrentham; George W. Wiggin, Franklin.

Trial Justices for Juvenile Offenders.

Charles H. Drew, Brookline; Frederick D. Ely, Dedham.

Commissioners of Insolvency.

Charles H. Deans, Medway; Frederick D. Ely, Dedham; George W. Wiggin, Franklin.

Masters in Chancery.

John V. Beal, Randolph; Thomas E. Grover, Canton; Isaac G. Reed, Hyde Park; Thomas L. Wakefield, Erastus Worthington, Dedham.

Commissioners to qualify Civil Officers.·

Jonathan H. Cobb, Jonathan Cobb, Chauncey C. Churchill, Dedham; Daniel A. Cook, Wrentham; Naaman L. White, Braintree.

Deputy Sheriffs.

John D. Bradlee, Milton; Harvey B. Coleman, Wrentham; Valentine R. Coombs, Medway; Augustus B. Endicott, Dedham; Washington French, Quincy; William E. Nason, Franklin; Abram C. Paul, Stoughton; John M. Twitchell, Hyde Park; George W. White, jr., Weymouth; Rufus C. Wood, Canton. William H. Warren, Randolph, held the office until his death, August 3d; John Long, of Randolph, was subsequently appointed to fill the vacancy.

. Special Coroner.

Rufus C. Wood, Canton.

Coroners.

Lewis Bass, Quincy; John D. Bradlee, Milton; Harvey B. Coleman, Wrentham; Valentine R. Coombs, Medway; George K. Daniell, Needham; Charles Hamant, Medfield; Ralph Houghton, Randolph; Charles Sturtevant, Hyde Park; E. F. E. Thayer, Braintree; Nathaniel Wales, Stoughton.

Public Administrator.

Ira Cleveland, Dedham.

BELLINGHAM.

[Incorporated Nov. 27, 1719, from parts of Dedham, Wrentham and Mendon.]

TOWN OFFICERS.

[Annual Town Meeting, March 6, 1876.]

Moderator. — David Lawrence.
Town Clerk and Treasurer. — Rev. Joseph T. Massey.
Selectmen and Overseers of the Poor. — Martin Rockwood, George F. Wales, Sabin Holbrook.
Assessors. — Amos H. Holbrook, Jeraul O. Wilcox, Savel Metcalf.
Constable and Collector of Taxes. — Henry A. Whitney.
Highway Surveyors. — F. A. Sherburne, Martin Rockwood, Irving Wales, Seneca Burr, S. A. Adams, Willard I. Fisk, Orin Chilson, George Nelson, Edgar M. Scott, Samuel Darling, Edgar A. Sherburne, Charles Partridge, George F. Wales, Orin Fisk, Savel Metcalf.
Sextons. — Whipple O. Chilson, Samuel A. Adams, V. B. Rockwood.

VALUATION AND TAX.

Valuation of real estate,	$412,968 00	Items of tax —	
" " personal est.,	108,897 00	State tax,	$540 00
		County tax,	444 66
Total valuation,	$521,865 00	Town grant,	$5,000 00
		Overlayings,	185 62
Rate of tax,	$10.50 on $1,000		
Number of polls,	345	Total tax,	$6,170 28

APPROPRIATIONS.

Town charges,	$2,000 00	Highways,	$1,000 00
Schools,	1,800 00		
		Total,	$4,800 00

ASSETS AND LIABILITIES, MAY 1, 1876.

ASSETS.		LIABILITIES.	
School-houses,	$7,500 00	School-houses,	$3,000 00
Other public buildings,	4,000 00	Other debts,	5,650 00
Public grounds,	-400 00		
Other real estate,	3,500 00	Total,	$8,650 00
Other assets,	500 00		
Total,	$15,900 00		

PROPERTY EXEMPT FROM TAXATION.

Baptist Church. — Building and land,	$4,000 00

SCHOOL STATISTICS.

SCHOOL COMMITTEE.

Roland Hammond, M.D., *Chairman and Superintendent;* George H. Thayer, *Secretary;* Hiram A. Cook, George A. Crooks, F. R. Smith, George D. Rockwood, George F. Wales, C. H. Cutter, John N. Rhodes.

SCHOOLS.

No. 1. — Mrs. Emma N. Metcalf,		24	scholars.
" 2. — Miss Eliza F. Bond,		31	"
" 3. — " Mattie Pickering,		10	"
" 4. — " Mary J. Rhodes,		27	"
" 5. — " L. O. Hayward,		40	"
" 6. — " A. H. Adams,		22	"
" 8. — " Inez L. Sherburne,		20	"
" 9. — " Clara E. Warfield,		35	"
Total,		209	"

BRAINTREE.

[*Incorporated May* 13, 1640.]

TOWN OFFICERS.

[Annual Meeting, March 6, 1876.]

Moderator. — Francis A. Hobart.

Town Clerk. — Samuel A. Bates.

Selectmen, Assessors, and Overseers of the Poor. — Joseph R. Frazier, Abijah Allen, Samuel W. Hollis. Oct. 19, vacancy, caused by death of Joseph R. Frazier, filled by choice of David H. Bates, who was chosen chairman.

Treasurer. — Jonathan French.

Auditors. — B. F. Dyer, N. F. T. Hayden, Eben Denton.

Collector of Taxes. — David H. Bates.

Surveyors of Highways. — Thomas Hill, B. J. Loring, J. B. Wood.

Constables. — Horace Faxon, Samuel L. Dyer, Robert Gillespie, N. Martin Hobart, E. B. Jordan, William F. Locke, Michael M. Hawke, Thomas Penniman, B. J. Loring, Jr., J. Frank Bates, P. B. Anglim, Joseph A. Arnold, Thomas B. Stoddard.

VALUATION AND TAX.

Valuation of real est.,	$2,096,675 00	Items of tax —	
" " per. "	747,675 00	State tax,	$2,700 00
		County tax,	2,223 29
Total valuation,	$2,844,350 00	Town grant,	26,364 71
		Total tax,	$31,288 00

Rate of tax, $10.20 on $1,000
Number of polls,   1,138

APPROPRIATIONS.

Schools,	$6,800 00	Centennial celebration,	$600 00
Highways,	3,500 00	Janitor for Town hall & libr'y,	450 00
Interest on debt,	3,500 00	Public library,	350 00
Poor,	3,500 00	Repairs of Union and Middle	
Building of Middle street,	1,500 00	street school-houses,	350 00
Incidentals,	1,500 00	Incidentals for schools,	300 00
Town officers,	1,200 00	Decoration day,	150 00
Debt,	1,000 00	Seats Iron-Works school-house,	75 00
Fire department,	850 00	Total,	$25,625 00

In addition to the above, the Town appropriated for schools from Town School Fund, $400; from State School Fund, $306; and from Dog Tax, $510 — in all, $1,216.

ASSETS AND LIABILITIES, MAY 1.

ASSETS.		LIABILITIES.	
School-houses,	$35,060 00	Public library,	$10,000 00
Public library,	30,000 00	Trust funds,	16,000 00
Other public buildings,	24,000 00	Other debts,	42,212 00
Public grounds,	5,000 00	Total,	$68,212 00
Cemeteries,	300 00		
Other real estate,	4,215 00		
Fire apparatus,	4,000 00		
Trust funds,	$16,000 00		
Other assets,	7,000 00		
Total,	$125,575 00		

PROPERTY EXEMPT FROM TAXATION.

First Congregational Society. — Building and lot,		$21,000 00
Union Religious " " "		20,600 00
South Parish " " "		14,500 00
Methodist Episcopal " " "		3,500 00
Baptist " " "		1,300 00
Braintree Lyceum Corporation. — Hall and reading-room,		750 00
Total,		$61,650 00

SCHOOL STATISTICS.

SCHOOL COMMITTEE.

Naaman L. White, *Chairman;* Dr. Noah Torrey, *Secretary;* Dr. James M. Cutting, Rev. Fisk Barrett, George H. Arnold, S. W. Hollis.

SCHOOLS.

High. — Charles E. Stetson, *Principal;* Miss Martha Reed, *Assistant,*	63	scholars.
Pond Grammar. — Miss Mary Fennersy,	45	"
Union Grammar. — Miss Ella F. White,	26	"
Iron-Works Grammar. — Miss Sarah A. Hammett,	43	"
Pond Intermediate. — Miss Lizzie M. Thompson,	38	"
Union Intermediate. — Miss S. Lizzie Burnham,	33	"
Iron-Works Intermediate. — Miss Joanna W. Penniman,	39	"

Pond Primary. — Miss S. Ella Torrey,	37 scholars.
Union Primary. — Miss Inez M. Rogers,	45 "
Iron-Works Primary. — Miss Alice M. Mason,	39 "
East. — Miss Victoria P. Wild,	44 "
Middle. — Miss Lottie E. Allen,	33 "
South-east. — Miss Alice M. Cushing,	14 "
South. — Miss Margarette E. C. Bannon,	16 "
South-west. — Miss Helen A. Williams,	17 "
West. — Miss Avis A. Thayer,	14 "
Total,	546 "

FIRE DEPARTMENT.

ENGINEERS.

John Cavanagh, *Chief;* William Allen, *Clerk;* C. W. Proctor, James T. Stevens, William M. Richards, Thomas South, Josephus Shaw, Thomas Penniman, Benj. J. Loring.

Union No. 1. — Thomas O. Sullivan, *Foreman.*

Butcher Boy No. 2. — George Sumner, *Foreman.*

Wompatuck Hook & Ladder Co. — A. F. Hannaford, *Foreman;* William Cavanaugh, *Clerk.*

BROOKLINE.

[*Incorporated November* 13, 1705.]

TOWN OFFICERS.

[Annual Meeting, March 20, 1876.]

Moderator. — William I. Bowditch.

Town Clerk. — Benjamin F. Baker. (25th year of continuous service.)

Selectmen, Overseers of the Poor, and Surveyors of Highways. — William I. Bowditch, Horace James, James M. Codman, Francis W. Lawrence, Marshall Russell.

Assessors. — Thomas B. Hall, Frederick W. Prescott, William Lincoln.

Treasurer and Collector. — Moses Withington.

Board of Health. — Dr. T. E. Francis, Dr. Robert Amory, Desmond Fitzgerald.

Water Board. — Edward S. Philbrick, Charles K. Kirby, Oliver Whyte.

Commissioners of Sinking Fund. — J. C. Abbott, William A. Wellman, Charles D. Head.

Trustees of Walnut-Hill Cemetery. — William I. Bowditch, Charles S. Sargent, George Crafts, Charles H. Stearns, Theodore Lyman, Nathaniel G. Chapin, Desmond Fitzgerald. Benjamin F. Baker, *Clerk;* Moses Withington, *Treasurer, ex-officiis.*

Constables. — J. P. Sanborn, W. Y. Gross, George F. Johnson, B. C. Clark, S. D. Edwards, T. S. Pettengill, Eben W. Reed, D. C. Murray, G. F. Dearborn, Eben Morse, John C. Morse.

VALUATION AND TAX.

Valuation of real est.,	$16,804,000 00	Items of tax —	
" " per. est.,	10,686,300 00	State tax,	$28,450 00
		County tax,	23,433 49
Total valuation,	827,490,300 00	Town grant,	283,498 51
Rate of tax,	$12.20 on $1,000		
Number of polls,	1,748	Total tax,	$335,382 00

APPROPRIATIONS.

Interest on town debt,	$90,000	Care of Town hall,	$2,500
Sinking fund,	55,000	Hook-and-ladder apparatus and	
Schools,	38,000	hose-carriage,	2,500
Construction of sewers,	30,000	Care of sewers,	2,000
Extension of water works,	25,000	Repair of town buildings,	2,000
Highways,	23,000	Interest on new issue of water	
Police,	16,000	scrip,	1,250
Lighting Town hall and streets,	16,000	Engineering on sewers,	1,000
Town officers,	11,000	State aid,	1,000
Contingencies,	10,000	Disabled soldiers and families	
Watering streets,	8,000	of deceased soldiers,	1,000
Fire department,	7,500	Clerk of Selectmen,	750
Making five new streets,	5,250	Evening schools,	500
Maintenance of water works,	5,000	Lamp-posts,	500
Abatement of taxes,	5,000	State aid to B. Cusick,	350
Poor,	4,000	Decoration day,	300
Public library,	4,000	Cemetery,	200
Building bridge on Brighton st.,	3,500	Maps and plans for water works,	200
Health department,	3,000	Preparing tax-list, etc.,	200
Sidewalks,	3,000	Ringing bell,	175
Stone-crusher and shed,	2,800		
Supt. of Streets and engineering,	2,500	Total,	$383,975

ASSETS AND LIABILITIES, MAY 1.

ASSETS.		LIABILITIES.	
School-houses,	$111,500	Public library,	$18,500
Public library,	95,000	Other public buildings,	150,000
Other public buildings,	359,950	Public grounds and park,	98,300
Public grounds and parks,	78,000	Cemeteries,	53,000
Cemeteries,	50,000	Water works,	500,000
Water works,	500,000	Sewerage,	74,000
Fire apparatus,	66,825	Trust funds,	10,000
Trust funds,	10,000	Other debts,	474,500
Other assets,	89,700		
Total,	$1,360,975	Total,	$1,378,300

PROPERTY EXEMPT FROM TAXATION.

Harvard Orthodox Society. —	Church and land,		$80,000
St. Paul's Episcopal "	" "		50,000
Sears Chapel. —	" "		40,000
Lawrence Testimonial, Episcopal. —	" "		35,000
Baptist Society. —	" "		35,000
Unitarian "	" "		20,000
Swedenborgian Society. —	" "		15,000
Beals' Free Church. —	" "		14,000
Roman Catholic Church. —	" "		10,000
Total,			$299,000

SCHOOL STATISTICS.

SCHOOL COMMITTEE.

J. Elliot Cabot, *Chairman;* Rev. Warren Goddard, *Secretary;* George Brooks, *Treasurer;* Wm. H. Lincoln, Rev. Howard N. Brown, Francis Hunnewell, W. T. R. Marvin, Michael Driscoll, William Hobbs.

SCHOOLS.

High. — John E. Hoar, *Principal;* Fred Lauton, Misses Abby
   W. Deane, Bessie P. Kirby, Minnie Laighton, *Assistants,*   103 scholars.
Pierce. — D. H. Daniels, *Principal;* Misses Virginia A. Clark-
   son, Alice Peaslee, Mary M. Hammond, Etta D. Paul, Mary
   P. Frye, Margaret E. Malone, Harriet F. Woods, Emma
   S. Beede, *Assistants,*   288   "
Heath-street. — Miss Carrie L. Rideout, *Principal;* Misses Mary
   J. Collingwood, Eleanor W. Collingwood, M. E. Hyde,
   Assistants,   141   "
Ward. — David Bentley, *Principal*; Misses Sarah W. Loker,
   Frederika Swanton, Hattie A. Dalrymple, M. B. Magoon,
   Emma L. Wiswall, Carrie W. Gookin, Annie L. Richard-
   son, Jennie Hintz, *Assistants,*   338   "
Harvard-street. — Misses Sarah D. Newton, Emma L. Stevens,   73   "
Boylston-street. — Misses Mary Shea, Emma T. Lewis,   89   "
Lawrence. — Miss Susie M. Rowe,   30   "
Longwood. — Miss Alice H. Abbott,   17   "
Newton-street. — Miss L. P. Rollins,   12   "

       Total,   1,091   "

Teacher of Music. — Wm. S. Tilden.
Teachers of Sewing. — H. A. Nevers, Anna H. Pope.
Truant Officer. — George F. Dearborn.

FIRE DEPARTMENT.

ENGINEERS.

Wm. B. Sears, *Chief;* Moses Jones, G. H. Johnson, J. S. Woods; W. A. Good-
win, *Clerk.*
Steam Fire Engine. — Leo Bertsch, *Engineer;* Edward Phillips, *Driver;* John A.
Ayer, *Call-fireman.*
Hose No. 1. — George Harvey, *Foreman;* George Palmer, *Assistant;* Howard
Turner, *Clerk.* 6 hosemen.
Hose No. 2. — C. E. Delano, *Foreman;* W. H. Lyon, 1*st Assistant;* G. H. Del-
ano, *Clerk.* 8 hosemen.
Hook and Ladder No. 1. — A. E. Kenrick, *Foreman;* E. F. Palmer, *Assistant
Foreman;* M. F. Kenrick, *Clerk.* 12 ladder-men.

POLICE.

Alonzo Bowman, *Chief;* P. H. Cusick, *Deputy;* Harris R. Head, *Sergeant.*

Patrolmen. — Burton R. Willis, Mears Orcutt, Burnham C. Clark, Patrick Dillon, Thomas J. Murray, Wm. W. O'Connell, Charles B. McCausland, Patrick Johnson, George F. Martin, Edward Russell, George F. Dearborn, Albert S. Page, Alonzo B. Langley.

CANTON.

[*Incorporated Feb. 23, 1797, from northerly part of Stoughton.*]

TOWN OFFICERS.

[Annual Meeting, April 3, 1876.]

Moderator. — Daniel T. V. Huntoon.
Town Clerk. — Andrew Lopez.
Selectmen, Assessors, Overseers of the Poor, and Surveyors of Highways. — William Horton, Edward R. Eager, William W. Brooks.
Treasurer. — Francis W. Deane.
Collector. — William W. Brooks.
Auditors. — Elijah A. Morse, Frederic Endicott, Edwin Wentworth.
Fire-Wards. — Frank M. Ames, James S. Shepard, George B. Hunt, J. W. Wattles, Robert Draper, Charles F. Cushman, Albion W. Kinsley, Isaac Horton, N. S. White, R. C. Wood, Ellis Tucker, Charles Draper, George F. Sumner.
Constables. — Rufus C. Wood, George M. Davenport, Samuel H. Capen, Lucius Edson, Charles N. Draper, Patrick F. Brady.

VALUATION AND TAX.

		Items of tax —	
Valuation of real estate,	$1,930,780 00	State tax,	$3,120 00
" " personal est.,	1,174,051 00	County tax,	2,579 03
		Town grant,	32,687 03
Total valuation,	$3,104,831 00	Overlayings,	901 95
Rate of tax,	$12.00 on $1,000		
Number of polls,	1,015	Total tax,	$39,288 00

APPROPRIATIONS.

Schools,	$11,000 00	Street lamps,	$600 00
Poor,	5,000 00	Barn at Poor farm,	600 00
Widening Washington st.,	4,500 00	Sidewalks,	500 00
Highways and bridges,	4,000 00	Evening schools,	400 00
Contingent expenses,	3,000 00	Cemeteries,	300 00
School-houses and incid'tals,	1,975 00	Incidentals,	250 00
Interest,	800 00	Decoration day,	150 00
Public library,	800 00		
York st.,	700 00	Total,	$35,175 00
Police,	600 00		

ASSETS AND LIABILITIES, MAY 1.

ASSETS.		LIABILITIES.	
School-houses,	$45,200	Debts,	$2,000
Other public buildings,	1,000		
Cemeteries,	2,000		
Other real estate,	5,617		
Fire apparatus,	5,000		
Total,	$58,817		

PROPERTY EXEMPT FROM TAXATION.

First Congregational Society. — Meeting-house and land,			$5,000
" Universalist " " "			4,000
Baptist " " "			6,000
Orthodox " " "			6,000
Roman Catholic " "			7,000
Total,			$28,000

SCHOOL STATISTICS.

SCHOOL COMMITTEE.

Geo. Frederic Sumner, *Chairman;* Arthur C. Kollock, *Secretary;* J. W. Wattles, Isaac .Horton, Edwin Wentworth, Jesse Fenno, George E. Downes, Thomas Lonergan, Rev. John Flatly.
Superintendent. — Frederic Endicott.

SCHOOLS.

High. — Mr. Clarence H. Berry, *Principal. Assistants,* Miss Annie E. Chace, for first two terms; Miss Mary L. Prescott, since September 1, 35 scholars.

District No. 1. *Grammar.* — Mr. George W. Capen. *Primary.* — Miss Charlotte Tucker, 80 "

District No. 2. — Miss Ellen McKendry, first two terms; Miss Helen G. Kinsley, since September 1, 40 "

District No. 3. *Grammar.* — Mr. John Everett, to March 1; Mr. Arthur B. Morong, to summer vacation; Mr. Bradford W. Drake, since September 1. Miss Ella M. Hill, *Assistant. Intermediate.* — Misses Alice H. Lowry, Lucie A. Hall. *First Primary.* — Misses Eldora A. Drake, Emma P. Bense. *Second Primary.* — Misses Carrie L. Shattuck, M. Ella Deane, 380 "

District No. 4. — Miss S. Jennie Deane, till middle of spring term; Miss Eliza A. Sumner, since, 35 "

District No. 5. — Miss Mary J. Holmes, 40 "

District No. 6. *Grammar.* — Mr. Jeremiah E. Earle. *Primary.* — Miss E. Florence Faunce, 100 "

District No. 7. *Intermediate.* — Mrs. Abby J. Snow. *Primary.* — Miss Mary Scollard, 90 "

Total, 800 "

Special Teacher of Music. — Mr. Henry J. Whittemore, of Hyde Park.

There are two Evening Schools: one in District No. 3, Mr. Bradford W. Drake, and Misses Alice H. Lowry and Miss Snow, teachers; and one in District No. 6, Mr. Jeremiah E. Earl, teacher. In No. 3 the average attendance is 45; in No. 6, 14.

COHASSET.

[*Incorporated April 26, 1770, from Second Precinct of Hingham.*]

TOWN OFFICERS.

[Annual Meeting, March 6, 1876.]

Moderator. — John Q. A. Lothrop.
Town Clerk. — Newcomb B. Tower.
Selectmen, Assessors, and Overseers of the Poor. — J. Q. A. Lothrop, Louis N. Lincoln, Philander Bates.
Treasurer and Collector. — Abraham H. Tower, Jr.
Fire-Wards. — J. Q. A. Lothrop, J. Foster Doane, Philip Fox, Isaac W. Beal, Alson S. Richardson.
Highway Surveyors. — Louis N. Lincoln, Philander Bates, J. Q. A. Lothrop, Louis T. Cushing, Richard Wells.
Constables. — Louis N. Lincoln, Andrew W. Williams, David B. Lincoln, John L. Pratt, Isaiah Lincoln, Ezra Brown, J. Foster Doane.

VALUATION AND TAX.

		Items of tax —	
Valuation of real estate,	$1,466,505 00	State tax,	$2,304 00
" " personal est.,	872,687 00	County tax,	1,897 21
		Town grant,	19,550 00
Total valuation,	$2,339,192 00	Overlayings,	812 79
Rate of tax,	$10.00 on $1,000		
Number of polls,	586	Total tax,	$24,564 00

APPROPRIATIONS.

Schools,	$5,000 00	Miscellaneous,	$800 00
Highways,	3,000 00	Roads and bridges,	700 00
Poor,	2,500 00	Removing snow,	400 00
Interest,	1,200 00	Repairs on school-houses,	400 00
Abatement of taxes,	1,200 00	Printing and Fire department,	400 00
Payment of debt,	1,000 00	Town house and B'd of Health,	100 00
Town officers,	1,000 00		
Building Doane st.,	1,000 00	Total,	$19,550 00
Widening sts. and sidewalks,	850 00		

ASSETS AND LIABILITIES, MAY 1.

ASSETS.		LIABILITIES.	
School-houses,	$14,500 00	School-houses,	$5,000 00
Other public buildings,	16,000 00	Other public buildings,	3.000 00
Public grounds and park,	6,000 00	Trust funds,	1,000 00
Cemeteries,	3,000 00	Other debts,	7,000 00
Other real estate,	6,000 00		
Fire apparatus,	1,500 00	Total,	$16,000 00
Trust funds,	1,000 00		
Other assets,	3,269 00		
Total,	$51,269 00		

PROPERTY EXEMPT FROM TAXATION.

First Cong. Unitarian Soc.	— Building and land,	$5,000;	organ,	$1,000,			$6,000
Second " Orthodox "	"	"	4,500;	"	600,		5,100
Beechwood " "	"	"	3,000;	"	100,		3,100
Methodist "	"	"	2,500;	"	100,		2,600
Roman Catholic "	"	"	3,000;	"	———		3,000
Totals,		$18,000;		$1,800,			$19,800

SCHOOL STATISTICS.

SCHOOL COMMITTEE.

Levi N. Bates, *Chairman;* M. A. Stevens, *Secretary;* John Q. A. Lothrop. *Superintendent.* —Rev. Samuel Osgood.

SCHOOLS.

High. — Miss Drusilla S. Lothrop, *Principal;* Mr. E. P. Collier, *Assistant,*	60	scholars.
North Grammar. — Miss Martha A. Bates,	25	"
North Primary. — Miss Susan L. Stoddard,	29	"
Centre Grammar. — Miss Annie A. Souther,	38	"
Centre Primary. — Miss Lizzie C. Bates,	37	"
South Grammar. — Miss Elizabeth D. Tower,	42	"
South Primary. — Miss Myra L. Beal,	41	"
Beechwoods Grammar. — Mr. L. Webster Bates,	27	"
Beechwoods Primary. — Miss Georgianna Bates,	34	"
Jerusalem. — Miss Anna Fox,	15	"
Harbor. — Miss Charlotte M. Whittington,	35	"
King-street. — Misses Addie F. Beal and Roberta Nichols,	22	"
Total,	405	"

DEDHAM.

[*Incorporated September 8, 1636.*]

TOWN OFFICERS.

[Annual Meeting, March 6, 1876.]

Moderator. — Frederick D. Ely.

Town Clerk. — Charles II. Farrington.

Selectmen, Assessors, Overseers of the Poor, and Board of Health. — Ezra W. Taft, Augustus B. Endicott, Benjamin Wetherbee, Howard Colburn, Charles C. Sanderson.

Treasurer. — Lewis H. Kingsbury.

Collector. — Henry C. Bonney.

Auditors. — Chauncey C. Churchill, William Bullard, Augustus B. Endicott.

Road Commissioners. — Nathaniel Noyes, George F. Richards, Elijah W. Bonnemort.

Constables. — Christopher T. Bailey, George E. Morse, Philander S. Young, Peter Gaffney, H. A. Atwood, J. V. Abbott, Eustis Baker, John Dean.

VALUATION AND TAX.

Valuation of real estate,	$3,975,192 00	Items of tax —	
" " personal est.,	1,985,120 00	State tax,	$5,994 00
		County tax,	4,935 71
Total valuation,	$5,960,312 00	Town grant,	55,449 89
		Overlayings,	2,121 40
Rate of tax,	$11.00 on $1,000		
Number of polls,	1,467	Total tax,	$68,501 00

APPROPRIATIONS.

School-teachers' salaries,	$18,000 00	Removing snow,	$1,000 00
General repairs highways,	8,000 00	Incidental expenses,	1,000 00
Stone arch bridge over Charles river,	5,100 00	Bridge on Canton street,	900 00
Fire department,	3,500 00	Insurance, etc., school-houses,	900 00
Poor out of Almshouse,	3,200 00	Public library,	850 00
Lighting streets,	2,700 00	Additional police,	800 00
Town officers,	2,400 00	Abatement of taxes,	800 00
Care and repair of school-houses,	2,200 00	Keeper of lock-up,	500 00
Special repairs on highways, including sidewalks and curbstones,	2,000 00	Reservoir at East Dedham,	500 00
Poor in Almshouse,	2,000 00	Cemeteries,	350 00
Constables and special police,	1,700 00	Interest on money borrowed in anticipation of taxes,	300 00
Fire-alarm bell at East Dedham,	1,500 00	Supplies for lock-up,	250 00
Fuel for schools,	1,300 00	Decoration day,	150 00
Printing, advertising and stationery,	1,100 00	Rent of Oakdale school-room,	150 00
Collection of taxes,	1,100 00	Printing By-laws,	100 00
		Total,	$64,350 00

ASSETS AND LIABILITIES, MAY 1.

ASSETS.		LIABILITIES.	
School-houses,	$59,300 00	Trust funds,	$1,300 00
Public library,	2,500 00		
Other public buildings,	50,000 00		
Other real estate,	9,300 00		
Fire apparatus,	17,100 00		
Trust funds,	1,300 00		
	$139,500 00		

PROPERTY EXEMPT FROM TAXATION.

Temporary asylum for discharged female prisoners.— Land and bldgs.,			$10,400 00
St. Mary's School and Asylum. — " "			8,484 00
Dedham Public Library.— Books,			2,500 00
First Church and Society.— House, pews and furniture,		$11,000	
Chapel,		1,000	
Land,		4,792	
			16,792 00
Allin Evangelical Society.— House, inc. furniture,		$12,000	
Land,		2,750	
			14,750 00
St. Paul's Church (Episcopal).— House, pews and furniture,		$25,000	
Chapel,		5,000	
Land,		2,295	
			32,295 00
St. Mary's Church (Roman Catholic).— Building,		$4,000	
Land,		1,560	
			5,560 00
Unitarian Church, West Dedham.— Building and furniture,		$5,500	
Land,		200	
			5,700 00
Baptist Church, West Dedham.— House, pews and furniture,		$4,000	
Chapel,		400	
Land,		100	
			4,500 00
Baptist Church, East Dedham.— House, pews and furniture,		$4,000	
Land,		428	
			4,428 00
Methodist Church, East Dedham.— House, pews and furniture,		$2,000	
Land,		320	
			2,320 00
Norfolk Agricultural Society.— Land at Readville,			17,500 00
			$125,229 00

SCHOOL STATISTICS.

SCHOOL COMMITTEE.

Rev. Calvin S. Locke, *Chairman;* C. C. Churchill, *Secretary;* Rev. Edward Crowninshield, Rev. Daniel Goodwin, Miss Ellen H. Crehore, Frank M. Bailey.

SCHOOLS.

High. — Carlos Slafter, *Principal;* Misses Martha A. Smith, Maria T. Delano, *Assistants,*   75 scholars.

Ames. — Joseph H. Noyes, *Principal;* Misses Abbie T. Crane, Josie M. Prince, Mary L. Talbot, Hattie W. Whiting, Mary F. Hodges, Henrietta Adams, *Assistants,*   275   "

Avery. — Henry E. Crocker, *Principal;* Misses Annie J. Barton,
Mary A. Alden, Mary S. Morse, Martha M. Davis, Annie G.
Fish, Mary E. Keelan, Annie L. Farrington, *Assistants.*   280 scholars.
Colburn. — James N. Parker, *Principal;* Misses Sarah A. Ellis,
Sarah L. Cheney, *Assistants,*   90   "
Quincy. — Misses Melissa D. Robinson, Mary Hutchins,   75   "
Endicott. — William T. Hart,   25   "
Dexter. — Miss Lucy A. Calder,   30   "
Fisher. — Misses Sarah L. Norris, Lucy E. Allen,   20   "
Oakdale. — Miss Louisa Harris,   36   "
Burgess. — Miss Ella E. Ward,   12   "
Union. — Miss Hattie E. Colburn,   20   "
                                                              ———
Total,   938   "
Teacher of Music. — Mr. C. E. Whiting,

FIRE DEPARTMENT.

ENGINEERS.

Chief Engineer, George F. Richards; *Asst. Engineers*, Francis Soule. H. A.
Atwood, George A. Guild, Ebenezer Gould; *Clerk*, George A. Guild.

ENGINEERS AND OFFICERS.

Relief Steam Fire-Engine Co. No. 1, Dedham Village. — *Foreman*, F. C.
Field; *Asst. Foremen*, T. J. Mack, E. Ramsdell; *Clerk*, J. B. Calder.
Hero Engine Co. No. 1 (Hand Engine), Upper Village. — *Foreman*, W. B. Lin-
coln; *Asst. Foreman*, C. DeMayn; *Clerk*, Albert Smith.
Lion Engine Co. No. 2 (Hand Engine), West Dedham. — *Foreman*, D. F. Hodg-
don; *Clerk*, Warren Kingsbury.
Niagara Engine Co. No. 3 (Hand Engine), East Dedham. — *Foreman*, John
Wardle; *Asst. Foreman*, William Fardy; *Clerk*, William Blakslee.
Norfolk Engine Co. No. 6 (Hand Engine), West Dedham. — *Foreman*, Joseph
Houghton; *Asst. Foreman*, E. A. Walley; *Clerk*, J. B. Baker.
Franklin Engine Co. No. 8 (Hand Engine), West Dedham. — *Foreman*, Daniel
W. Parker; *Clerk*, Howard Colburn.
Rescue Hook and Ladder Co. No. 1, Dedham Village. — *Foreman*, Charles H.
Barron; *Asst. Foreman*, H. A. Phipps; *Clerk*, T. C. Pierce.

DOVER.

*[Incorporated as a District, July 7, 1784, and as a Town, March 31, 1836. For-
merly part of Dedham.]*

TOWN OFFICERS.

[Annual Meeting, March 6, 1876.]

Moderator. — George Scott.
Town Clerk. — Abner L. Smith (resigned April 18, and his son, Charles H.
Smith, was appointed by the Selectmen).
Selectmen and Overseers of the Poor. — John Humphrey, Barnabas Paine, Henry
J. Winchenbach.

Assessors. — Amos W. Shumway, Ephraim Wilson, William Tisdale.
Treasurer and Collector. — Aaron Bacon.
Highway Surveyors. — No. 1. Ephraim Wilson; 2. A. K. Tisdale; 3. W. A.
Howe; 4. C. Kenrick; 5. Josiah Whiting; 6. W. Tisdale; 7. Henry
Goulding; 8. F. G. Gay.
Sexton. — Asa Talbot.
Constables. — Abner L. Smith, W. A. Howe.

VALUATION AND TAX.

Valuation of real estate, $394,693 00
"   " personal est., 40,562 00

Total valuation, $435,255 00
Rate of tax, $15.50 on $1,000
Number of polls, 182

Items of tax:—
State tax, $432 00
County tax, 355 73
Town grant, 6,323 27

Total tax, $7,111 00

APPROPRIATIONS.

Town charges, $2,000 00
Schools, 1,000 00
Highways, $900 00
Debt, 800 00

$4,700 00

ASSETS AND LIABILITIES, MAY 1.

ASSETS.
School-houses, $5,200 00
Public grounds, 300 00
Cemeteries, 400 00

$5,900 00

LIABILITIES.
Debts, $2,475 00

PROPERTY EXEMPT FROM TAXATION.

Unitarian Society. — House and land, $2,100 00
Orthodox "   "   "   " 1,050 00
Baptist "   "   "   " 650 00

$3,800 00

SCHOOL STATISTICS.

SCHOOL COMMITTEE.

Miss Hannah E. Chickering, *Chairman and Superintendent;* Joseph A. Smith,
Mrs. George D. Everett.

FOUR SCHOOLS OF MIXED GRADE.

Centre. — Miss Helen W. Sutherland, 40 scholars.
North. — Miss Alice M. Richards, 33 "
East. — Miss Lucy E. Allen, 23 "
West. — Miss Nellie Cleaves, 20 "

Total, 116 "

In addition to above, eight attend school in Dedham, and three attend High
schools elsewhere.

Whole number of children in town, between 5 and 15, as returned by Assessors,
May 1, was 120.

FOXBOROUGH.

[Incorporated June 10, 1778, from parts of Wrentham, Walpole, Stoughton and Sharon.]

TOWN OFFICERS.

[Annual Meeting, March 20, 1876.]

Moderator. — Charles F. Howard.

Town Clerk. — James F. Leonard.

Selectmen, Assessors, and Overseers of the Poor. — James F. Leonard, Newland F. Howard, Henry G. Warren.

Treasurer. — Eli Phelps.

Auditors. — C. W. Hodges, Charles F. Howard, Otis Cary.

Collector of Taxes. — George S. Wheeler.

Highway Surveyors. — Harvey Leonard, James A. Morse, Albert Fisher, Edward O. Nichols, Ezra Pickens, George W. Beal, William H. Stratton, Orin Wetherell, Patrick McTernan, Benjamin F. Boyden, Terrence Skelly, Michael Gary, John Welsh, Warren S. Bacon, Joseph Comey.

Fire Engineers. — Charles F. Howard, C. W. Lane, L. P. Faught, E. O. Nichols, John T. Carpenter, M. Ryan.

Constables. — Edward O. Nichols, George S. Walcott.

VALUATION AND TAX.

Valuation of real estate,	$1,330,830 00	Items of tax —	
" " per. estate,	308,005 00	State tax,	$1,746 00
		County tax,	1,437 73
Total valuation,	$1,638,835 00	Town grant,	16,000 00
		Overlayings,	273 27
Rate of tax	$11.00 on $1,000		
Number of polls,	724	Total tax,	$19,457 00

APPROPRIATIONS.

Schools,	$6,000 00	Discount and abatement of	
Town debt,	5,000 00	taxes,	$1,000 00
Interest,	2,500 00	Repairs of public buildings,	516 00
Poor,	2,000 00	Fire-engine repairs,	100 00
Highways and bridges,	1,100 00		
Town officers,	1,000 00		$19,216 00

ASSETS AND LIABILITIES, MAY 1.

ASSETS.		LIABILITIES.	
School-houses,	$20,000 00	School-houses,	$20,000 00
Public library,	1,000 00	Cemetery,	1,000 00
Other public buildings,	4,000 00	Fire apparatus,	5,000 00
Public grounds and parks,	5,000 00	Other debts,	6,500 00
Cemeteries,	1,000 00		
Other real estate,	20,500 00	Total,	$32,500 00
Water works,	1,000 00		
Fire apparatus,	5,000 00		
Other assets,	5,200 00		
Total,	$64,700 00		

PROPERTY EXEMPT FROM TAXATION.

Orthodox Society. — Building,	$13,000	
Furniture,	1,000	
Land,	1,200	
		$15,200 00
Baptist Society. — Building,	$6,500	
Furniture,	500	
Land,	1,200	
		8,200 00
Universalist Society. — Building,	$4,000	
Furniture,	800	
Land,	800	
		5,600 00
Roman Catholic Society. — Building,	$2,500	
Land,	400	
		2,900 00
Union Chapel. — Building,	$900	
Land,	200	
		1,100 00
Town house and school house connected therewith. — Bldg.,	$25,000	
Land	1,500	
		26,500 00
Six school houses. — Buildings,	$4,500	
Land,	800	
		5,300 00
Memorial Hall. — Building,		6,000 00
Engine house. — "		700 00
Cemeteries. — Land,		1,000 00
Public library. — Books and fixtures,		1,000 00
Almshouses. — Buildings and land,		4,500 00
School-house, 5th district, not occupied. — Building,	$2,000	
Land,	1,000	
		3,000 00
Total,		**$57,150 00**

SCHOOL STATISTICS.

SCHOOL COMMITTEE.

James E. Carpenter, *Chairman;* Edwin W. Clarke, *Secretary;* S. Payson Hodges.

SCHOOLS

High. — *Principal,* W. Edgar Horton, A. M.; Miss Sarah T. Cary, *Assistant,*	42	scholars.
Everett. — Miss Ella A. Blake,	40	"
Quaker Hill. — Miss Ida G. Decker,	32	"
Paine. — Miss Lucretia P. Townsend,	37	"
Pratt. — Miss Mercie B. Nickerson,	71	"
Centre Grammar. — Mr. Frank M. Copeland,	39	"
Centre First Intermediate School. — Miss Isabel E. Johnson,	49	"
Centre Second Intermediate. — Miss Ella J. Carleton,	43	"
Centre First Primary. — Miss Mary E. Anthony,	38	"
Centre Second Primary. — Miss Susan E. Nichols,	42	"
Plympton. — Miss Lizzie S. Rea,	39	"
Cary. — Miss Elizabeth N. Brayton,	48	"
Total,	**520**	"

FRANKLIN.

[Incorporated March 2, 1778, from westerly part of Wrentham.]

TOWN OFFICERS.

[Annual Meeting, March 6, 1876.]

Moderator. — James M. Freeman.
Town Clerk and Collector. — George W. Wiggin.
Selectmen, Overseers of Poor, and Highway Surveyors. — Henry R. Jenks, Peter Adams, Edmund Hartshorn.
Assessors. — Stephen W. Richardson, Asa A. Fletcher, Joseph Harrold.
Treasurer. — James M. Freeman.
Auditor — Waldo Daniels.
Constables. — Lewis R. Whitaker, William E. Nason, Hugh McParland.

VALUATION AND TAX.

Valuation of real est.,	$1,102,925 00	Items of tax : —	
" " per. estate,	394,215 00	State tax,	$1,494 00
		County tax,	1,230 22
Total valuation,	$1,497,140 00	Town grant,	17,627 78
Rate of tax,	$12.50 on $1,000	Total tax,	$20,352 00
Number of polls,	819		

APPROPRIATIONS

Schools,	$6,000 00	Abatement and collection of	
Roads and bridges,	4,000 00	taxes,	$500 00
Poor,	2,500 00	Fire department,	300 00
New fire-engine,	1,800 00	Printing and stationery,	200 00
Miscellaneous expenses,	1,500 00	Public library,	200 00
Interest,	1,000 00		
Town officers,	1,000 00	Total,	$19,000 00

ASSETS AND LIABILITIES, MAY 1.

ASSETS.		LIABILITIES.	
School-houses,	$15,000 00	School-houses,	$3,000 00
Other public buildings,	5,500 00		
Public grounds and park,	2,500 00		
Other real estate,	2,800 00		
Fire apparatus,	4,000 00		
	$29,800 00		

PROPERTY EXEMPT FROM TAXATION.

Dean Academy Corporation. —	Personal,	$163,300;	real,	$148,500,	$311,800 00
First Congregational Parish. —	"	4,000;	"	26,000,	30,000 00
" Universalist Society. —	"	4,500;	"	25,800,	30,300 00
Methodist Episcopal "	"	1,500;	"	10,800,	12,300 00
Baptist "	"	1,500;	"	10,600,	12,100 00
Union Congregational Parish. —	"	75;	"	2,500,	2,125 00
Roman Catholic Society. —	"	500;	"	10,500,	11,000 00
					$409,625 00

Franklin Library Association. — Fund, $3,250
                              Library,   1,000
                                              ——— $4,250

                                                   $175,625   ———————
          Total, $589,250 00

SCHOOL STATISTICS.

SCHOOL COMMITTEE.

Rev. S. W. Squire, *Chairman;* William F. Ray, *Secretary;* Dr. William B. Nolen.

SCHOOLS.

High. — Miss Mary A. Bryant,	32 scholars.
High Grammar. — Miss Juliette D. Stanley,	25 "
Sub-Grammar. — Miss Mary A. Holbrook,	40 "
Intermediate. — Miss Clara L. Warren,	56 "
No. 1 Primary. — Miss Agnes S. Jones,	56 "
No. 2 Primary. — Miss Annie S. Harrold,	54 "
No. 3 Primary. — Miss Anna L. Bean,	53 "
King-street. — Miss Isa Smiley,	13 "
City Mills. — Miss Emma Rounds,	19 "
Latie No. 6. — Miss Effie A. Dunbar,	48 "
North-west. — Miss Emily Albee,	51 "
Unionville No 8. — Mr. M. H. Nason,	52 "
South Franklin. — Miss Eva Morse,	38 "
Mount No. 10. — Miss Ella E. Squire,	13 "
	———
Total,	550 "

HOLBROOK.

[*Incorporated Feb. 29, 1872, from part of Randolph.*]

TOWN OFFICERS.

[Annual Meeting, April 3, 1876.]

Moderator. — Francis Gardner.

Town Clerk and Treasurer. — John Underhay.

Selectmen, Assessors, and Overseers of Poor. — Charles H. Belcher, Willard F.
          Gleason, Newton White.

Auditors. — George W. Paine, J. T. Southworth, Richmond T. Pratt.

Collector of Taxes. — Samuel L. White.

Fire Engineers. — S. D. Chase, James W. White.

Highway Surveyors. — Samuel L. White, Thurston P. White, John A. Blood,
          William B. Belcher, William Armstrong, George W. Wilde.

Constables. — Samuel L. White, Frederick Bigelow, Freeman Bard, Henry C.
          Dorman.

VALUATION AND TAX.

Valuation of real estate,	$741,340 00	Items of tax —		
" " personal est.,	199,020 00	State tax,		$1,548 00
		County tax,		1,027 69
Total valuation,	$940,360 00	Town grant,		11,549 31
Rate of tax,	$14.00 on $1,000	Total tax,		$14,125 00
Number of polls,	530			

APPROPRIATIONS.

Schools,	$5,000 00	Insurance,	$600 00
Town debt,	5,000 00	Fire department,	600 00
Poor,	3,000 00	Public library,	500 00
Interest,	1,200 00	Bridges, etc.,	400 00
Highways,	1,000 00	Cemeteries,	100 00
General expenses,	1,000 00		
Town officers,	800 00	Total,	$20,000 00
Repairs of Town hall,	800 00		

ASSETS AND LIABILITIES, MAY 1.

ASSETS.		LIABILITIES.	
School-houses,	$10,000 00	Debts,	$11,000 00
Public library,	8,000 00		
Other public buildings,	29,000 00		
Fire apparatus,	800 00		
Total,	$47,800 00		

PROPERTY EXEMPT FROM TAXATION.

Winthrop Religious Society. — Church and land,		$25,000 00
Brookville Baptist Church. — " "		2,000 00
Public Library. — Bldg. and land, $4,000; books and furniture, $4,000,		8,000 00
Total,		$35,000 00

SCHOOL STATISTICS.

SCHOOL COMMITTEE.

Thomas H. West, Dr. J. B. Kingsbury, Z. A. French.

SCHOOLS.

Sumner-Hill Grammar. — Mr. Walter C. Hill, of Stoneham, was principal the first two terms of the year. Present principal, Mr. Charles H. Goldthwait, of Salem; Mrs. Ellen W. Thayer, assistant during the year, — 65 scholars.

Sumner Sub-Grammar. — Miss Roxie E. Dickinson, of Amherst, 38 "

Sumner Intermediate. — Miss F. Emma Sherman, of Weymouth, 59 "

Brookville Intermediate. — Miss Mary A. Bosworth, of Quincy, teacher the first two terms; now under charge of Miss Lucy J. Beebe, of South Wilbraham, 35 "

Brookville Primary. — Miss E. Gertrude Bosworth, of Quincy, 45 "

Franklin Primary. — Miss Mary H. French; Miss Clara P.
French, *Assistant;* both of Holbrook,   111 scholars.
Lincoln Mixed. — Miss Hattie N. Bailey, of Scituate, teacher first
    two terms; now in charge of Miss Mary A. Tobey, of Milford,   50   "
Roberts Mixed. — Miss Louise Bronsdon,   50   "

    Total,   453   "

HYDE PARK.

[*Incorporated April 22, 1868, from part of Dedham, Dorchester and Milton.*]

TOWN OFFICERS.

[Annual Meeting, March 6, 1876.]

Moderator. — Fergus A. Easton.
Town Clerk. — Henry B. Terry.
Selectmen, Overseers of Poor, Surveyors of Highways, and Board of Health. —
    Edwin R. Walker, George Sanford, J. D. McAvoy.
Assessors. — R. P. Moseley, Joel F. Goodwin, John M. Twitchell.
Treasurer. — Henry S. Bunton.
Collector. — Henry A. Rich.
Auditors. — D. W. C. Rogers, G. Fred Gridley, John A. Boyle.
Commissioners of Sinking Fund. — Henry Grew, Alpheus P. Blake, William J.
    Stuart.
Constables. — Charles Jacobs, E. W. Moffatt, W. H. Cumminger, John A. Soule,
    J. B. Neal, E. G. Currier, Jeremiah Corbett.

VALUATION AND TAX.

Valuation of real est., $5,860,765 00

  "   " personal est.,   685,002 00

    Total valuation, $6,545,767 00

Rate of tax, $13.00 on $1,000
Number of polls,   1,506

Items of tax —
    State tax, $6,282 00
    County tax,   5,172 86
    Town grant,   76,652 14

        Total tax, $88,107 00

APPROPRIATIONS.

Expenses of last year unp'd, $8,072 18
Interest,   17,500 00
Schools,   15,000 00
State and county taxes,   13,000 00
Incidentals,   5,000 00
Fire department,   4,500 00
Sinking fund,   4,000 00
Highways,   4,000 00
Poor,   3,500 00

Salaries, $2,700 00
Discount on taxes,   2,500 00
School incidentals,   2,000 00
Police,   1,500 00
Unp'd damages on River st.,   1,375 00
Public library,   700 00
Evening schools,   400 00

        Total, $85,747 18

ASSETS AND LIABILITIES, MAY 1.

ASSETS.		LIABILITIES.	
School-houses,	$144,250 00	Total indebtedness,	$250,700 00
Public library,	5,000 00		
Other public buildings,	22,500 00		
Fire apparatus,	20,000 00		
Other assets (sinking fund included),	75,306 00		
Total,	$267,056 00		

PROPERTY EXEMPT FROM TAXATION.

Baptist Church. — Furniture and organ,		$3,500 00	
Building,		20,000 00	
Land,		10,200 00	
			$33,700 00
Methodist Church. — Furniture and organ,		$3,500 00	
Building,		20,000 00	
Land,		3,750 00	
			27,250 00
Orthodox Church. — Furniture and organ,		$3,500 00	
Building,		12,000 00	
Land,		15,400 00	
			30,900 00
Episcopal Church. — Furniture and organ,		$1,500 00	
Building,		4,000 00	
Land,		16,766 00	
			22,266 00
Unitarian Cong. Church. — Furniture,		$1,500 00	
Building,		12,000 00	
Land,		1,816 00	
			15,316 00
Roman Catholic Church. — Furniture,		$200 00	
Building,		600 00	
Land,		3,200 00	
			4,000 00
Norfolk Agricultural Society. — Buildings,		$5,000 00	
Land,		10,000 00	
			15.000 00
Harvard College. — Land,		$1,750 00	1,750 00
Total,			$150,182 00

SCHOOL STATISTICS.

H. M. Cable, *Chairman;* W. H. H. Andrews, *Secretary;* H. C. Chamberlain,
E. M. Lancaster, Rev. W. J. Corcoran, R. W. Husted.

SCHOOLS.

High. — Mr. J. F. Elliott, *Principal;* Miss S. L. Barnes, *First
Assistant;* Miss E. P. Parsons, *Second Assistant,*   90 scholars.
Grew. — Mr. Geo. M. Fellows, *Principal;* Misses F. J. Emer-
son, L. Dunbar, M. A. Alexander, Genevieve Brainard,
S. S. Lancaster, *Assistants,*   300   "

Blake. — Mr. H. F. Howard, *Principal;* Misses Ida M. Pratt,
  E. A. George, J. S. Hammond, Belle N. Roper, H. M.
  Oliver, *Assistants,*   260 scholars.
Greenwood. — Mr. J. L. Curtis, *Principal;* Misses L. A. Cur-
  rier, H. J. Folsom, M. E. Libbey, C. P. Barnes, *Assistants,*   230   "
Damon. — Mr. E. W. Cross, *Principal;* Misses L. D. Bunker,
  S. A. Crosby, Julia C. Donovan, C. E. Walker, *Assistants,*   225   "

        Total,   1,105   "

FIRE DEPARTMENT.

ENGINEERS.

Chief Engineer, William U. Fairbairn; *Assistant Engineers,* L. A. Runnells,
Charles W. Paul.

ENGINES AND OFFICERS.

Goodwill Steam Fire Engine Co. No. 1. — *Foreman,* Henry B. Briggs; *Assist-
ant Foreman,* Albert Flagg; *Clerk,* J. C. Sanford; *Treasurer,* William H.
Darling; *Engineman,* P. McClellan.
Rough and Ready Steam Fire Engine Co. No. 2 — *Foreman,* Malcolm Rogers:
Assistant Foreman, William Holtham; *Clerk and Treasurer,* H. A. Bur-
nett; *Engineman,* William Henry Cumminger.
Splicer Hose Co. No. 1. — *Foreman,* John B. Guinazzo; *Assistant Foreman,*
Jeremiah Mings; *Clerk,* James A. Guinan; *Treasurer,* John B. Guinazzo.
Norfolk Hook-and-Ladder Co. No. 1. — *Foreman,* E. A. Hawley; *Assistant
Foreman,* Peter Bussey; *Clerk and Treasurer,* T. L. Pratt; *Steward of
the Department,* Joshua Wilder.

MEDFIELD.

[*Incorporated May 23, 1651.*]

TOWN OFFICERS.

[Annual Meeting, March 6, 1876.]

Moderator. — Isaac Fiske.
Town Clerk. — Rev. Charles C. Sewall.
Selectmen, Assessors, and Overseers of the Poor. — Benjamin F. Shumway, Alonzo
  B. Parker, Hamlet Wight.
Treasurer — Isaac Fiske.
Auditor. — Charles Hamant.
Collector. — Ralph A. Battelle.
Board of Health. — J. H. Richardson, James Hewins, J. B. Hale.
Highway Surveyors. — William P. Hewins, Charles H. Russell, Hamlet Wight,
  H. P. Tabor, G. W. Kingsbury, F. S. Wight.
Constables. — Charles Hamant, Hinsdale F. Bullard, R. W. Sherman.

VALUATION AND TAX.

Valuation of real est.,	$689,047 00	Items of tax —		
" " personal est.,	278,850 00	State tax,	$1,008 00	
		County tax,	830 03	
Total valuation,	$967,897 00	Town grant,	9,984 97	
Rate of tax,	$11.50 on $1.000	Total tax,	$11,823 00	
No. of polls,	344			

APPROPRIATIONS.

Schools,	$2.300 00	Poor,	$1,000 00
Town debt,	2,000 00	Public library,	100 '00
Interest,	1,600 00		
General expenses,	1,500 00	Total,	$9,700 00
Highways,	1,200 00		

ASSETS AND LIABILITIES, MAY 1.

ASSETS.		LIABILITIES.	
School-houses,	$7,000 00	Debts,	$15,193 00
Public library,	1,000 00		
Other public buildings,	25,000 00		
Other real estate,	4,000 00		
Fire apparatus,	1,000 00		
Total,	$38,000 00		

PROPERTY EXEMPT FROM TAXATION.

Unitarian Society. — Building, land and furniture,		$10,000 00
Baptist " " " " "		9,000 00
Orthodox " " " " "		8,000 00
Total,		$27,000 00

SCHOOL STATISTICS.

SCHOOL COMMITTEE.

J. B. Hale, *Chairman;* Rev. A. M. Crane, *Secretary;* W. F. Guild, J. H. Gould, A. E. Mason.

SCHOOLS.

Centre School, Upper Department. — Mr. Wm. E. Marshall,	32	scholars.
Centre School, Grammar Department. — Miss Susan J. Woods,	30	"
Centre School, Primary Department. — Miss Esther Emerson,	33	"
North School, Mixed. — Miss Sarah C. Littlefield,	37	"
South School, Mixed. — Miss Ida C. Whiting,	21	"
Total,	153	"

MEDWAY.

[Incorporated Oct. 24, 1713, from part of Medfield.]

TOWN OFFICERS.

[Annual Meeting, March 6, 1876.]

Moderator. — David A. Partridge.
Town Clerk and Treasurer. — Orion A. Mason.
Selectmen and Surveyors of Highways. — Willard P. Clark, Joseph Bullard, . Edward Eaton.
Assessors. — Wales Kimball, Willard P. Clark, Edward Clark.
Overseers of Poor. – David Daniels, George R. Drake, Charles A. Bigelow.
Auditor. — S. J. Axtell.
Collector of Taxes. — Edward Clark.
Constables. — R. K. Colcord, Sylvester Howard, Timo. O'Brien, J. W. Tuttle, II. B. Woodman, Amos Whiting.

VALUATION AND TAX.

Valuation of real estate, $1,433,515 00		Items of tax —	
" " personal est., 329,695 00		State tax,	$1,836 00
		County tax	1.511 84
Total valuation,	$1,763,210 00	Town grant,	23,412 16
Rate of tax,	$14.00 on $1,000	Total tax,	$26,760 00
Number of polls,	1,038		

APPROPRIATIONS.

Schools,	$7,000 00	Engine-house, West Medway,	$500 00
Roads and bridges,	4,000 00	Lock-up, East Medway,	300 00
Debt and interest,	4,000 00	Decoration day,	100 00
Incidental expenses,	3,500 00		
Support of poor,	2,500 00	Total,	$22,900 00
Fire department,	1,000 00		

ASSETS AND LIABILITIES, MAY 1.

ASSETS.		LIABILITIES.	
School-houses,	$30,000 00	Debts,	$15,366 00
Public library,	350 00		
Other public buildings,	3,100 00		
Cemeteries,	1,000 00		
Other real estate,	8,000 00		
Water works,	2,500 00		
Fire apparatus,	5,000 00		
Other assets,	4,000 00		
Total,	$53,950 00		

PROPERTY EXEMPT FROM TAXATION.

First Congregational Society. — Personal,	$1,500 ;	real,	$5,000,		$6,500 00
Second " " "	1,000 ;	"	9,000,		10,000 00
Third " " "	1,500 ;	"	6,000,		7,500 00
Baptist " "	400 ;	"	4,000,		4,400 00
Methodist "		"	3,500,		3,500 00
Episcopal "		"	3,000,		3,000 00
Roman Catholic "		"	3,000,		3,000 00

$37,900 00

Dean Library Associat'n. — Books and furn., $800; other prop., $2,800, 3,600 00

Total, $41,500 00

SCHOOL STATISTICS.

SCHOOL COMMITTEE.

Seth J. Axtell, Jr., *Chairman ;* Charles H. Deans, *Secretary ;* William A. Jencks, Charles F. Daniels, Waldo B. Hixon, Charles A. Brigham, Anson Daniels, J. Warren Clark, Elias T. Fisher.

SCHOOLS.

No. 1, East Medway. — Dr. P. C. Porter, Miss A. C. Grant,	84 scholars.
" 2, " Miss H. S. Cobb, Miss H. A. Jones,	66 "
" 3, " Miss L. M. Bradish,	32 "
" 4, West Medway. — Mr. Fred. Holland, Misses Richardson, K. L. Haseltine, H. Z. Allen,	199 "
" 5, West Medway. — Miss E. F. Whitmore,	33 "
" 6. " Mrs. S. H. Fisher,	41 "
" 7, Medway Village. — Mr. G. B. Towle, Misses N. B. Bullard, E. D. Richards, L. C. Jackman, L. C. Coolidge,	213 "
" 8, West Medway. — Miss A. B. Adams,	27 "
" 9, " Mrs. H. E. Hixon, Mrs. M. F. Hixon,	116 "
Total,	811 "

FIRE DEPARTMENT.

ENGINEERS.

George R. Drake, W. H. Campsy, E. H. Tyler, T. M. Daniels, Daniel Hammond, R. K. Colcord.

ENGINES AND OFFICERS.

No. 1, Torrent, Henry Woodman, *Foreman ;* No. 2, Rapid, Geo. M. Farrington, *Foreman ;* No. 3, Union, Oliver Clark, *Foreman ;* No. 4, Niagara, Elihu Fuller, *Foreman ;* No. 5, Reserve, Sewall Clark, *Foreman.*

MILTON.

[*Incorporated May 7, 1662.*]

TOWN OFFICERS.

[Annual Meeting, March 6, 1876.]

Moderator. — Joseph McKean Churchill.
Town Clerk. — Henry B. Martin.
Selectmen, Assessors, Overseers of Poor, and Surveyors of Highways. — Samuel
   Babcock, Henry S. Russell, T. Edwin Ruggles.
Treasurer. — Charles Breck.
Collector. — Simeon Emerson.
Auditors. — Edward J. Kendall, Edward Cunningham.
Trustees of Cemetery. — Oliver W. Peabody, Robert M. Todd, Samuel Babcock,
   John Tolman, Albert K. Teele.
Fire-Wards. — William S. Leavitt, *Chief;* R. L. Chapman, David W. Tucker,
   Otis Skinner, John B. Badger, J. W. Bradlee, John H. Burt, Anthony
   Gardner, N. T. Davenport.
Constables. — Samuel C. Hebard, Jonas W. Jewett, C. F. Cook, E. F. Hopkins,
   Calvin Sanford, Elbridge Blackman, Joseph Noble.

VALUATION AND TAX.

Valuation of real est.,	$3,267,800 00	Items of tax —	
" " personal est.,	4,626,500 00	State tax,	$7,704 00
		County tax,	6,343 79
Total valuation,	$7,894,300 00	Town grant,	37,156 21
Rate of tax,	$6.30 on $1,000	Total tax,	$51,204 00
Number of polls,	735		

APPROPRIATIONS.

Schools,	$12,000 00	Fire department,	$500 00
Highways, inc. Supt.'s salary,	10,000 00	Collection of taxes,	500 00
Town officers,	3,500 00	Interest,	500 00
Poor,	3,000 00	Printing and stationery,	400 00
Police,	2,000 00	Abatement of taxes,	300 00
Cemetery,	2,000 00	Decoration day,	100 00
Public library,	1,200 00		
Miscellaneous expenses,	1,000 00	Total,	$37,000 00

ASSETS AND LIABILITIES, MAY 1.

ASSETS.		LIABILITIES.	
School-houses,	$22,500 00	Trust funds,	$1,500 00
Public library,	10,000 00		
Other public buildings,	6,000 00		
Public grounds and park,	6,000 00		
Cemeteries,	10,000 00		
Other real estate,	12,000 00		
Fire apparatus,	2,000 00		
Trust funds,	1,500 00		
Total,	$70,000 00		

PROPERTY EXEMPT FROM TAXATION.

First Congregational Society.— House and land,	$18,000 00
" Evangelical " " "	10,000 00
Second " " " "	7,000 00
Trustees of Milton Acadamy.— " "	12,000 00
Total,	$47,000 00

SCHOOL STATISTICS.

SCHOOL COMMITTEE.

Rev. Timothy F. Clary, *Chairman;* J. Walter Bradlee, *Secretary;* Jason Houghton, R. C. Watson, E. D. Wadsworth, Charles E. C. Breck.

SCHOOLS.

High. — Mr. S. D. Hunt, Miss M. E. Wright,	31	scholars.
East, Grammar Department. — Mr. O. A. Andrews,	26	"
East, Intermediate Department. — Miss G. F. Penniman,	43	"
East, Primary Department. — Miss A. G. Mayhew,	49	"
Pleasant St. — Miss A. G. Pierce,	39	"
North, Grammar Department. — Mr. P. A. Gay,	21	"
North, Primary Department. — Miss Hattie Hutchinson,	39	"
Centre, Grammar Department. — Mr. C. Boylston,	28	"
Centre, Primary Department. — Miss E. C. Emerson,	35	"
South, Mixed Department. — Miss Fannie G. Morse,	26	"
West, Grammar Department. — Mr. J. W. Clark,	46	"
West, Primary Department. — Miss L. W. Vose,	42	"
Total,	425	"

NEEDHAM.

[*Incorporated November 5, 1711, from part of Dedham.*]

TOWN OFFICERS.

[Annual Meeting, March 6, 1876.]

Moderator. — Emery Grover.

Town Clerk and Treasurer. — Solomon Flagg (27th year of service).

Selectmen, Overseers of the Poor, and Auditors. — Joseph E. Fiske, James Mackintosh, Mark Lee.

Assessors. — Charles C. Greenwood, Mark Lee, Lyman K. Putney.

Collector. — Dexter Kingsbury.

Superintendent of Roads. — Augustus Stevens.

Town Agents. — Galen Orr, George K. Daniell.

Fire-Wards. — William S. Ware, Andrew Burnett, George H. Gay, William H. Mackintosh, Marshall Newell, T. W. Ferguson, John Dunn, Bill Burrill, 2d, Hugh McLeod, William E. Hurd, Henry Blackman, A. W. Mann, Israel Hunting.

Constables. — Thomas W. Ferguson, John Purcell, Sylvester McIntosh, George E. Eaton, W. H. Norton, Wm. G. Hart.

VALUATION AND TAX.

Valuation of real estate, $3,849,193 00
" " personal est., 998,743 00

Total valuation, $4,847,936 00

Rate of tax, $11.50 on $1.000
Number of polls, 1,389

Items of tax —
State tax, $4,392 00
County tax, 3,616 55
Town grant, 50,520 45

Total tax, $58,529 00

APPROPRIATIONS.

Schools,	$13,500 00	Miscellaneous expenses,	$1,200 00
Highways,	8,000 00	Printing,	600 00
Interest,	5,500 00	Salary Collector of Taxes,	600 00
New school-house at Charles		Extinguishing fires,	500 00
River Village,	5,000 00	Abatement of taxes,	400 00
Incidentals for schools,	3,300 00	Fire-proof safe in Town	
Poor,	3,000 00	house,	300 00
Town officers,	3,000 00	Removing snow,	200 00
Discount on taxes,	3,000 00	Purchase of banner used at	
Lyon's bridge (new),	*2,700 00	Lexington, April 19, 1875,	122 00
Improvements on certain			
streets,	1,375 00	Total,	$52,297 00

ASSETS AND LIABILITIES, MAY 1.

ASSETS.		LIABILITIES.	
School-houses,	$94,500 00	School-houses,	$51,725 00
Other real estate,	16,800 00	Other debts,	23,025 00
Other assets,	5,800 00		
		Total,	$74,750 00
Total,	$117,100 00		

PROPERTY EXEMPT FROM TAXATION.

First Parish. — Meeting-house,	$2,500 00	
Land,	400 00	
		$2,900 00
Wellesley Cong. Society. — Meeting-house,	$20,000 00	
Land,	1,600 00	
		21,600 00
Grantville Society. — Meeting-house,	$5,000 00	
Land,	1,000 00	
		6,000 00
Evangelical Ch. and Soc. — Meeting-house,	$2,250 00	
Land,	500 00	
		2,750 00
First Baptist Society. — Meeting-house,	$7,000 00	
Land,	1,900 00	
		8,900 00
Unitarian Soc. of Grantville. — Chapel,	$2,250 00	
Land,	800 00	
		3,050 00

* $6,000 appropriated for bridge : $3,300 to be taken from other sources, $2,700 only to be assessed.

Methodist Epis. Ch. Soc. — Meeting-house (unfinished), $4,500 00
          Land,   600 00
                                           $5,100 00
St. John's Church, Catholic. — Meeting-house, $10,000 00
          Stable,   600 00
          Land,   1,600 00
                                        12.200 00

   Total valuation of church property, $62,500 00

Wellesley College. — College buildings, $650,000 00
       7 dwelling houses,   13,100 00
       Gas-house,   1,500 00
       Stone building,   500 00
       5 barns,   8,150 00
       Greenhouses,   3,500 00
       320¼ acres land,   44,000 00
                                      720,750 00
   Personal estate, consisting of library, furniture
      in college buildings, neat atctle, etc.,   56,963 00
Appleton Temporary Home. — Buildings, $12,000 00
          Land,   4,500 00
                                      16,500 00
      Household furniture and library,   4,500 00

   Total valuation of property used for educational and charitable
    purposes, exempt from taxation, $861,213 00

SCHOOL STATISTICS.

SCHOOL COMMITTEE.

Joseph E. Fiske, *Chairman;* Charlotte Kingsbury, *Secretary;* Solomon Flagg, Mrs. Harriet C. May, Emory Grover, Edward La Croix.

SCHOOLS.

East High. — Miss F. A. Caldwell,   35 scholars.
West High. — Mr. C. E. Washburn,   36   "
Plain Grammar. — Miss Edith Phillips,   36   "
Plain Intermediate. — Miss Belle Jenkins,   42   "
Plain Primary. — Miss Sarah J. Pickering,   36   "
Highlandville Grammar. — Mrs. E. J. Coggins,   36   "
Highlandville Intermediate. — Miss A. L. Bowen,   27   "
Highlandville Primary. — Miss E. B. Richardson,   40   "
Highlandville Sub-Primary. — Miss Ida, L. Morton,   29   "
Centre Grammar. — Miss Isabella Kinnee,   23   "
Centre Primary. — Miss A. E. Hoffsees,   27   "
East Grammar. — Miss Mary Longfellow,   26   "
East Primary. — Miss Eunice Guptill,   43   "
North Grammar. — Miss Nellie S. Watkins   25   "
North Intermediate. — Miss Mary E. Mason,   34   "
North Primary. — Miss Alice Phillips,   32   "
Grantville Grammar. — Miss Mary Field,   23   "
Grantville Primary. — Miss Ella F. Bass,   50   "

Wellesley Grammar — Miss C. E. Cameron,	20 scholars.
Wellesley Intermediate. — Miss Mary L. Clarke,	22 "
Wellesley Primary. — Miss Elmira Townsend,	44 "
Unionville Mixed. — Miss Fannie E. Kingsbury,	20 "
C. R. Village Mixed. — Miss Annie S. Ball,	33 "
Greendale Mixed. — Miss Fannie Longfellow,	18 "
Total,	747 "

NORFOLK.

[*Incorporated Feb.* 23, 1870, *from parts of Wrentham, Franklin, Medway and Walpole.*]

TOWN OFFICERS.

[Annual Meeting, March 6, 1876.]

Moderator. — Daniel J. Holbrook.
Town Clerk. — Silas E. Fales.
Selectmen and Overseers of Poor. — Levi Mann, Henry Trowbridge, Henry K. W. Pond.
Assessors. — Horatio Kingsbury, Saul B. Scott, Andrew R. Jones.
Treasurer. — Henry Southland.
Collector of Taxes. — William Ward.
Surveyors of Highways. — Jacob F. Pond, Walter H. Fisher, Nathaniel D. Kingsbury, Andrew R. Jones.
Constables. — Asa B. Ware, James A. Guild.

VALUATION AND TAX.

Valuation of real est.,	$351,975 00	Items of tax —	
" " personal est.,	74,525 00	State tax,	$558 00
		County tax,	459 48
Total valuation,	$426,500 00	Town tax,	5,999 52
Rate of tax,	$16.00 on $1,000	Total tax,	$7,017 00
No. of polls,	256		

APPROPRIATIONS.

General expenses,	$2,800 00	Roads and bridges,	$800 00
Schools,	1,400 00		
Poor,	1,000 00	Total,	$6,000 00

ASSETS AND LIABILITIES, MAY 1.

ASSETS.		LIABILITIES.	
School-houses,	$4,465 00	Debt,	$2,500 00
Other assets,	300 00		
Total,	$4,765 00		

PROPERTY EXEMPT FROM TAXATION.

Two meeting-houses and land, $4,500 00

SCHOOL STATISTICS.

SCHOOL COMMITTEE.

Sidon Adams, Silas E. Fales, Sylvester F. Bucklin.

SCHOOLS.

Centre. — Messrs. J. Webster Coombs, Edward J. Keith, Walter
N. Smith, Miss Emma C. Ware, one term each, 36 scholars.
North. — Miss Malvina V. Scott, one term; Miss Addie E. Win-
ship, two terms, 25 "
Felting Mills. — Mr. Edward J. Keith, one term; Miss Malvina
V. Scott, two terms, 31 "
River End. — Mrs. Ednah M. Guild, 23 "
Pondville. — Miss Ella E. Fales, one term; Miss Gifford, two
terms, 11 "

Total, 126 "

NORWOOD.

[*Incorporated Feb. 23, 1872, from parts of Dedham and Walpole.*]

TOWN OFFICERS.

[Annual Meeting, March 6, 1876.]

Moderator. — Warren E. Locke.
Town Clerk. — Francis Tinker.
Selectmen, Assessors, Overseers of Poor, and Board of Health. — Samuel E. Pond,
Tyler Thayer, George H. Morse.
Treasurer. — L. Waldo Bigelow.
Collector of Taxes. — Caleb Ellis.
Auditors. — Willard Gay, George Everett, William C. Fisher.
Highway Surveyors. — William C. Fisher, Isaac Ellis, Joseph W. Roby, Nathan
A. Johnson, Albert Dean, George H. Morse, Sylvester Hawes.
Constables. — Samuel Howard, Sumner Bagley, George E. Draper.

VALUATION AND TAX.

Valuation of real est.,	$1,380.119 00	Items of tax —	
" " personal est.,	444,172 00	State tax,	$1,692 00
		County tax,	1.393 96
Total valuation,	$1,824,291 00	Town grant,	19,000 00
		Overlayings,	420 04
Rate of tax,	$11.70 on $1,000		
Number of polls,	582	Total tax,	$22,506 00

APPROPRIATIONS.

Schools,	$6,500 00	Reservoir on R.R. avenue,	$300 00
Highways,	3,500 00	Bridge over Hawes brook,	300 00
Poor,	1.700 00	Land damages on Dean street,	225 00
Town officers,	1.000 (0	Retaining-wall on Walpole st.,	205 00
Fire department,	750 00	Lighting street lamps,	200 00
Walpole street,	600 00	Retaining-wall on Wash'gton st.,	200 00
Washington st. land damages,	550 00	Printing and stationery,	150 00
Removing snow,	500 00	Retaining-wall on Walpole st.,	95 00
Incidental expenses,	500 00	Addition to salary of Collector,	75 00
Widening Wilson street,	500 00	Cemetery,	50 00
Widening Dean street,	400 00		
Bal. land damages, Walpole st.,	400 00	Total,	$19,000 00
Public library,	300 00		

ASSETS AND LIABILITIES, MAY 1.

ASSETS.		LIABILITIES.	
School-houses,	$15,000 00	Trust funds,	$6,000 00
Public library,	1.250 00		
Real estate,	100 00		
Fire apparatus,	4,000 00		
Trust funds,	6,000 00		
Total,	$26,350 00		

PROPERTY EXEMPT FROM TAXATION.

Universalist Society.—	Personal, $1,000;	real, $15,000,	$16,000 00
Baptist	"	"	500;	"	9,000,	9,500 00
St. Catherine's (R. Catholic) Society.—	"	300;	"	7,000,	7,300 00
Congregational	"	"	500;	"	4,100,	4,600 00
School-houses,						6,500 00
Total,						$43,900 00

SCHOOL STATISTICS.

SCHOOL COMMITTEE.

Dr. Francis M. Cragin, *Chairman;* Samuel E. Pond, *Secretary;* Rev. Joseph P. Bixby.

SCHOOLS.

Everett, High School Department. — Horace T. Atwood, *Principal:* Miss Marion Endicott, *Assistant,*   41 scholars.

Everett Grammar. — Miss Sarah P. Hamilton,	39 "
Everett First Intermediate. — Miss S. Louisa Rhodes,	49 "
Everett Second Intermediate. — Miss Maria L. Wheelock,	48 "
Everett First Primary — Miss Carrie M. Morse,	49 "
Everett Second Primary. — Miss A. Elizabeth Park,	52 "
Balch Grammar. — Miss Millie J. Blaisdell,	26 "
Balch Intermediate. — Miss Viola F. Littlefield,	33 "
Railroad Avenue Primary. —Miss Abbie A. White,	48 "
Total,	385 "

QUINCY.

[*Incorporated Feb.* 23, 1792, *from North Precinct of Braintree.*]

TOWN OFFICERS.

[Annual Meeting, March 6, 1876.]

Moderator. — John Quincy Adams.
Town Clerk. — George L. Gill.
Selectmen, Assessors, Overseers of Poor, and Surveyors of Highways. — John Q.
A. Field, Edmund B. Taylor, Henry F. Barker.
Treasurer. — Horace B. Spear.
Auditors. — William B. Wooster, Edward B. Souther, J. P. Jordan, Charles H.
Porter, H. A. Keith.
Constables. — E. H. Richardson, Charles H. S. Newcomb, William C. Seelye,
Levi Stearns, Edw. A. Spear, Alonzo Glines, Samuel T. Allen, W. M.
French, Benj. Watson, Charles A. Follett, Leon C. Badger, Geo. H. Locke,
George B. Pray, Joseph T. French.

VALUATION AND TAX.

Valuation of real estate,	$5,745,180 00	Items of tax —	
" " person'l est.,	1,787,965 00	State tax,	$7,020 00
		County tax,	5,780 56
Total valuation,	$7,533,145 00	Town grant,	97,229 44
Rate of tax,	$14.00 on $1,000	Total tax,	$110,030 00
Number of polls,	2,283		

APPROPRIATIONS.

Schools,	$25,000 00	Removing snow and misc.	
Highways,	8,000 00	street expenses,	$1,000 00
Interest on debt,	6,500 00	Mount Wollaston Cemetery,	1,000 00
Poor,	6,000 00	Hose-carriage,	800 00
Discount and abatement of		Fourth of July celebration,	600 00
taxes,	5,000 00	Fire dept., deficiency of last	
Fire department,	4,500 00	year,	500 00
Alteration of Coddington		Repairs of Town buildings,	500 00
school building,	3,500 00	Survey of bounds of high-	
Incidental expenses of schools,	3,225 00	ways, etc.,	400 00
Public library,	3,200 00	Safe for records,	400 00
Street lights,	2,800 00	Copying old records,	250 00
Town officers,	2,750 00	Expenses under vagrant law,	200 00
Miscellaneous street ex-		Lawsuit,	200 00
penses,	2,480 00	Decoration day,	200 00
Superintendent of Schools,	2,000 00	Old cemetery,	100 00
Miscellaneous town expenses,	2,000 00	Reservoir,	75 00
New streets at Wollaston			
Heights,	1,850 00	Total,	$86,530 00
Bridges,	1,500 00		

ASSETS AND LIABILITIES, MAY 1.

ASSETS.		LIABILITIES.	
School-houses,	$76,000 00	Trust funds,	$82,000 00
Public library,	5,000 00	Other debts,	58,299 00
Other public buildings,	30,000 00		
Cemeteries,	20,000 00	Total,	$140,299 00
Other real estate,	10,000 00		
Fire apparatus,	5,000 00		
Trust funds,	82,000 00		
Other assets,	7,000 00		
Total,	$235,000 00		

PROPERTY EXEMPT FROM TAXATION.

Trustees of Woodward School Fund. — Personal,	$61,000 00
National Sailors' Home. — Personal, $1,200; real, $33,000,	34,200 00
Sailors' Snug Harbor. — " $500; " $33,250,	33,750 00
Adams Temple and School Fund,	28,000 00
Coddington School Fund (towns of Braintree and Randolph),	1,000 00
Catholic Society. — Land and buildings,	32,000 00
Unitarian " " "	27,000 00
Orthodox " " "	20,000 00
Episcopal " " "	13,000 00
Roman Catholic Society. — " "	7,000 00
Universalist " " "	6,500 00
Congregational " Wollaston. — " "	6,400 00
Baptist " " " "	6,000 00
Methodist " Quincy Point. — " "	5,500 00
Methodist Episcopal Society, " "	3,800 00
Methodist " Wollaston. — " "	3,400 00
Quincy Reform Club. — " "	2,300 00
Total,	$290,850 00

SCHOOL STATISTICS.

SCHOOL COMMITTEE.

John Quincy Adams, *Chairman ;* James Slade, *Secretary;* Charles F. Adams, Jr., Edwin W. Marsh, Charles L. Badger, Dr. William B. Duggan. *Superintendent.* — Francis W. Parker.

SCHOOLS.

High. — Harrison A. Keith, *Principal;* Evelyn L. Holbrook, *Assistant,*   64 scholars.

Adams. — George P. Aldrich, *Principal;* Misses Georgie Patterson, Eliza C. Sheehan, Mary L. Flint, Esther B. Hall,* Annie C. French, Hattie F. Thayer,* Mary M. Devlin, Lizzie A. Williams, Charlotte M. Frost, *Assistants,*   421 "

Coddington. — J. Henry Wardwell,* Seth S. Crocker, *Principals;* Misses Ellen McKean, Mary E. Dearborn, Mary E. Dinegan, Elizabeth E. Morse, Julia E. Underwood, Lydia L. Follett, *Assistants,*   216 "

* Resigned. Taught part of year.

Quincy. — Sylvester Brown, *Principal;* Misses Mary W. Woods, Elgina M. Plummer, Cora I. Young, *Assistants,*   198 scholars.
Washington. — I. Freeman Hall, *Principal;* Misses Mary Marden, Jennie Bates,* Hattie G. Piper,* Ella M. Ames, S. Addie Souther, Caroline E. Morse, *Assistants,*   244   "
Willard. — Henry F. Woodman, *Principal;* Misses Vessie Woodman,* Kate T. Clark,* Mary T. W. Dewing, Mary L. Pierce, Emily A. Bosworth, Emeline A. Newcomb, Nellie Fegan, Mary A. Spear, Katie Desmond, *Assistants,*   485   "
Wollaston. — Miss Harriet H. Morse, *Principal;* Misses Cora F. Nichols, Belle A. Thomas, *Assistants,*   126   "

Total,   1,784   "

FIRE DEPARTMENT.

ENGINEERS.

E. A. Spear, *Chief;* J. H. Elcock, *Clerk;* A. M. Litchfield, J. W. Hall, H. M. Federhen, J. T. Penniman.

ENGINES AND OFFICERS.

Tiger, No. 2 (South Quincy). — *Foreman,* G. H. Osborn; *Clerk,* A. S. Litchfield; *Steward,* Andrew W. Dunbar.
Granite, No. 3 (West Quincy). — *Foreman,* Peter F. Farrell; *Clerk,* Otis Thayer; *Steward,* J. Lyons.
Vulture, No. 4 (Quincy Point). — *Foreman,* Charles F. Lapham; *Clerk,* Waldo N. Ford; *Steward,* Waldin Hall.
Hook-and-Ladder, No. 1 (South Quincy).— *Foreman and Steward,* J. M. Glover; *Clerk,* J. A. Beard.
W. M. French Hose Co. (Sea St.) — *Foreman,* J. E. Maxim; *Clerk,* E. W. Underwood; *Steward,* M. M. C. Chubbuck.
Chemical Engine Co. (Wollaston Heights). — *Foreman,* John M. Call; *Clerk,* Seth F. Dame; *Steward,* Albert G. Olney.

RANDOLPH.

[Incorporated March 9, 1793, from part of Braintree.]

TOWN OFFICERS.

[Annual Meeting, April 3, 1876.]

Moderator. — Daniel Howard.
Town Clerk and Treasurer. — Hiram C. Alden.
Selectmen, Assessors, and Overseers of Poor. — John T. Flood, Seth Mann, 2d, Sidney French.
Collector. — Edson M. Roel.

* Resigned. Taught part of year.

Trustees Stetson School Fund. — Daniel Howard, Charles Howard, Dr. T. T.
Cushman; Seth Turner, *Secretary of Board.*
Auditors. — Frank Morton, Franklin Porter, Edgar Howard.
Highway Surveyors. — J. H. Wales, P. E. Wilbur, Jedediah French, J. G.
Abbott, Jackson Belcher, M. P. Pike, Edson M. Roel.
Constables. — William H. Warren, John Long, T. Farrell, H. H. Francis, J. C.
Neary, J. Frizell, George Wilder.

VALUATION AND TAX.

Vaulation of real est.,	$1,453.900 00	Items of tax —	
" " personal est.,	650,610 00	State tax,	$2,466 00
		County tax,	2,030 60
Total valuation,	$2,104,510 00	Town grant,	24,396 40
Rate of tax,	$12.60 on $1.000	Total tax,	$28,893 00
Number of polls,	1,188		

APPROPRIATIONS.

Town expenses, inc. town officers,		Stetson school,	$1,000 00
poor and incidentals,	$8.000 00	Centennial celebration,	300 00
Schools,	7,600 00	Decoration day,	100 00
Town debt,	3,000 00		
Highways,	3,000 00	Total,	$25,400 00
Fire department,	2,400 00		

ASSETS AND LIABILITIES, MAY 1.

ASSETS.		LIABILITIES.	
School-houses,	$32.950 00	Trust funds,	$19,100 00
Public library,	45,000 00	Other debts,	23,720 00
Other public buildings,	32,700 00		
Fire apparatus,	2,125 00	Total,	$42,820 00
Trust funds,	19,100 00		
Total,	$131,875 00		

PROPERTY EXEMPT FROM TAXATION.

Turner Library,	$4,000 00
First Baptist Church. — Building and land,	2,500 00
" Cong. " " "	2,000 00
St. Mary's Catholic Church. — Building and land,	2,000 00
Methodist Chapel, Tower Hill. — Building and land,	1,000 00
Total,	$11,500 00

SCHOOL STATISTICS.

SCHOOL COMMITTEE.

Rev. James E. O'Brien, *Chairman;* Winslow Battles, *Secretary;* Michael A.
Donovan.

SCHOOLS.

No. 1, *Ungraded.* — Miss Ellen Henny,	40 scholars.
No. 2, *Grammar.* — Mr. Thomas H. West,	46 "
" *Sub-Grammar.* — Miss Sarah E. Shankland,	40 "

No. 2, *First Intermediate.* — Miss Annie Veazie,	40	scholars.
" *First Primary.* — Miss Isabel G. Driscoll,	44	"
" *First Primary.* — Miss Mary Malloy,	44	"
" *Second Primary.* — Miss Mary E. Wren,	38	"
" *Third Primary.* — Miss Emma D. Stetson,	38	"
" *Fourth Primary.* — Miss Kate E. Sheridan,	40	"
No. 3, *Ungraded.* — Miss Annie M. Wilde,	48	"
No. 4, *Grammar.* — Miss M. A. N. Fuller,	38	"
" *Sub-Grammar.* — Miss Alice A. Smith,	36	"
" *First Primary.* — Miss Cora F. May,	28	"
" *Second Primary.* — Miss Antoinette T. Smith,	36	"
No. 5, *Ungraded.* — Miss Isabel C. Beal,	26	"
No. 6, *Sub-Grammar.* — Miss Sarah V. Wilde,	30	"
" *Primary.* — Miss Emma H. King,	28	"
Total,	640	"

Stetson School, under charge of Board of Trustees, consisting of Daniel Howard, Charles Howard, Dr. T. T. Cushman, and Seth Turner; Mr. V. H. Dean, *Principal*; Miss Minnie Jones, *Assistant*; 70 scholars.

FIRE DEPARTMENT.

ENGINEERS.

Levi Wilbur, *Chief;* Edward E. Lothrop, *Clerk;* Louis Gores, John Dooley, Jr.

ENGINES AND OFFICERS.

Independence No. 2. — *Foreman,* William Brennan; *Clerk,* Joseph Donovan; *Steward,* John B. McGrane.

Fearless No. 3. — *Foreman,* Myron W. Hollis; *Clerk,* Royal T. Mann; *Steward,* William A. English.

Fire King No. 5. — *Foreman,* James H. Wales; *Clerk,* Michael J. Green; *Steward,* John T. Cartwright.

Hook-and-Ladder No. 1. — *Foreman,* Charles A. Wales; *Clerk,* Weston P. Alden; *Steward,* John T. Cartwright.

SHARON.

[*Incorporated June* 20, 1765.]

TOWN OFFICERS.

[Annual Meeting, April 3, 1876.]

Moderator. — Charles D. Hixon.
Town Clerk and Treasurer. — Otis Johnson.
Selectmen, Assessors, and Overseers of the Poor. — Lewis W. Morse, William C. Myrick, Benjamin Gannett.
Auditors. — Sanford Waters Billings, William R. Mann.

Collector of Taxes. — Sanford Waters Billings.

Highway Surveyors. — James II. McManies, George Richards, Oren J. Foster, Elbridge G. Harwood, Nathan Cobb, Abijah Tisdale, Warren M. Holmes, Oliver II. Whittemore, Edwin P. Davis, Robert Foreman, John B. Hearteg, Charles T. Howard, Leprelette Morse, Benjamin Rhoades, Charles A. Willett.

Trustees of Sharon Friend School Fund. — J. M. Bullard, D. W. Pettee, Benjamin Rhoades, George R. Mann, Charles T. Howard.

Trustees of Dorchester and Surplus Revenue School Fund. — Barnabas D. Capen, Lewis W. Morse.

Constables. — William Richards, Thomas Decatur.

VALUATION AND TAX.

Valuation of real estate,	$814,534 00	Items of tax —	
" " personal est.,	252,378 00	State tax,	$954 00
		County tax,	785 56
Total valuation,	$1,066,912 00	Town grant,	7,625 44
Rate of tax,	$8.00 on $1,000	Total tax,	$9,365 00
Number of polls,	417		

APPROPRIATIONS.

Current expenses and poor,	$2,500 00	School-houses,	$150 00
Schools,	1,800 00	Carpenter's road,	100 00
Highways and bridges,	1,500 00	Decoration day,	25 00
Interest,	1,000 00		
Text-books,	200 00	Total,	$7,275 00

ASSETS AND LIABILITIES, MAY 1.

ASSETS.		LIABILITIES.	
School-houses,	$10,540 00	Trust funds,	$5,360 00
Real estate,	4,400 00	Debt, including war debts,	11,415 00
Trust funds,	5,360 00		
Other assets,	3,000 00	Total,	$16,775 00
Total,	$23,300 00		

PROPERTY EXEMPT FROM TAXATION.

Orthodox Society. — Building, $5,000;		land, $500,			$5,500 00
Unitarian "	"	4,000;	"	1,000,	5,000 00
Baptist "	"	3,000;	"	250,	3,250 00
Rom. Cath. "	"	600;	"	100,	700 00
Bay-street "	Chapel and land.				200 00
Centre School-house. — Building, $4,000;		land, $1,000,			5,000 00
West "	"	2,100;	"	30,	2,130 00
South "	"	1,000;	"	20,	1,020 00
East "	"	1,900;	"	50,	1,950 00
North, "	"	1,000;	"	40,	1,040 00
Town farm. "	"	1,000;	"	2,500,	3,500 00
Total,					$29,290 00

STATISTICS. **41**

SCHOOL STATISTICS.

SCHOOL COMMITTEE.

John M. Bullard, *Chairman ;* Sanford Waters Billings, *Secretary and Treasurer;* Lewis W. Morse, George W. Capen, Mary L. Young, Darius W. Foss.

SCHOOLS.

Centre Grammar. — Willard A. Estey, *Principal ;* Misses Carrie
  A. Long and Lizzie B. Ladd, *Assistants,*   76 scholars.
Centre Primary. — Miss Mary L. Young,   47   "
North. — Miss Carrie E. Bullard,   22   "
South. — Miss Ella J. Howard,   24   "
East. — Miss Mary J. Gannett,   48   "
West. — Mr. Melville G. Smith,   43   "

    Total   260   "

STOUGHTON.

[Incorporated Dec. 22, 1726, from part of Dorchester.]

TOWN OFFICERS.

[Annual Meeting, March 13, 1876.]

Moderator. — George H. Goward.
Town Clerk. — Henry C. Kimball.
Selectmen, Assessors, and Overseers of Poor. — George Talbot, George W. Robbins, Newell S. Atwood.
Treasurer. — Charles Jones.
Auditors. — Jabez Talbot, Jr., Levi M. Flint, Adam Capen, Jr.
Board of Health. — Nath'l Wales, Simeon Tucker, W. E. C. Swan, Elisha Hawes, S. S. Gifford.
Collector. — M. H. Ballou.
Surveyors of Highways. — Nathaniel M. Warren, Isaac Blanchard.
Constables. — M. H. Ballou, Cornelius Gerry, Lysander Wood.

VALUATION AND TAX.

Valuation of real estate,	$1,774,200 00	Items of tax—	
" " personal est.,	684,850 00	State tax,	$3,760 00
		County tax,	2,564 16
Total valuation,	$2,459,050 00	Town tax,	35,812 84
Rate of tax,	$16.10 on $1,000		
Number of polls,	1,272	Total tax,	$42,137 00

APPROPRIATIONS.

Schools,	$12,000 00	Fire department,	$1,500 00
Interest and discount,	6,300 00	State aid,	1,500 00
Town debt,	5,000 00	Printing and stationery,	250 00
Roads and bridges,	4,000 00	Lock-up,	200 00
Poor,	3,000 00		
Miscellaneous,	2,000 00	Total,	$37,350 00
Town officers,	1,600 00		

ASSETS AND LIABILITIES.

ASSETS.		LIABILITIES.	
School-houses,	$54,200 00	Debts,	$30,335 00
Public library,	1,500 00		
Other public buildings,	3,000 00		
Real estate,	5,600 00		
Fire apparatus,	1,000 00		
Total,	$65,300 00		

PROPERTY EXEMPT FROM TAXATION.

Universalist Society. — Building and land,	$18,000 00
Cong. " " "	13,000 00
St. Michael " " "	12,000 00
Baptist " " "	10,500 00
Methodist " " "	10,000 00
St. Mary " " "	9,800 00
Methodist Society, North Stoughton. — Building and land,	3,000 00
Total,	$76,300 00

SCHOOL STATISTICS.

SCHOOL COMMITTEE.

Albert Johnson, *Chairman;* Samuel Paul, *Secretary;* William H. Tucker, Henry C. Kimball.

Superintendent. — Henry C. Kimball.

SCHOOLS.

High. — Mr. William E. Pulsifer, *Principal;* Miss Amelia M. Clifton, *Assistant,*	50	scholars.
Gifford Grammar. — Mr. Samuel S. Young, *Principal,*	36	"
Gifford Primary. — Miss Helen T. Littlefield,	53	"
Gifford Intermediate. — Miss Lucy A. Upham,	48	"
Gifford Sub-Grammar. — Miss Sophia H. French,	56	"
Smith — Miss Hattie F. Packard,	20	"
Adams Grammar. — Mr. Francis Capen,	42	"
Adams Primary. — Miss Alice A. Kimball,	51	"
Tolman. — Mr. Charles D. Capen,	37	"
Atherton. — Miss Alice Howard,	26	"
Park. — Miss Evelyn F. Penniman,	47	"
Dennis. — Miss Eliza Porter,	53	"
Drake Grammar. — Mr. Isaac Swan,	62	"
Drake Sub-Grammar. — Miss Rebecca F. Leach,	36	"
Drake First Intermediate. — Miss Sarah C. Tuttle,	44	"
Drake Second Intermediate. — Miss Abbie B. Bryden,	46	"
Drake First Primary. — Miss Jennie Curtis,	58	"
Drake Second Primary. — Miss Elizabeth Jones,	49	"
Centre Sub-Grammar. — Miss Azubah G. Capen,	41	"
Centre Intermediate. — Miss Margaret A. Jones,	48	"
Littlefield. — Miss Mary M. Brett,	61	"
Capen. — Miss Annie M. Page,	45	"
Total,	1,033	"

FIRE DEPARTMENT.

ENGINEERS.

Thomas W. Bright, *Chief;* Levi M. Flint, *Clerk;* Ezra Stearns, Henry Tucker, Patrick McPoland.

ENGINES AND OFFICERS.

Pacific No. 1. — *Foreman,* Ellis Drake; *Clerk,* Clarance Mead.   50 members.
Ocean No. 2. — *Foreman,* James Murphy; *Clerk,* Peter Jordan.   50 members.
Bay State No. 3. — Not fully organized.
Ocean Hose Co. — *Foreman,* Matthew O'Dea; *Clerk,* James Carroll.   8 members.
Washington Hook-and-Ladder Co. — *Foreman,* George W. Dutton; *Clerk,* Frank Hill.   15 members.

WALPOLE.

[*Incorporated Dec.* 10, 1724, *from part of Dedham.*]

TOWN OFFICERS.

[Annual Meeting, March 6, 1876.]

Moderator. — Samuel Allen.
Town Clerk. — George P. Morey.
Selectmen and Overseers of Poor. — Henry S. Clarke, James G. Scott, Henry E. Craig.
Assessors. — James G. Scott, Charles Hartshorn, Elbridge P. Boyden.
Treasurer. — Samuel Allen.
Auditors. — H. W. Tilton, George E. Craig, James N. Thompson.
Collector of Taxes. — Charles H. Prescott.
Highway Surveyors. — David Fisher, Luman Gay, Edwin Everett, Simon Gould, Lewis L. Bowker, Almond F. Boyden.
Constables. — Isaac H. Bullard, Nathaniel Bird, Clinton Bagley.

VALUATION AND TAX.

		Items of tax —	
Valuation of real estate,	$1,094,951 00	State tax,	$1,494 00
" " personal est.,	282,537 00	County tax,	1,230 22
		Town grant,	14,500 15
Total valuation,	$1,377,488 00	Overlayings,	481 63
Rate of tax,	$12.00 on $1.000		
Number of polls,	588	Total tax,	$17,706 00

APPROPRIATIONS.

Schools,	$6,000 00	Public library,	$485 00
Support of poor and other town charges,	4,000 00	Copying records,	50 00
Roads and bridges,	3,500 00	Total,	$14,735 00
Hearse,	700 00		

ASSETS AND LIABILITIES, MAY 1.

ASSETS.		LIABILITIES.
School-houses,	$18,000 00	None.
Public library,	500 00	
Real estate,	3,000 00	
Total,	$21,500 00	

PROPERTY EXEMPT FROM TAXATION.

School-houses, furniture and land,		$18,000 00
Orthodox Society. — House,	$15,000 00	
Furniture,	1,500 00	
Land,	500 00	
		17,000 00
Unitarian Society. — House,	$12,000 00	
Furniture,	1,000 00	
Land,	1,000 00	
		14,000 00
Meth. Epis. Society (So. Walpole). — House,	$5,000 00	
Furniture,	500 00	
Land,	300 00	
		5,800 00
Roman Catholic Society. — House,	$5,000 00	
Furniture,	500 00	
Land,	300 00	
		5,800 00
Almshouse. — House,	$3,000 00	
Per. property at same,	1,500 00	
		4,500 00
Total,		$65,100 00

SCHOOL STATISTICS.

SCHOOL COMMITTEE.

Andrew Washburn, *Acting Chairman ;* Mrs. M. M. Allen, *Secretary ;* Loring Johnson, John N. Smith, Mrs. M. B. Johnson, Miss Mary R. Bird.

SCHOOLS.

High. — Mr. A. H. K. Blood, *Principal ;* Miss Alice E. Bentley, Assistant,	40 scholars.
Centre Grammar. — Miss Mary Morey,	50 "
Centre Intermediate. — Miss Lucy D. Morton,	35 "
Centre Primary. — Miss J. Ella Bacon,	56 "
East Grammar. — Miss Frances N. Perkins,	25 "
East Primary. — Miss Alice A Polleys,	30 "
South Grammar. — Miss L. A. Lewis,	27 "
South Primary. — Miss Lillie J. Smith,	28 "
North (not graded). — Miss Charlotte E. Eaton,	40 "
West (not graded). — Miss Winifred O'Brien,	10 "
Total,	341 "

WEYMOUTH.

[Incorporated September 2, 1635.]

TOWN OFFICERS.

[Annual Meeting, March 6, 1876.]

Moderator. — Noah Vining.

Town Clerk, — Francis Ambler.

Selectmen and Overseers of the Poor. — Noah Vining, John W. Bartlett, Thomas H. Humphrey, Francis Ambler, William Nash.

Assessors. — Noah Vining, Elias Richards, Cornelius T. Robbins, William W. Raymond, Oran White.

Treasurer and Collector. — Oran White.

Auditors. — Elias S. Beals, Thomas B. Porter, Elias Richards.

Fire-Wards. — Seth W. Bicknell, Charles Chubbuck, Joseph Peaks, Robert McIntosh.

Surveyors of Highways, — George Bennett, John H. Thompson, John R. H. Williams, James Moore, Avery S. Howe.

Constables. — R. N. Cushing, Wilmot Cleverly, Andrew J. Garey, G. W. French, B. H. Everett, John H. Whelan, Geo. W. White, Jr., B. F. Robinson, S. M. Holbrook, Robert Coleraine, I. N. Tirrell, C. C. Tinkham, Freeman B. Vinson, Franklin Whitten, Noble Morse.

VALUATION AND TAX.

Valuation of real est.,	$3,673,246 00	Items of tax —	
" " personal est.,	1,917,914 00	State tax,	$6,084 00
		County tax,	5,009 82
Total,	$5,591,160 00	Town grant,	55,962 18
Rate of tax,	$11.00 on $1,000		
Number of polls,	2,775	Total tax,	$67,056 00

APPROPRIATIONS.

Schools,	$22,500 00	Repairs of school-house,	$1,500 00
Highways and bridges,	8,000 00	Miscellaneous expenses,	1,200 00
Poor,	8,000 00	Superintendent of schools,	1,100 00
Interest,	4,000 00	Printing,	600 00
Town officers,	2,900 00	Decoration day,	300 00
Abatement and discount on taxes,	2,500 00	Total,	$54,600 00
New school-house at Weymouth Neck,	2,000 00		

ASSETS AND LIABILITIES, MAY 1.

ASSETS.		LIABILITIES.	
School-houses,	$113,000 00	School-houses,	$27,892 00
Other public buildings,	19,500 00	Other debts,	16,000 00
Other real estate,	5,500 00		
Fire apparatus,	9,000 00	Total,	$43,892 00
Other assets,	5,055 00		
Total,	$152,055 00		

PROPERTY EXEMPT FROM TAXATION.

Estimated value of school-houses and lots,		$113,000 00
" " " Almshouse and farm, 60 acres land,		12,000 00
Church of the Sacred Heart. — Church,	$28,000 00	
Land, ¼ acre,	2,000 00	
Organ,	100 00	
		30,100 00
Union Congregation, S.W. — Church,	$24,000 00	
Land, 1 acre,	2,500 00	
Organ, etc.,	2,500 00	
		29,000 00
Second Cong. Parish, S.W. — Church,	$22,000 00	
Land, 1¼ acre,	3,000 00	
Organ, etc.,	2,000 00	
		27,000 00
Catholic Church, E.W. — Church,	$18,000 00	
Land, 60 rods,	400 00	
		18,400 00
Methodist Church, E.W. — Church,	$14,000 00	
Land, ¾ acre,	1,500 00	
Organ, etc.,	2,500 00	
		18,000 00
Congregational Church, E.W. — Church,	$11,000 00	
Land, ½ acre,	1,000 00	
Organ, etc.,	1,600 00	
		16,600 00
Baptist Church. — Church,	$12,000 00	
Land, ¼ acre,	800 00	
Organ, etc.,	1,800 00	
		14,600 00
Pilgrim Church, N.W. — Church,	$10,000 00	
Land, ½ acre,	700 00	
Organ, etc.,	1,000 00	
		11,700 00
Catholic Church, S.W. — Church,	$10,000 00	
Land, 1 acre,	1,000 00	
Organ,	300 00	
		11,300 00
Second Universalist Church, S. W. — Church,	$8,000 00	
Land, ½ acre,	1,500 00	
Organ, etc.,	1,800 00	
		11,300 00
First Universalist Church. — Church,	$7,000 00	
Land, ¼ acre,	1,500 00	
Organ, etc.,	1,200 00	
		9,700 00
First Parish Church, N.W. — Church,	$8,000 00	
Land, ½ acre,	500 00	
Organ, etc.,	1,000 00	
		9,500 00

Universalist Church, N.W. — Church,	$3,300 00	
Land, 40 rods,	400 00	
Organ,	400 00	
		$4,100 00
Episcopal Church. — Church,	$2,500 00	
Land, ¼ acre,	500 00	
Organ,	400 00	
		3,400 00
Agricultural and Industrial Society. — Hall,	$2.000 00	
Land, 33 acres,	3,000 00	
		5,000 00
Pratt & Herring School funds,	$10,000 00	
		10,000 00
Total,		$354,700 00

SCHOOL STATISTICS.

SCHOOL COMMITTEE.

Dr. C. C. Tower, *Chairman;* Mrs. Elizabeth C. Hawes, *Secretary;* Henry Dyer, James Humphrey, John H. Stetson, Samuel W. Reed.
Superintendent, F. B. Gamwell.

SCHOOLS.

Ward One.

Athens Grammar. — Mr. Edward N. Dyer,	36	scholars.
Athens Intermediate. — Miss Mary L. Ells,	50	"
Athens Primary. — Miss Mabel F. Harlow,	58	"
Adams Grammar. — Miss Eliza French,	30	"
Adams Intermediate. — Miss Louie Briggs,	30	"
River-street Intermediate. — Miss Clarabelle Pratt,	30	"

Ward Two.

Commercial-street Upper Grammar. — Mr. Lucius Brown, *Principal;* Miss Martha J. Hawes, *Assistant,*	60	"
Commercial-street Lower Grammar — Miss Ellen G. Parrott,	40	"
Commercial-street Primary — Miss Josephine Raymond,	40	"
Grant-street Primary. — Miss Ella M. Burgess,	42	"
High-street Lower Intermediate. — Miss Lizzie R. Healey,	40	"
High-street Primary. — Miss Carrie L. Farren,	51	"
Middle-street Intermediate. — Miss Hattie J. Farren,	50	"
Middle-street Primary. — Mrs. A. F. Gardner,	64	"
Pleasant-street Intermediate. — Miss Abbie A. Burrill,	50	"
Pleasant-street Primary. — Miss Annie H. Vining,	65	"
School-street Upper Intermediate. — Miss Marianna Holbrook,	50	"

Ward Three.

North High. — Mr. Geo. W. Shaw, *Principal;* Miss Sarah B. Goodwin, *Assistant,*	65	"
Broad-street Lower Intermediate. — Miss Emma F. Parker,	45	"
Broad-street Upper Primary. — Miss Hannah E. Ward,	50	"

Mt. Pleasant Upper Grammar. — J. W. Armington,   38 scholars.
Mt. Pleasant Middle Grammar. — Miss Nettie W. Knights,   36 "
Mt. Pleasant Lower Grammar. — Miss Carrie A. Blanchard,   42 "
Mt. Pleasant Upper Intermediate. — Miss Abbie L. Loud,   54 "
Perkins Middle Primary. — Miss Mary L. Hunt,   45 "
Perkins Lower Primary. — Miss Clara F. Perry,   55 "
Tremont Middle Intermediate. — Mrs. Flora A. Tilden,   50 "

Ward Four.

Main-street Grammar. — Miss S. L. Vining,   32 "
Main-street Intermediate. — Miss Maria C. Holbrook,   50 "
Main-street Primary. — Mrs. Ellen J. French,   33 "
Pratt Intermediate, Pleasant street. — Miss Sarah E. Spilstead,   50 "
Pratt Grammar, Pleasant street. — Mr. Geo. C. Torrey, *Prin-*
     cipal; Miss Lizzie Dyer, Assistant,   60 "
Washington-street Intermediate. — Miss Ellena S. Spilstead,   60 "

Ward Five.

South High. — Mr. Geo. B. Vose, *Principal; Miss Alice R.*
     Rogers, *Assistant,*   65 "
Central-street Lower Grammar. — Miss Lizzie C. Whitman,   40 "
Central-street Upper Intermediate. — Miss S. C. Vining,   50 "
Central-street Lower Intermediate. — Mrs. Maria A. Morrell,   50 "
Central-street Primary. — Mrs. S. J. Rogers,   42 "
Pond-street Intermediate. — Miss Maria Torrey,   40 "
Randolph-street Intermediate. — Miss Emily V. White,   25 "
Torrey-street Upper Grammar. — Mr. Louis A. Cook, *Principal;*
     Miss Mary Logue, *Assistant,*   55 "
Union-street Intermediate. — Mrs. Emma J. Smith,   35

          Total,   1,953 "

FIRE DEPARTMENT.

WEYMOUTH FIRE DISTRICT.

Engineers. — Charles E. Bicknell, *Chief;* Herbert L. White, William S. Wallace, James T. Pease, John H. R. Williams.
Amazon No. 2. — Gustavus Leach, *Foreman;* F. M. Drown, *1st Assistant;* L. N. White, *2d Assistant;* Darius Smith, *Clerk;* W. F. Leach, *Steward.*   60 men.

SOUTH WEYMOUTH FIRE DISTRICT.

Engineers. — Alvah Raymond, Jr., *Chief;* William H. Hosking, J. M. Whitcomb, William Nash.
Conqueror Engine Company. — George W. Bates, *Foreman;* Franklin Derby, *1st Assistant;* Adson H. Belcher, *2d Assistant;* Noah F. Vining, *Clerk.*   50 men.
Extinguisher Engine Company. — Walter H. Joy, *Foreman;* W. D. Lovell, *Clerk.*
Hook-and-Ladder Company. — William H. Bates, *Foreman.*

WRENTHAM.

[*Incorporated October* 15, 1673.]

TOWN OFFICERS.

[Annual Meeting, March 6, 1876.]

Moderator. — Abraham W. Harris.
Town Clerk. — Samuel Warner. (22d year of service.)
Selectmen and Overseers of the Poor. — George M. Warren, George Sheldon, Harvey B. Coleman.
Assessors. — Gardner H. Starkey, Lowell R. Blake, J. S. Clarke.
Treasurer. — F. N. Plimpton.
Collector of Taxes. — George W. Porter.
Surveyors of Highways. — Marcellus D. Hawes, Horace A. Pond, James W. White, Lowell R. Blake, G. Hartshorne Fisher, John F. Coleman, Gardner H. Starkey.
Constable. — Alonzo Cook.

VALUATION AND TAX.

Valuation of real est.,	$985,093 00	
" " per. est.,	185,479 00	
Total valuation,	$1,170,572 00	
Rate of tax,	$14.50 on $1,000	
Number of polls,	606	

Items of tax —
State tax,	$1,170 00
County tax,	963 43
Town grant,	16,049 57
Total tax,	$18,183 00

APPROPRIATIONS.

Schools,	$6,780 20	School-house debts,	$1,000 00
Highways,	2,500 00	Other town expenses,	1,000 00
Poor,	3,100 00		
Interest,	1,400 00	Total,	$15,780 20

ASSETS AND LIABILITIES, MAY 1.

ASSETS.		LIABILITIES.	
School-houses,	$19,300 00	School-houses,	$10,000 00
Other public buildings,	3,000 00	Other public buildings,	3,000 00
Other real estate,	5,000 00	Other real estate,	1,000 00
Trust funds,	2,000 00	Trust funds,	2,000 00
Other assets,	643 00	Other debts,	6,182 00
Total,	$29,943 00	Total,	$22,182 00

PROPERTY EXEMPT FROM TAXATION.

Congregational Church. — Building,		$10,000 00	
	Organ,	2,000 00	
	Land,	500 00	
			$12,500 00
Episcopal Church. — Building,		$5,000 00	
	Land,	500 00	
			5,500 00

Baptist Church. — Building,	$3,000 00	
Land,	300 00	
		$3,300 00
Universalist Church. — Building,	$2,000 00	
Land,	100 00	
		2,100 00
Total,		$23,400 00

SCHOOL STATISTICS.

SCHOOL COMMITTEE.

Rev. William R. Tompkins, *Chairman;* J. C. Whiting, *Secretary;* Rev. T. P. Briggs.

SCHOOLS.

Centre High. — Mr. C. W. Fearing,	37	scholars.
Centre Grammar. — Miss E. A. Gerould,	35	"
Centre Primary. — Miss C. J. Randall,	30	"
Plainville Grammar. — Mr. O. D. Crockett, *Principal;* Miss Annie Hitchcock, *Assistant,*	55	"
Plainville Primary. — Miss M. F. Cowell,	50	"
Sheldonville Grammar. — Mr. C. G. Smith,	28	"
Sheldonville Primary. — Miss Annie Ware,	20	"
Shepardville Mixed. — Mr. J. H. Shannon,	30	"
Willard's Mixed. — Miss Carrie P. Lymber,	30	"
South-street Mixed. — Miss M. J. Belcher,	25	"
Guinea-street Mixed. — Miss —— Ray,	15	"
West Wrentham Mixed. — Miss C. W. Heaton,	27	"
Blake's Hill. — Mr. Jencks,	20	"
Total,	402	"

Aggregate of Polls, Property, Taxes, etc., as assessed May 1, 1876.

Towns.	Total number of Polls.	Total Tax on Polls.	Total Value of Personal Estate.	Total Value of Real Estate.	Total Valuation, May 1, 1876.	Total Tax for State, County, City & Town purposes, including High-way Tax.	Rate of Total Tax per $100.	Total number of Dwelling-houses.	Total number of Horses.	Total number of Cows.	Total number of Sheep.	Total number of Acres of Land taxed in the City or Town.
Bellingham	315	$690	$108,897	$412,968	$521,865	$6,170	$1 05	262	187	317	4	10,785
Braintree	1,138	2,276	747,675	2,095,675	2,841,350	31,288	1 02	780	342	379	39	8,101
Brookline	1,718	3,196	10,686,300	16,804,000	27,490,300	335,382	1 22	1,122	618	276	..	3,751
Canton	1,015	2,030	1,171,051	1,930,780	3,104,831	39,388	1 20	687	268	353	30	11,412
Cohasset	586	1,172	872,687	1,466,505	2,339,192	24,564	1 00	508	207	209	33	5,837
Dedham	1,467	2,934	985,120	3,975,192	5,960,312	68,501	1 10	1,113	529	288	1	12,410
Dover	182	364	40,562	391,693	435,255	7,111	1 50	138	110	738	8	8,986
Foxborough	724	1,418	308,005	1,330,830	1,638,835	19,457	1 10	593	289	314	2	12,020
Franklin	819	1,658	394,215	1,102,925	1,497,140	20,352	1 25	513	369	302	2	15,366
Holbrook	530	1,060	199,020	741,310	910,360	11,125	1 40	323	150	512	..	4,558
Hyde Park	1,506	3,012	685,062	5,860,765	6,545,767	88,107	1 30	1,189	243	138	..	2,800
Medfield	344	688	278,850	680,047	967,897	11,823	1 15	244	187	54	2	8,051
Medway	1,038	2,076	329,695	1,433,515	1,763,210	26,760	1 40	710	333	381	..	12,977
Milton	735	1,470	4,626,500	3,267,800	7,894,300	51,204	63	514	520	658	4	7,880
Needham	1,389	2,778	998,743	3,819,193	4,817,936	58,529	1 15	890	589	450	49	13,539
Norfolk	256	512	74,525	351,975	426,500	7,017	1 60	187	737	461	..	8,929
Norwood	582	1,164	441,172	1,384,119	1,824,291	22,506	1 17	369	217	271	..	6,270
Quincy	2,283	4,566	1,787,965	5,745,180	7,533,145	110,030	1 40	1,639	674	340	3	8,639
Randolph	1,188	2,376	650,610	1,451,900	2,101,510	28,893	1 26	757	302	495	..	5,814
Sharon	417	834	252,378	814,534	1,066,912	9,365	80	301	217	221	..	13,873
Stoughton	1,272	2,514	684,850	1,774,200	2,459,050	42,137	1 61	867	411	229	..	11,749
Walpole	588	1,176	282,537	1,094,951	1,377,488	17,706	1 20	457	348	316	..	12,402
Weymouth	2,775	5,550	1,917,914	3,673,246	5,591,160	67,056	1 10	1,714	842	476	..	9,516
Wrentham	606	1,212	185,479	985,033	1,170,572	18,183	1 45	537	361	480	24	13,143
Totals	23,533	$47,066	$29,715,752	$62,629,426	$92,345,178	$1,125,554	..	16,474	9,210	8,921	201	234,691

RELIGIOUS SOCIETIES.

BELLINGHAM.

FIRST BAPTIST CHURCH. Organized Nov., 1737. — *Pastor*, Rev. Joseph T. Massey, settled, 1834; *Deacons*, Sanford W. Allen, Elias Cook; *Clerk*, Addison H. Allen; *Treasurer*, Ellis Bullard; *Parish Committee*, Ruel F. Thayer, Ellis Bullard, Andrew A. Bates. Number of members, 83. *Supt. of Sunday School*, Addison H. Allen. 9 teachers, 89 scholars.

NORTH BELLINGHAM BAPTIST CHURCH. Organized 1867. — Rev. H. F. H. Miller, of Roslindale, supplies. *Deacons*, Roswell Bent, J. E. Pond; *Clerk*, S. F. Coombs; *Parish Committee*, Roswell Bent, J. E. Pond, William H. Humes. Number of members, 30. *Supt. of Sunday School*, S. F. Coombs. 4 teachers, 54 scholars.

BRAINTREE.

FIRST CONGREGATIONAL SOCIETY (Trinitarian). Organized Sept. 10, 1707. — *Pastor*, Rev. Thomas A. Emerson, settled May 7, 1874; *Deacons*, Nath'l Hayward, Elias Hayward, Henry M. Hollis, J. Ward Childs; *Clerk of Society*, William F. Locke; *Clerk of Church*, A. B. Keith; *Treasurer*, Alvah Butler; *Parish Committee*, Josephus Shaw, E. Watson Arnold, Thomas W. Sampson. Number of members, 155. *Supt. of Sunday School*, J. Ward Child. 25 teachers, 210 scholars.

UNION RELIGIOUS SOCIETY OF WEYMOUTH AND BRAINTREE (Trinitarian). Organized Feb. 11, 1811. — *Pastor*, Rev. Lucien H. Frary, settled April 13, 1875; *Deacons*, Jacob Loud, of Weymouth, Levi W. Hobart, Gilbert Nash, and Charles T. Crane, of Braintree; *Clerk of Society and Church*, Charles T. Crane; *Treasurer*, John J. Loud; *Parish Committee*, Gilbert Nash, Augustus J. Richards, George W. Shaw. Number of members, 161. *Supt. of Sunday School*, Gilbert Nash. 17 teachers, 171 scholars.

SOUTH CONGREGATIONAL SOCIETY (Trinitarian). Organized Nov. 18, 1829. — *Pastor*, Rev. Albion H. Johnson, settled April 1, 1875; *Deacons*, Atherton T. Wild, Jacob S. Dyer; *Clerk of Society and Church*, Noah Torrey; *Treasurer*, Benjamin Dyer; *Parish Committee*, Joseph Dyer, Jr., F. A. Hobart, Elisha Thayer. Number of members, 56. *Supt. of Sunday School*, Albion H. Johnson. 16 teachers, 125 scholars.

ELM STREET BAPTIST CHURCH. Organized July 13, 1869. — *Pastor*, none; church closed at present; *Deacons*, Perley Stedman, Elias Holbrook; *Parish Committee*, Perley Stedman, Elias Holbrook, William M. Fernald, Elisha Goodwin; *Clerk of Church*, William F. Fernald; *Treasurer*, Elias Holbrook. Number of members, 30. *Supt. of Sunday School*, William F. Fernald. 6 teachers, 35 scholars.

METHODIST EPISCOPAL CHURCH (So. BRAINTREE). Organized Feb. 22, 1874. — *Pastor*, Rev. Edward M. Taylor, settled April 1876; *Stewards*, James S. Baker, Louis F. Gomez, Wm. Frank Morrison, Henry H. Snow; *Recording Steward*, James S. Baker. Number of members, 25. *Supt. of Sunday School*, Edward M. Taylor. 6 teachers, 75 scholars.

BROOKLINE.

FIRST PARISH OF BROOKLINE (Unitarian). Organized 1705. — *Pastor*, Rev. Howard N. Brown, settled 1873; *Deacons*, Benjamin B. Davis, Abijah W. Goddard; *Clerk of Society*, Charles H. Stearns; *Treasurer*, Edward S. Philbrick; *Parish Committee*, Frank C. Cabot, Charles D. Head, Charles P. Ware, Miss Martha C. Stevenson, Miss S. B. R. Clark. Number of members, 75. *Supt. of Sunday School*, Rev. Howard N. Brown. 15 teachers, 70 scholars.

FIRST BAPTIST SOCIETY. Organized June 5, 1828. — *Pastor*, Rev. Henry C. Mabie, settled Jan. I, 1876; *Deacons*, Thomas Griggs, George Brooks, Austin W. Benton, George F. Joyce; *Clerk of Society*, David Bentley; *Clerk of Church*, George F. Joyce; *Treasurer*, David Bentley; *Parish Committee*, The Pastor and Deacons, and David Bentley, Henry G. Seaverns, George W. Stearns, Charles H. James, Osavius Verney; *Prudential Committee of the Society*, Edward C. Wilson, Moses C. Warren, David S. Coolidge, Peter W. Pierce, Thomas B. Griggs. Number of members, 250. *Supt. of Sunday School*, George Brooks. 33 teachers and officers, 210 scholars.

HARVARD CONGREGATIONAL SOCIETY (Trinitarian). Organized 1844. — *Pastor*, Rev. Reuen Thomas, settled May 4, 1873; *Deacons*, William Lincoln, Horatio S. Burdett, Edward I. Thomas, William H. Cooley; *Clerk of Society*, Horace E. Abbott; *Clerk of Church*, Charles W. Wrightington; *Treasurer of Society*, Charles W. Scudder; *Treasurer of the Church*, Henry B. Eager; *Standing Committee of Society*, William H. Wilder, Horatio S. Burdett, Oliver H. Hay, Henry Mason, John A. Howard, Henry N. Clark, Charles W. Scudder; *Standing Committee of Church*, Rev. Reuen Thomas, William Lincoln, Horatio S. Burdett, Edward I. Thomas, William H. Cooley, Langdon S. Ward, Oliver H. Hay, Henry B. Eager, Charles W. Wrightington. Number of members, 282. *Supt. of Sunday School*, Charles G. Chase. 31 teachers, 250 scholars.

ST. PAUL'S CHURCH (Episcopal). Organized July, 1849. — *Rector*, Rev. Leonard Kip Storrs, settled Jan. 1, 1876; *Wardens*, James S. Amory, Henry S. Chase; *Vestrymen*, The Wardens, and A. Lowell, C. K. Fay, Thomas Parsons, Edward E. Floyd, George E. Stedman; *Clerk*, Clement K. Fay; *Treasurer*, Henry S. Chase. Communicants, 197. *Supt. of Sunday School*, The Rector. 13 teachers, 135 scholars.

ST. MARY'S OF THE ASSUMPTION (Roman Catholic). Organized 1850. — *Pastor*, Rev. Laurence J. Morris, settled July, 19, 1873; *Clerk and Treasurer of Society*, Rev. L. J. Morris; *Clerk of Church*, James Driscoll, Jr. Number of members, 2,000. Sisters of Notre Dame have charge of Sunday School. 28 teachers, 475 scholars.

CHRIST CHURCH, at Longwood (Independent), closed for public worship. — Organized June 18, 1862. — C. V. Cotting, *Clerk and Treasurer.*

CHURCH OF OUR SAVIOUR (Episcopal). Organized March, 1868. — No settled Rector; *Wardens*, William R. Lawrence, Samuel L. Bush; *Clerk*, J. M. Clark; *Treasurer*, Francis W. Lawrence; *Vestrymen*, Amos A. Lawrence, Mitchell Clark, Robert Amory, T. J. Lee, A. P. Howard, F. W. Lawrence, Henry Lincoln, S. H. Gregory, S. D. Hayes. Communicants, 85. *Supt. of Sunday School*, T. J. Lee. 12 teachers, 50 scholars.

BROOKLINE SOCIETY OF THE NEW JERUSALEM CHURCH. Organized 1856. — *Pastor*, Rev. Warren Goddard, Jr., settled March, 1874; *Clerk of Society and Church*, Daniel H. Rogers; *Treasurer*, Abram L. Cutter; *Parish Committee*, W. A. Wellman, James W. Edgerly, Albert Mason, A. L. Cutter, D. H. Rogers. Number of members, 30. *Supt. of Sunday School*, Albert Mason. 6 teachers, 42 scholars.

METHODIST EPISCOPAL CHURCH. Organized 1873. — *Pastor*, Rev. Henry Witham
supplies ; *Parish Committee*, William Wood, William Heath, L. F. Johnson; *Clerk
of Church*, William Heath; *Treasurer*, William Wood. Number of members, 30.
Supt. of Sunday School, Enoch E. Doran. 6 teachers, 63 scholars.

CANTON.

FIRST CONGREGATIONAL PARISH (Unitarian). Organized 1717. — *Pastor*, Rev.
William Henry Savery, settled June 8, 1873; *Deacons*, Asa Shephard, J. Mason
Everett, Billings Hewitt; *Clerk of Society*, Larra W. Sumner; *Treasurer*, Charles H.
French; *Parish Committee*, J. Mason Everett, Elijah Bent, Billings Hewitt. *Supt.
of Sunday School*, Frank M. Ames. 20 teachers, 150 scholars.
EVANGELICAL CONGREGATIONAL CHURCH. Organized 1828. — *Pastor*, Rev. John
W. Savage, settled 1874. *Deacons*, Ezra S. Brewster, Elijah A. Morse; *Clerk of
Society*, George A. Mitchell; *Clerk of Church*, Jeremiah Kollock; *Treasurer*,
Arthur C. Kollock. Number of members, 90. *Supt. of Sunday School*, George A.
Mitchell. 14 teachers, 109 scholars.
ST. JOHN'S (Roman Catholic). Organized 1845. — *Pastor*, Rev. John Flatley, settled
July, 1861. Number of members, 1,400. *Superintendent of Sunday School*, P. F.
Brady. 20 teachers, 300 scholars.
FIRST UNIVERSALIST PARISH. Organized 1859. — *Pastor*, Rev. Edwin Davis,
settled Dec. 1, 1870; *Deacons*, Francis W. Deane, Abner T. Upham; *Clerk of
Church and Society*, Virgil J. Messenger; *Treasurer*, Joseph W. C. Seavey; *Parish
Committee*, William H. Little, John Hall, Joseph W. C. Seavey. Number of mem-
bers, 33. *Supt. of Sunday School*, William H. Little. 13 teachers, 100 scholars.
FIRST CANTON BAPTIST SOCIETY. Organized May 5, 1873. — *Pastor*, Rev.
Clifton Fletcher, settled July 2, 1873; *Deacons*, Willard Shepard, Hugh McPher-
son; *Clerk of Church and Society*, W. Henry Bense; *Treasurer of Society*, Aaron E.
Tucker; *Parish Committee*, William Bense, William H. Bullard, Sr., George W.
Coombs. Number of members, 144. *Supt. of Sunday School*, Hugh McPherson.
10 teachers, 75 scholars.

COHASSET.

FIRST PARISH IN COHASSET (Unitarian). Organized 1721. — *Pastor*, Rev. Joseph
Osgood, settled Oct. 26, 1842; *Deacons*, Newcomb Bates, Newcomb B. Tower; *Clerk
of Society*, Daniel N. Tower; *Clerk of Church*, Joseph Osgood; *Treasurer*, Newcomb
B. Tower; *Parish Committee*, John Q. A. Lothrop, Abraham H. Tower, Jr., Edward
E. Tower. Number of members, 50. *Supt. of Sunday School*, Abraham H. Tower,
Jr. 15 teachers, 68 scholars.
METHODIST EPISCOPAL CHURCH (NORTH COHASSET). Organized 1823. — *Pastor*,
Rev. James O. Thompson, settled March 30, 1874; *Stewards*, Osgood Eaton, Jr.,
Daniel Beal, Welcome Beal, Arthur Beale, Gardiner M. Jones; *Treasurer*, Osgood,
Eaton, Jr. Number of members, 47. *Supt. of Sunday School*, Osgood Eaton, Jr.
10 teachers, 65 scholars.
SECOND CONGREGATIONAL CHURCH (Trinitarian). Organized Oct., 1824. —
Pastor, Rev. Moody A. Stevens, settled April 18, 1871; *Deacons*, Bela Bates,
Philander Bates; *Clerk of Society*, John Bates; *Clerk of Church and Treasurer*,
Philander Bates; *Parish Committee*, John Warren Bates, Thomas Wilcutt, Robert
Pratt. Number of members, 119. *Supt. of Sunday School*, Philander Bates. 16
teachers, 135 scholars.
BEECHWOODS CHURCH, Cohasset, united with EVANGELICAL CONGREGATIONAL
SOCIETY, of Hingham. — *Pastor*, Rev. Edward C. Hood, settled Oct. 1, 1873;

Clerk of Society, Jacob O. Sanborn; *Clerk of Church,* Arthur W. Noyes, of Hingham Centre; *Treasurer,* Tobias O. Gardner; *Parish Committee,* Henry E. Spaulding, Isaac N. Damon, James M. Tileston. Number of members, 46. *Supt. of Sunday School,* Tobias O. Gardner. 12 teachers, 77 scholars.

ST. ANTHONY'S CHURCH (Roman Catholic). Organized 1875. — *Pastor,* Rev. Peter J. Leddy, settled Aug. 1, 1876; *Sexton,* Joseph St. John. Number of members, 300. *Supt. of Sunday School,* Joseph St. John. 7 teachers, 60 scholars.

DEDHAM.

FIRST CHURCH (Unitarian). Organized 1638. — *Pastor,* Rev. Seth C. Beach, settled Dec. 29, 1875; *Deacons,* Jonathan H. Cobb, Nathaniel Smith; *Clerk of Society,* Jonathan Cobb; *Clerk of Church,* Pastor; *Treasurer of Society,* Henry W. Richards; *Treasurer of Church,* Jonathan H. Cobb; *Parish Committee,* Alfred Hewins, Nathaniel Smith, Sanford Carroll; *Supt. of Sunday School,* Geo. C. Stearns. 19 teachers, 100 scholars.

ALLIN EVANGELICAL SOCIETY. Originally part of First Church, but separated and established as a new church Feb., 1822. — *Pastor,* Rev. Charles M. Southgate, settled Dec. 16, 1875; *Deacons,* Calvin Guild, Martin Draper, Theodore L. Brown; *Clerk of Society,* James O. Yatman; *Clerk of Church,* Wyllys Van Wagenen; *Parish Committee,* Edward P. Burgess, Nathaniel Morse, Henry C. Bigelow; *Treasurer,* Chauncey C. Churchill. Number of members, 257. *Supt. of Sunday School,* Theodore L. Brown. 37 teachers, 315 scholars.*

THIRD PARISH (Unitarian), WEST DEDHAM. Organized Jan. 1, 1736. — *Pastor,* Rev. Edward Crowninshield, settled Jan. 1, 1873; *Clerk of Society,* John E. Whiting; *Treasurer,* Joseph Fisher; *Parish Committee,* John E. Whiting, Daniel W. Parker, Henry L. Pettee; *Supt. of Sunday School,* the Pastor; teachers in Sunday School, 8, with 45 scholars.

ST. PAUL'S EPISCOPAL CHURCH. Organized 1756. — *Rector,* Rev. Daniel Goodwin, settled Nov. 1, 1874; *Assistant,* Rev. William F. Cheney, in charge of Chapel of the Good Shepherd at Oakdale; *Wardens,* Ira Cleveland, Thomas L. Wakefield; *Vestrymen,* Rufus E. Dixon, Lewis H. Kingsbury, Silas D. Bacon, Frederick D. Ely, Richard Codman; *Clerk of Vestry and Parish,* John F. Wakefield; *Treasurer,* Thomas L. Wakefield. Number of communicants, 193. *Supt. of Sunday School,* the Rector. In Parish Sunday School, 14 teachers, 115 scholars. In Mission Sunday School, 12 teachers, 115 scholars.

FIRST BAPTIST CHURCH (WEST DEDHAM). Organized Nov. 23d, 1824. — *Pastor,* Rev. Samuel C. Chandler, settled Sept. 1, 1874; *Deacons,* Willard Draper, James B. Baker; *Clerk of Society,* Ebenezer Gay; *Clerk of Church,* Nathaniel Noyes; *Treasurer,* John A. White; *Parish Committee,* Nathaniel Noyes, Charles Fuller, Greenwood Fuller. Number of members, 75. *Supt. of Sunday School,* Francis W. Draper. 12 teachers, 90 scholars.

EAST DEDHAM BAPTIST SOCIETY. Organized 1843. — *Pastor,* Rev. Charles H. Cole, settled, 1875; *Deacons,* James Newsome, George F. Shaw; *Clerk and Treasurer of Society,* James Newsome; *Clerk of Church,* George F. Shaw; *Parish Committee,* James Newsome, S. M. Ruggles, George Godding. Number of members, 60. *Supt. of Sunday School,* Charles Lewis. 10 teachers, 100 scholars.

METHODIST EPISCOPAL SOCIETY (EAST DEDHAM). Organized 1843. — *Pastor,* Rev. William A. Cottle, settled April 1, 1876; *Stewards,* John Adams, Frank M. Bailey,

---

* Includes two mission schools.

56

Charles F. Kimball, Henry E. Crocker, Frederic Bradley, Alexander H. Watson; *Trustees of Church*, John Adams, Wm. N. Tapley, John Sully, S. M. Norris, Frank M. Bailey, H. E. Crocker, Frederic Bradley, Charles F. Kimball; *Treasurer*, Frank M. Bailey. Number of members, 42. *Supt. of Sunday School*, Frank M. Bailey. 9 teachers, 90 scholars.

ST. MARY'S (Roman Catholic). Organized 1865. — *Pastor*, Rev. John P. Brennan; Rev. Dennis J. O'Donovan, *Assistant*. Number of members in the parish of Dedham and Norwood, 1,800. *Supt. of Sunday School*, Rev. D. J. O'Donovan. 12 teachers, 200 scholars.

BALCH SOCIETY OF ISLINGTON (Trinitarian). Organized June, 1875. — *Pastor*, Rev. Charles B. Smith, settled June 1, 1874; *Clerk and Treasurer*, Alonzo B. Wentworth; *Parish Committee*, Sylvanus Ballou, N. E. Smith, John Dean; *Supt. of Sunday School*, the Pastor. 2 teachers, 40 scholars.

DOVER.

DOVER FIRST PARISH (Unitarian). Organized 1749. — *Pastor*, Rev. Calvin S. Locke, of Dedham, supplies; *Deacons*, Joseph A. Smith, Asa Talbot; *Clerk of Society*, Ansel K. Tisdale; *Treasurer of Society*, Aaron Bacon; *Parish Committee*, John Humphrey, Mrs. George D. Everett, Deacon Asa Talbot. Number of members, 30. *Supts. of Sunday Schools*, George Scott, Frank Smith. 5 teachers, 40 scholars.

ORTHODOX CONGREGATIONAL SOCIETY. Organized Dec. 27, 1838. — *Pastor*, Rev. John Wood, settled April 1, 1875; *Clerk of Society*, George L. Howe; *Clerk of Church*, Ithamar Whiting; *Treasurer*, Leonard Draper; *Parish Committee*, Frederick H. Wight, Barnabas Paine, George McKenzie. Number of members, 27. *Supt. of Sunday School*, George L. Howe. 7 teachers, 50 scholars.

MISSION CHURCH (AT CHARLES RIVER VILLAGE). Connected with above Society.— Rev. John Wood, *Pastor*. *Supt. of Sunday School*, Joseph Nickerson. 6 teachers, 47 scholars.

BAPTIST CHURCH. Organized 1838. — No settled pastor; *Deacon*, John Kenrick; *Clerk of Church*, Timothy Soule; *Parish Committee*, John Kenrick, Alexander Soule, Timothy Bailey. *Supt. of Sunday School*, John Kenrick. 5 teachers, 23 scholars.

FOXBOROUGH.

ORTHODOX CONGREGATIONAL SOCIETY. Organized Nov. 25, 1779. No pastor at present; *Deacons*, Charles W. Morse, Thomas B. Bourne, Edwin B. Leonard; *Clerk and Treasurer of Society*, Allen H. Messenger; *Clerk and Treasurer of Church*, Horace Carpenter; *Parish Committee*, Leonard C. Bliss, Albert Fisher, Jr., Edwin B. Leonard. Number of members, 210. *Supt. of Sunday School*, Deacon Charles N. Morse. 25 teachers, 265 scholars.

FIRST BAPTIST SOCIETY. Organized March 11, 1816. — *Pastor*, Rev. William H. Spencer, settled Sept. 8, 1869; *Deacons*, John Comey, Elisha White, Ebenezer Wade Allen; *Clerk of Church and Society*, Ebenezer W. Allen; *Treasurer*, William Carpenter; *Parish Committee*, Elisha White, William Hart, George Allen Thayer. Number of members, 211. *Supt. of Sunday School*, Elbridge G. P. Gay. 25 teachers, 210 scholars.

FIRST UNIVERSALIST SOCIETY. Organized Nov. 5, 1846. — *Pastor*, Rev. William W. Hayward, settled January 1, 1875; *Deacons*, Chester Morse, Mrs. Edmund Boyden; *Clerk of Society*, George S. Walcott; *Clerk of Church*, James A. Morse;

Treasurer, Salmon Turner; *Parish Committee*, Charles C. Sumner, C. Warren Lane, George S. Wheeler. Number of members, 40. *Supt. of Sunday School*, C. Warren Lane. 8 teachers, 110 scholars.

ST. JOSEPH'S ROMAN CATHOLIC CHURCH. Organized 1872. — *Pastor*, Rev. Francis Gouesse, settled Nov. 17, 1872. Number of members, 250. *Supt. of Sunday School*, Mary Kirwan. 2 teachers, 25 scholars.

FRANKLIN.

FIRST CONGREGATIONAL SOCIETY (Trinitarian). Organized Feb., 1738. — *Pastor*, Rev. Henry C. Crane, settled Nov., 1874; *Deacons*, Joseph T. Bacon, Peter Adams, Thaddeus H. Shepherdson, George W. Bacon, Osmyn A. Stanley, Albert L. Clark; *Clerk of Society*, William E. Nason; *Clerk of Church*, Erastus E. Baker; *Treasurer*, Albert L. Clark; *Parish Committee*, Osmyn A. Stanley, Peter Adams, Thomas B. Allen. Number of members, 277. *Supt. of Sunday School*, Thaddeus H. Shepherdson. 18 teachers, 180 scholars.

UNION CONGREGATIONAL SOCIETY (Trinitarian). Organized Sept. 13, 1853. — *Pastor*, Rev. Josiah Merrill, settled Oct., 1867; *Deacons*, Paul B. Clark, Willard C. Whiting; *Clerk of Society*, Sabin Hubbard; *Clerk of Church*, Paul B. Clark; *Treasurer*, George M. Wadsworth; *Parish Committee*, Albert A. Newell, Paul B. Clark, H. B. Miller. Number of members, 24. *Supt. of Sunday School*, Willard C. Whiting. 5 teachers, 44 scholars.

FIRST UNIVERSALIST SOCIETY. Organized 1857. — *Pastor*, Rev. A. St. John Chambré, settled July 1, 1872; *Clerk of Society*, George W. Wiggin; *Treasurer*, James M. Freeman; *Parish Committee*, James P. Ray, Joseph G. Ray, Enoch Waite. Number of members, 70. *Supt. of Sunday School*, Rev. A. St. John Chambré. 16 teachers, 135 scholars.

FIRST BAPTIST CHURCH. Organized 1868. — *Pastor*, Rev. George W. Ryan, settled May, 1873; *Deacons*, William H. Davis, Alonzo G. Pike; *Clerk of Society and Church*, Hamilton P. Stewart; *Treasurer*, Alonzo G. Pike; *Parish Committee*, William H. Davis, Alonzo G. Pike, Alfred G. Metcalf, H. P. Stewart, James Follansbee. Number of members, 46. *Supt. of Sunday School*, Rev. George W. Ryan. 8 teachers, 60 scholars.

METHODIST EPISCOPAL SOCIETY. Organized June, 1872. — *Pastor*, Rev. John N. Short, settled April, 1874; *Stewards*, W. W. Haslam, Charles S. Bassett, Alfred Everett, Joseph T. Hutchinson, Charles Badger, William H. Howe, William B. Teed, Lepreletto L. Fisher, Daniel W. Whiting; *Clerk of Society and Church and Treasurer*, Charles S. Bassett. Number of members, 75. *Supt. of Sunday School*, Charles S. Bassett. 8 teachers, 100 scholars.

ST. PATRICK'S ROMAN CATHOLIC CHURCH. Organized 1872. — *Pastor*, Rev. Francis Gouesse, settled Nov. 17, 1872. Number of members, 500. *Supt. of Sunday School*, John L. Fitzpatrick. 8 teachers, 60 scholars.

HOLBROOK.

WINTHROP SOCIETY. Organized Dec. 30, 1856. — No settled pastor; *Deacons*, Newton White, Elisha Holbrook; *Clerk of Society*, E. Frank Lincoln; *Clerk of Church*, Seth C. Sawyer; *Treasurer*, E. Frank Lincoln; *Parish Committee*, Charles H. Belcher, Seth C. Sawyer, Z. Aaron French. Number of members, 165. *Supt. of Sunday School*, Newton White. 26 teachers, 216 scholars. There is also a Sunday School established near the railroad station in Holbrook, which is conducted mostly by members of the Winthrop church, called the Union Sunday School. It was organized June 9, 1868. *Superintendent*, William Gray. 8 teachers, 55 scholars. It has a library of about 1,000 volumes.

BAPTIST CHURCH AT BROOKVILLE. Organized May 30, 1868. —No settled pastor; *Deacons*, George A. Snell, Rodney Howard; *Clerk of Parish*, M. B. Faxon; *Clerk of Church*, George A. Snell; *Treasurer*, Freeman Bard; *Parish Committee*, Albert Leonard, S. H. Scudder, Freeman Bard. Number of members, 43; *Supt. of Sunday School*, Albert Leonard; *Clerk of Sunday School*, Henry Luddon. 13 teachers, 76 scholars.

HYDE PARK.

FIRST BAPTIST SOCIETY. Organized June, 1858. — No settled pastor; *Deacons*, T. H. Videto, Charles F. Gerry, N. H. Tucker, Oliver P. Horne; *Clerk of Society*, Samuel L. White; *Clerk of Church*, Thomas C. Evans; *Treasurer*, Theodore H. Videto; *Parish Committee*, Amos Webster, T. H. Videto, Isaac C. Plummer, John Jigger, Samuel L. White. Number of members, 270. *Supt. of Sunday School*, Thomas C. Evans. 20 teachers, 196 scholars.

CHRIST CHURCH (Episcopal). Organized Feb. 14, 1861. — *Rector*, Rev. Robert B. Van Kleeck, D.D., settled June 10, 1874; *Wardens*, Eben B. Page, Charles W. W. Wellington; *Vestrymen*, B. H. Hardy, William H. Hoogs, Robert H. Vivian. Asa Adams, Samuel N. Piper; *Clerk*, Asa Adams; *Treasurer*, Samuel N. Piper. Communicants, 140. *Supt. of Sunday School*, Henry Hyde Smith. 15 teachers, 110 scholars.

FIRST CONGREGATIONAL CHURCH (Trinitarian). Organized May 7, 1863. — *Pastor*, Rev. Perley B. Davis, settled April 10, 1867; *Deacons*, Zenas Allen, Enoch E. Blake, Ellery Piper, Elliot O. Taylor; *Clerk of Society*, Edwin R Walker; *Clerk of Church*, Henry S. Bunton; *Treasurer*, Charles F. Holt; *Parish Committee*, Joseph B. Quimby, Thomas Chamberlain, Henry D. Noyes, Joseph Farwell. Number of members, 337. *Supt. of Sunday School*, Edward S. Hathaway. 29 teachers, 356 scholars.

METHODIST EPISCOPAL CHURCH. Organized Feb. 10, 1867. — *Pastor*, Rev. J. Swinburne Weedon, April 14, 1876; *Trustees*, John Terry, C. W. Knowles, A. H. Holway, A. R. Whittier, G. L. Stocking, W. H. Norris, Oliver A. Neal, B. F. Radford, Charles Haley; *Stewards*, Richard W. Husted, C. A. Houso, J. P. Higgins, T. C. Holmes, Henry A. Silver, Palmer Morritt; *Clerk of Church*, W. H. Norris; *Treasurer*, A. H. Holway. Number of members, 250. *Supt. of Sunday School*, Richard W. Husted. 25 teachers, 250 scholars.

SECOND CONGREGATIONAL SOCIETY (Unitarian). Organized 1868. — *Pastor*, Rev. Francis C. Williams, settled 1869; *Clerk of Society*, B. H. Jones; *Treasurer*, H. B. Phelps; *Parish Committee*, Theodore D. Weld, B. C. Vose, B. H. Jones, H B. Phelps, Thomas Watson, Jr., I. B. Samuels, George Sanford, T. P. Swift. Number of members, 100. *Supt. of Sunday School*, B. C. Vose. 10 teachers, 100 scholars.

CHURCH OF THE EPIPHANY (Roman Catholic). Organized Oct., 1870. — *Pastor*, Rev. William J. Corcoran, settled Oct., 1870. Number of members, 700. *Supt. of Sunday School*, Rev. J. W. Corcoran. 20 teachers, 120 scholars.

ADVENT SOCIETY. Organized 1874. — *Pastor*, Rev. Thomas M. Preble, settled 1874; *Deacon*, Joseph Merrill; *Clerk of Society*, George Garren; *Treasurer*, Daniel F. Kendall; *Parish Committee*, Joseph G. Hamblin, Daniel F. Kendall, Joseph Merrill; *Supt. of Sunday School*, Henry L. Fuller.

MEDFIELD.

FIRST CONGREGATIONAL SOCIETY (Unitarian). Organized 1650. — *Present Pastor*, Rev. Charles Chauncey Sewall supplies; *Deacons*, John Ellis and George M. Smith, *pro tem.; Clerk of Society*, Samuel Ellis; *Treasurer*, Hamlet Wight; *Parish Committee*, Daniel D. Curtis, Moses Hartshorn, Hamlet Wight. Number of members, 37. *Supt. of Sunday School*, Charles C. Sewall. 12 teachers, 85 scholars.

BAPTIST CHURCH. Organized Aug. 18, 1776. — *Pastor*, Rev. Alvin M. Crane, settled Aug. 18, 1872; *Deacons*, Seth R. Maker, Wm. Bennett Grover; *Clerk of Church*, Charles R. Dunn; *Treasurer and Collector*, Thomas L. Barney; *Executive Committee*, William S. Tilden, Jacob R. Cushman, J. B. Hale. Number of members, 130. *Supt. of Sunday School*, William S. Tilden. 14 teachers, 100 scholars.

SECOND CONGREGATIONAL (Evangelical). Organized Feb. 6, 1828. — *Pastor*, Rev. William H. Cobb, settled December, 1876; *Deacons*, Benjamin Chenery, Francis S. Wight; *Clerk of Society*, Isaac Fiske; *Clerk of Church*, Benjamin Chenery; *Treasurer*, Isaac Fiske; *Parish Committee*, William Chenery, Andrew J. Johnson, John H. Gould. Number of members, 115. *Supt. of Sunday School*, Francis S. Wight. 7 teachers, 50 scholars.

MEDWAY.

FIRST PARISH, EAST MEDWAY (Trinitarian). Organized Feb. 3, 1748 — *Pastor*, Rev. E. O. Jameson, settled Nov. 15, 1871; *Deacons*, Elbridge Clark, William Daniels, Horatio Jones; *Clerk of Society*, George B. Fisher; *Clerk of Church*, William Daniels; *Treasurer*, Elisha A. Jones; *Parish Committee*, J. D. Clark, Horatio Jones, Edwin Metcalf. Number of members, 136. *Supt. of Sunday School*, William Daniels. 226 teachers and scholars.

SECOND CONGREGATIONAL SOCIETY, WEST MEDWAY (Trinitarian). Organized Oct. 4, 1750. — *Pastor*, Rev. James M. Bell, settled Sept. 26, 1876; *Deacons*, Anson Daniels, Edmund Shumway, Austin Metcalf; *Clerk of Society*, Sumner Robbins; *Clerk of Church*, Cyrus Albert Adams; *Treasurer*, Sumner Robbins; *Parish Committee*, Joshua Seavey, Joseph Bullard, Addison Smith. Number of members, 388. *Supt. of Sunday School*, Warren C. Adams. 20 teachers, 180 scholars.

BAPTIST SOCIETY (WEST MEDWAY). Organized March 11, 1819. — *Pastor*, Rev. Seth J. Axtell, Jr., settled Dec. 1, 1870; *Deacons*, Wales Kimball, John S. Smith, Horace C. Messenger; *Clerk of Society and Church*, Elbridge G. Ware; *Treasurer*, George S. Rice; *Parish Committee*, Wales Kimball, George S. Rice, Charles F. Harding. Number of members, 100. *Supt. of Sunday School*, Rev. Seth J. Axtell, Jr. 15 teachers, 120 scholars.

EVANGELICAL CONGREGATIONAL SOCIETY, (MEDWAY VILLAGE.) Organized 1837. *Pastor*, Rev. Rufus K. Harlow, settled Feb. 13, 1872; *Deacons*, Milton M. Fisher, John W. Richardson; *Clerk of Society*, Fred. L. Fisher; *Clerk of Church*, R. K. Harlow; *Treasurer*, Francis Cummings; *Parish Committee*, Edward Eaton, George W. Ray, Orion A. Mason. Number of members, 232. *Supt. of Sunday School*, Fred. L. Fisher. 15 teachers, 160 scholars.

METHODIST EPISCOPAL CHURCH (WEST MEDWAY). Organized 1860. — *Pastor*, Rev. Loranus Crowell, settled April, 1874; *Stewards*, Samuel Bancroft, William Creasy, J. T. Greenwood, Charles Cole, Charles Ford; *Clerk of Society and Church*, John T. Greenwood; *Treasurer*, Sylvanus J. Lawrence. Number of members, 95. *Supt. of Sunday School*, Aaron Brigham. 12 teachers, 115 scholars.

ST. CLAIR'S ROMAN CATHOLIC CHURCH. Organized 1864. — *Pastor*, Rev. P. J.

Quinlan, Holliston. Number of members, 800. *Supt. of Sunday School.* Patrick Connolly. 12 scholars.

ST. CLEMENT'S EPISCOPAL CHURCH, (EAST MEDWAY).—This has a chapel, but no legally organized society, and no pastor.

MILTON.

FIRST CONGREGATIONAL CHURCH (Unitarian). Organized April 24, 1678.— *Pastors*, Rev. John H. Morison, D.D., settled January, 1846; Rev. Frederick Frothingham, settled Oct. 1876; *Deacon*, Samuel Adams; *Clerk of Society*, Charles Breck; *Treasurer*, Charles Breck; *Parish Committee*, Amor L. Hollingsworth, Henry S. Russell, John Sias; *Supt. of Sunday School*, Henry Emmons. 6 teachers, 50 scholars.

FIRST EVANGELICAL SOCIETY (Trinitarian). Organized 1678. — Rev. Wm. C. Reed supplies; *Deacons*, Stillman L. Tucker, William H. Balkam, John A. Tucker; *Clerk of Society*, William H. Balkam; *Clerk of Church*, Stillman L. Tucker; *Treasurer*, John A. Tucker; *Parish Committee*, Stillman L. Tucker, Samuel Cook; Number of members, 90. *Supt. of Sunday School*, Herbert B. Tucker. 10 teachers, 60 scholars.

SECOND EVANGELICAL CONGREGATIONAL SOCIETY (E. MILTON). Organized June 18, 1846. — Rev. Robert F. Gordon has supplied since Sept., 1875; *Deacon*, Simeon Emerson; *Clerk of Church and Society*, Simeon Emerson; *Treasurer*, Nathaniel H. Beals; *Parish Committee*, Nathaniel H. Beals, E. B. Andrews, Orrin A. Andrews. Number of members, 25. *Supt. of Sunday School*, Rev. Robt. F. Gordon. 10 teachers, 60 scholars.

NEEDHAM.

FIRST PARISH (Unitarian). Organized 1711. — *Pastor*, Rev. Solon W. Bush supplies; *Deacons*, Otis Morton, one vacancy; *Clerk of Society*, John M. Harris; *Clerk of Church*, Otis Morton; *Treasurer*, Charles C. Greenwood; *Parish Committee*, Otis Morton, Edward A. Mills, Diana P. Washburn. Number of members, 30. *Supt. of Sunday School*, Otis Morton. 8 teachers, 75 scholars.

WELLESLEY CONGREGATIONAL SOCIETY (Trinitarian). Organized 1778. — *Pastor*, Rev. George G. Phipps, settled Jan. 23, 1868; *Deacons*, Augustus Fuller, Whitman S. Winsor; *Clerk of Society*, Solomon Flagg; *Clerk of Church*, Augustus Fuller; *Treasurer*, Frank Perry; *Parish Committee*, Augustus Stevens, Frank Perry, Andrew W. Fuller. Number of members, 155. *Supt. of Sunday School*, D. S. Short. 18 teachers, 132 scholars.

GRANTVILLE RELIGIOUS SOCIETY (Trinitarian). Organized 1847. — *Pastor*, Rev. Jonathan Edwards, settled March 1, 1876; *Deacons*, Ruel Ware, George D. Ware; *Clerk of Society*, Frank L. Fuller; *Clerk of Church*, Flavius J. Lake; *Treasurer*, Henry L. Sanderson; *Parish Committee*, Flavius J. Lake, Hugh McLeod, George D. Ware. Number of members, 85. *Supt. of Sunday School*, Henry L. Sanderson. 12 teachers, 90 scholars.

FIRST BAPTIST CHURCH. Organized 1854. — No settled pastor; *Deacons*, William Moseley, Edward J. Chadbourne; *Clerk*, Thomas Sutton; *Treasurer*, John Moseley. Number of members, 77. *Supt. of Sunday School*, John Moseley. 10 teachers, 85 scholars.

EVANGELICAL CONGREGATIONAL SOCIETY. Organized May 6, 1857. — *Pastor*, Rev. J. E. M. Wright, settled July, 1875; *Deacons*, Nelson S. Read, Alden Harlow; *Clerk of Society*, William H. Crocker; *Clerk of Church*, Alden Harlow; *Treasurer*,

Nathan Parker; *Parish Committee*, Nathan Parker, Levi Ladd, John J. Morgan. Number of members, 71. *Supt. of Sunday School*, Nelson S. Read. 13 teachers, 100 scholars.

UNITARIAN SOCIETY OF GRANTVILLE. Organized Feb. 8, 1871. — *Pastor*, Rev. Albert B. Vorse, settled May 5, 1871; *Clerk*, Charles Gavett; *Treasurer*, Rebecca Eaton; *Parish Committee*, John W. Shaw, Rebecca Eaton, David C. Perrin, Harriet P. Lane, William Henshaw. Number of members, 25. *Supt. of Sunday School*, the Pastor. 5 teachers, 40 scholars.

METHODIST EPISCOPAL SOCIETY, HIGHLANDVILLE. Organized Sept. 20, 1876. — *Pastor*, Rev. Gilbert R. Bent, settled April 1, 1874; *Trustees*, Mark Lee, C. Hiram Dewing, Wm. Carter, Alex. Lynes, C. G. Upham, John Lee; *Stewards of Church*, Mark Lee, John Tompson, Wm. Carter, Joseph Poyner, John Daim, C. G. Upham, Joseph Thorp, Joseph Langdale; *Clerk and Treasurer*, Mark Lee. Number of members, 70. *Supt. of Sunday School*, Mark Lee. 18 teachers, 100 scholars.

ADVENT SOCIETY. Organized 1872. — *Elder*, S. G. Lowe; *Deacon*, Lauren Kingsbury. Number of members, 15. 30 scholars in Sunday School.

ST. JOHN'S CHURCH (Roman Catholic). — *Pastor*, Rev. Michael Dolan.

NORFOLK.

CLEAVELAND RELIGIOUS SOCIETY (Trinitarian). Organized April 30, 1832. — *Pastor*, Rev. Ephraim N. Hidden supplies. *Deacons*, Levi Mann, Lathrop C. Keith; *Clerk of Society and Church*, Lathrop C. Keith; *Treasurer of Society*, Levi Blake; *Treasurer of Church*, Lathrop C. Keith; *Parish Committee*, Levi Mann, Silas E. Fales, Asa B. Ware. Number of members, 42. *Supt. of Sunday School*, Levi Mann. 8 teachers, 45 scholars.

BAPTIST SOCIETY. Organized 1842. — *Pastor*, Rev. T. W. Clark supplies. *Deacons*, Samuel P. Blake, Addison P. Morse; *Clerk of Society*, Addison P. Morse; *Clerk of Church*, William King; *Treasurer*, Addison P. Morse. Number of members, 42. *Supt. of Sunday School*, Henry H. Watson. 5 teachers, 40 scholars.

NORWOOD.

FIRST CONGREGATIONAL CHURCH AND SOCIETY (Trinitarian). Organized 1736. — *Pastor*, Rev. Joseph P. Bixby, settled Oct. 1, 1866; *Deacons*, Lewis H. Rhoades, Samuel Morrill; *Clerk and Treasurer of Society*, Francis Tinker; *Clerk of Church*, Pastor; *Parish Committee*, Sidney E. Morse, David S. Fogg, William Williamson. Number of members, 145. *Supt. of Sunday School*, Francis O. Winslow. 20 teachers, 165 scholars.

FIRST UNIVERSALIST SOCIETY. Organized 1828. — *Pastor*, Rev. George Hill, settled Feb. 1, 1865; *Deacons*, Willard Gay, John E. Hartshorn; *Clerk and Treasurer of Society*, Lewis Day; *Clerk of Church*, Charles E. Pond; *Parish Committee*, Abijah Wheelock, Charles E. Pond, William H. Pond. Number of members, 50. *Supt. of Sunday School*, Charles E. Pond. 17 teachers, 142 scholars.

NORWOOD BAPTIST CHURCH. Organized 1858. — Rev. I. H. Gilbert has supplied since Sept., 1876; *Deacon and Clerk*, Francis M. Baker; *Church Committee*, Henry C. Morse, S. B. Pullen, T. F. Guy; *Treasurer*, Henry B. Baker. Number of members, 75. *Supt. of Sunday School*, Edwin A. Morse. 9 teachers, 45 scholars.

ST. CATHERINE'S (Roman Catholic). Organized 1865. — *Pastor*, Rev. John P. Brennan, Rev. D. J. O'Donovan, *Assistant*. Number of members in the Parish of Dedham and Norwood, 1800. *Supt. of Sunday School*, Rev. D. J. O'Donovan. 6 teachers, 60 children.

62   NORFOLK COUNTY MANUAL.

QUINCY.

FIRST CONGREGATIONAL SOCIETY (Unitarian). Organized 1639. — No settled pastor; *Clerk of Society*, Wm. F. Whitney; *Treasurer*, J. F. Faxon; *Parish Committee*, John Q. A. Field, Horace B. Spear, Charles II. Porter; *Supt. of Sunday School*, Charles A. Howland. 30 teachers, 200 scholars.

CHRIST CHURCH (Episcopal). Organized 1704. — *Rector*, Rev. Reginald H. Howe, settled Dec. 1, 1871; *Wardens*, William L. Wainwright, Braintree, and William Greenough, Quincy; *Vestrymen*, Charles F. Shimmin, of Hingham, Peter Butler, of Quincy, Samuel G. Wyman, of Baltimore, Arthur L. Walker, of Braintree, G. S. Coffin, of Quincy; *Clerk and Treasurer*, William Greenough. Communicants, 100. *Supt. of Sunday School*, The Rector. 9 teachers, 120 scholars.

FIRST UNIVERSALIST SOCIETY. Organized March 10, 1831. — *Pastor*, Rev. George Wallace Whitney, settled April 1, 1872; *Clerk of Society*, John Moore; *Clerk of Church*, The Pastor; *Treasurer*, Urbane Cudworth, Jr.; *Parish Committee*, Ebenezer Bent, William II. Parker, Richard G. Elliot. Number of members, 76. *Supt. of Sunday School*, John Otis Hall. 24 teachers, 155 scholars.

METHODIST CHURCH, QUINCY POINT. Organized 1831. — *Pastor*, Rev. S. L. Beiler, settled April 1, 1875; *Clerk of Society and Treasurer*, E. S. Starbuck, Sr.; *Parish Committee*, E. S. Starbuck, Jr., J. E. Hall, Clarence Sampson. Number of members, 50. *Supt. of Sunday School*, E. S. Starbuck, Jr. 16 teachers, 125 scholars.

EVANGELICAL CONGREGATIONAL SOCIETY. Organized April 5, 1832. — *Pastor*, Rev. Edward Norton, settled June 16, 1874; *Deacons*, George L. Smalley, Elbridge Clapp; *Clerk of Society and Church*, James L. Baxter; *Treasurer*, Franklin Hardwick; *Parish Committee*, Charles W. Carter, John O. Jones, II. Walter Grey. Number of members, 151. *Supt. of Sunday School*, Charles W. Carter. 21 teachers, 285 scholars.

FIRST BAPTIST CHURCH. Organized Feb. 23, 1867. — No settled pastor; *Deacon*, Daniel II. Bills; *Clerk of Church*, Samuel Graves; *Treasurer*, Daniel II. Bills; *Church Committee*, D. II. Bills, Samuel Graves, Samuel E. Johnson, Robert Clark. Number of members, 53. *Supt. of Sunday School*, Frank II. Graves. 6 teachers, 40 scholars.

ST. JOHN'S CHURCH (Roman Catholic). *Pastor*, Rev. Francis A. Frigugliotti, settled Feb., 1868. Number of members, St. John's Church with St. Mary's, 2,200. *Supt. of Sunday School*, Cornelius Moynahan. 30 teachers, 250 scholars.

ST. MARY'S CHURCH, WEST QUINCY (Roman Catholic). — *Pastor*, Rev. Francis A. Frigugliotti, settled Feb., 1868. Number of members, as above. 20 teachers in Sunday School, 200 scholars.

FIRST BAPTIST CHURCH (WOLLASTON HEIGHTS). Organized July 13, 1871. — *Pastor*, Rev. Charles II. Rowe, settled April 1, 1874; *Deacons*, Howard Gannett, Jones Howe, Josiah Sparrow; *Clerk of Society and Church*, W. W. Marple; *Treasurer*, Howard Gannett; *Parish Committee*, Pastor, Deacons, Lucius A. Elliot, Thomas B. Emery, W. W. Marple. Number of members, 71. *Supt. of Sunday School*, Howard Gannett. 11 teachers, 106 scholars.

METHODIST EPISCOPAL CHURCH (WEST QUINCY). Organized July, 1873. — *Pastor*, Rev. Samuel Kelley, settled April 28, 1872; *Stewards*, Jonas Shackley, Mayo P. Fuller, Thomas Northcot, Hiram Glines; *Trustees*, Jonas Shackley, Mayo P. Fuller, Hiram Glines, Enoch II. Doble, Jonathan B. L. Bartlett, Alonso Glines, Frederic J. Fuller, Thomas Craig; *Clerk of Board of Trustees*, Thomas Craig; *Recording*

Steward, Mayo P. Fuller; *Treasurer of Board of Trustees*, Enoch II. Doble; *Treasurer of Church*, M. P. Fuller. Number of members, 30; *Supt. of Sunday School*, Thomas Craig. 20 teachers and officers, 150 scholars.

METHODIST EPISCOPAL CHURCH (WOLLASTON HEIGHTS). Organized Jan., 1874. — *Pastor*, Rev. Mark Trafton; *Clerk of Society*, Henry Braden; *Treasurer*, Benjamin C. Barbour. Number of members, 25. *Supt. of Sunday School*, Henry Braden. 5 teachers, 40 scholars.

FIRST CONGREGATIONAL CHURCH WOLLASTON HEIGHTS (Trinitarian). Organized Nov. 11, 1874. — *Pastor*, Rev. Francis N. Zabriskie, settled Sept. 15, 1876; *Deacons*, Annes A. Lincoln, Joseph W. Lovett; *Clerk of Society and Collector*, W. W. Bemis; *Treasurer*, A. A. Lincoln, Jr.; *Assessors*, William W. Bemis, Alfred W. Sprague, Horace A. Pinkham, John P. Haynes, Joseph W. Lovett. Number of members, 30. *Supt. of Sunday School*, A. A. Lincoln, Jr. 10 teachers, 80 scholars.

RANDOLPH.

FIRST CONGREGATIONAL CHURCH (Orthodox). Organized May 28, 1731. — *Pastor*, Rev. John C. Labaree, settled Dec. 14, 1865; *Deacons*, Oliver H. Leach, Joseph Graham; *Clerk of Society and Treasurer*, Alfred W. Whitcomb; *Clerk of Church*, John V. Beal; *Parish Committee*, Royal W. Turner, J. White Belcher, Benjamin Dickerman. Number of members, 166. *Supt. of Sunday School*, George H. Wilkins. 23 teachers, 200 scholars.

FIRST BAPTIST CHURCH. Organized 1819. — *Pastor*, Rev. Joseph C. Foster, settled Dec., 1872; *Deacons*, Daniel Alden, Austin Roel, Aaron A. Prescott, John May, *Clerk of Church and Treasurer*, Nathaniel Howard; *Parish Committee*, Seth Mann, 2d, Adoniram Smith, Charles Prescott. Number of members, 249. *Supt. of Sunday School*, John May. 17 teachers, 200 scholars.

ST. MARY'S ROMAN CATHOLIC CHURCH. Organized Dec. 1, 1848. — *Pastor*, Rev. James E. O'Brien, settled June 19, 1873; *Treasurer*, Rev. James E. O'Brien. Number of members, 1,800 in Randolph and Holbrook. *Supt. of Sunday School*, William Campbell, 35 teachers, 400 scholars.

SHARON.

FIRST CONGREGATIONAL SOCIETY (Unitarian). Organized 1740. — No settled pastor; *Clerk of Society*, Charles Winship; *Treasurer*, George W. Gay; *Parish Committee*, H. Augustus Lothrop, Albert G. Hixon, Lepreletto Morse.

BAPTIST CHURCH. Organized October, 1814. — *Pastor*, Rev. Lyman Partridge, settled July, 1, 1872; *Deacons*, Barnabas D. Capen, one vacancy; *Clerk*, Charles D. Hixon; *Treasurer*, Barnabas D. Capen; *Parish Committee*, Samuel D. Hitchcock, Albert L. Felt, Charles D. Hixon. Number of members, 63. *Supt. of Sunday School*, Charles D. Hixon. 8 teachers, 80 scholars.

CHRISTIAN SOCIETY (Trinitarian). Organized 1821. — *Pastor*, Henry C. Weston, settled Sept. 2, 1874; *Deacons*, Lewis W. Morse, D. Webster Pettee; *Clerk of Society*, William C. Myrick; *Clerk of Church*, Sanford Waters Billings; *Treasurer*, D. Webster Pettee; *Parish Committee*, Wm. R. Mann, Lewis W. Morse, George F. Gay. Number of members, 104. *Supt. of Sunday School*, Sanford Waters Billings. 14 teachers, 116 scholars.

METHODIST CHURCH. Organized 1876. — No settled pastor; *Clerk and Treasurer*, John Wiswall; *Parish Committee*, William H. Hitchcock, Darius Aspinwall, —— Burleigh. Number of members, 14. 4 teachers, 35 scholars in Sunday School.

64   *NORFOLK COUNTY MANUAL.*

STOUGHTON.

UNIVERSALIST CHURCH. Organized 1743. — *Pastor*, Rev. Henry B. Smith, settled 1876; *Deacons*, Albert Johnson, H. N. Tucker, Robert Porter; *Clerk of Society*, Jabez Talbot, Jr.; *Clerk of Church*, Albert Johnson; *Treasurer*, Consider Southworth; *Parish Committee*, J. Freeman Ellis, Robert Porter, Consider Southworth. Number of members, 85. *Supt. of Sunday School*, Francis Capen. 34 teachers, 242 scholars.

BAPTIST CHURCH (EAST STOUGHTON). Organized 1780. *Pastor*, Rev. T. M. Merriman, settled July, 1875; *Deacons*, Charles Packard, Marcus M. Porter; *Clerk of Society*, Samuel L. Crane; *Clerk of Church*, William T. Page; *Treasurer*, Marcus M. Porter; *Parish Committee*, William T. Page, Marcus M. Porter, Franklin Blanchard. Number of members, 70. *Supt. of Sunday School*, William T. Page. 9 teachers, 80 scholars.

FIRST CONGREGATIONAL CHURCH AND SOCIETY (Trinitarian). Organized Dec. 14, 1825. — *Pastor*, Rev. John Herbert, settled Dec. 21, 1876; *Deacons*, Ebenezer Drake, Nathaniel Gay; *Clerk of Society*, Levi M. Flint; *Clerk of Church*, William D. Ward; *Treasurer of Society*, John A. Sawyer; *Treasurer of Church*, Levi M. Flint; *Parish Committee*, Calvin P. Guild, William D. Ward, Edwin M. Norton. Number of members, 132. *Supt. of Sunday School*, Levi M. Flint. 22 teachers, 196 scholars.

CHURCH * OF THE IMMACULATE CONCEPTION (Roman Catholic). Organized 1854. — *Pastor*, Rev. Thomas Norris, settled June 23, 1872. Number of members, 800. *Supt. of Sunday School*, Rev. Thomas Norris. 12 teachers, 100 scholars.

FIRST METHODIST EPISCOPAL CHURCH. — *Pastor*, Rev. John Livsey, settled April, 1875; *Stewards*, Edwin Gay, Eliphalet Gay, Jonathan Capen, Nathan May, Isaac Capen, U. Capen Porter, Albert Holmes, George Richmond; *Clerk of Society*, Jason W. Drake; *Recording Steward*, Isaac Capen; *Treasurer of the Church*, Jonathan Capen; *Treasurer of Trustees*, Eliphalet Gay; *Trustees*, Edwin Gay, Eliphalet Gay, Jefferson May, Jason W. Drake, Jason Gill, Jonathan Capen, Albert Holmes, Nathan May. Number of members, 128. *Supt. of Sunday School*, Rev. John Livsey. 17 teachers, 176 scholars.

METHODIST EPISCOPAL SOCIETY (NORTH STOUGHTON). Organized Feb. 23, 1873. — *Pastor*, Rev. John Alfred Story, settled April 1, 1874; *Treasurer*, Herbert Raymond; *Trustees*, Jonathan Raymond, Abram Jones, William Adlington, Horace Wentworth, Jacob Luteman. Number of members, 45. *Supt. of Sunday School*, Benjamin Tucker. 9 teachers, 80 scholars.

ST. MICHAEL'S ROMAN CATHOLIC CHURCH (AT EAST STOUGHTON). — In charge of Rev. James E. O'Brien, of Randolph.

WALPOLE.

FIRST CONGREGATIONAL SOCIETY (Unitarian). Organized 1730. — *Pastor*, Rev. Frank P. Hamblett, settled July 1, 1876; *Deacons*, Newell Boyden, Horatio Boyden; *Clerk of Society*, James G. Scott; *Treasurer*, Washington Glover; *Parish Committee*, Newell Boyden, David E. Metcalf, George A. Kendall. Number of members, 50. *Supt. of Sunday School*, James H. Leland. 7 teachers, 50 scholars.

---

* With Mission Chapel at Sharon.

ORTHODOX CONGREGATIONAL CHURCH AND SOCIETY. Organized Nov. 13, 1826. — *Pastor,* Rev. Calvin G. Hill, settled Sept. 27, 1876; *Deacons,* Willard Lewis, Samuel E. Guild; *Clerk of Society,* Samuel Allen; *Clerk and Treasurer of Church,* John Noyes Sherman; *Treasurer of Society,* Melzar W. Allen; *Parish Committee,* Bradford Lewis, Loring Johnson, Samuel E. Guild. Number of members, 183. *Supt. of Sunday School,* Deacon Samuel E. Guild. 10 teachers, 95 scholars.

METHODIST EPISCOPAL SOCIETY (SOUTH WALPOLE). Organized April, 1819. — *Pastor,* Rev. Alfred C. Godfrey, settled April, 1875; *Stewards,* Caleb S. Ellis, Joseph E. Pond, Edson C. Boyden, Willard M. Nottage, Frank B. Kingman, Elbridge P. Boyden, Jeremiah Boyden, William C. Boyden; *Clerk and Treasurer,* Edson C. Boyden; *Trustees,* Joseph E. Pond, Caleb S. Ellis, Frank B. Kingman, Elbridge P. Boyden, Edson C. Boyden, Jeremiah Boyden, Isaac H. Bullard, Warren Shepard, Wm. C. Boyden. Number of members, 72. *Supt. of Sunday School,* Elbridge P. Boyden. 14 teachers, 100 scholars.

ST. FRANCIS (Roman Catholic). Organized 1872. — *Pastor,* Rev. Francis Gouesse, settled Nov. 17, 1872. Number of members, 600. *Supt. of Sunday School,* William Mahoney. 10 teachers, 70 scholars.

WEYMOUTH.

FIRST CONGREGATIONAL CHURCH, NORTH WEYMOUTH (Trinitarian). Organized 1623. — *Pastor,* Rev. Franklin P. Chapin, settled Oct. 22, 1873; *Deacons,* Francis E. Loud, Francis F. Forsaith, Elnathan Bates; *Clerk of Society,* Samuel Thompson; *Clerk of Church,* Rev. F. P. Chapin; *Treasurer of Society,* Israel Wildes; *Treasurer of Church,* Francis Loud; *Parish Committee,* Francis E. Loud, William White, Elnathan Bates. Number of members, 128. *Supt. of Sunday School,* Benjamin F. Richards. 13 teachers, 85 scholars.

SECOND CONGREGATIONAL SOCIETY, SOUTH WEYMOUTH (Trinitarian). Organized June 21, 1723. — *Pastor,* Rev. George F. Stanton, settled Oct. 27, 1870; *Deacons,* Jacob Loud, Jason Holbrook; *Clerk of Society,* George C. Torrey; *Clerk of Church,* Henry Dyer; *Treasurer,* B. Franklin White; *Parish Committee,* Augustine Loud, Henry Dyer, George W. Bates. Number of members, 138. *Supt. of Sunday School,* William Dyer. 27 teachers, 250 scholars.

METHODIST EPISCOPAL CHURCH (EAST WEYMOUTH). Organized 1823. — *Pastor,* Rev. Samuel L. Gracey, settled March, 1874; *Clerk of Society and Church,* Z. L. Bicknell; *Treasurer,* Leavitt Bates; *Stewards,* Cyrus Washburn, Bela French, Z. L. Bicknell, N. Goodspeed, J. N. L. Bicknell, Leavitt Bates, Jos. A. Cushing, Charles W. Rice, John W. Bates. *Supt. of Sunday School,* Z. L. Bicknell. 24 teachers, 230 scholars.

FIRST UNIVERSALIST SOCIETY. Organized July, 1836. — *Pastor,* Rev. L. S. Crossley; *Deacons,* Joseph W. Armington, Mary Jane LaForrest; *Clerk of Society and Church,* Henry A. Peterson; *Treasurer,* Martin K. Pratt; *Parish Committee,* Elias Richards, David L. Sterling, Peter H. Cushing, George S. Baker, Alexander Sherman, Thomas B. Porter, Joseph W. Armington, Albion Hall, George E. Porter, G. W. White, Jr., Edwin P. Worster, C. W. Stevens, C. P. Hunt. *Supt. of Sunday School,* Joseph W. Armington. 10 teachers, 50 scholars.

UNION CONGREGATIONAL SOCIETY, SOUTH WEYMOUTH (Trinitarian). Organized June 20, 1842. — *Pastor,* Rev. James McLean, settled March, 1872, resigned July 1, 1876; *Deacons,* John S. Cobb, Josiah Reed; *Clerk of Society,* Noah F. Vining; *Clerk of Church and Treasurer,* Orin B. Bates; *Parish Committee,* Josiah Reed, Alfred Tirrell, James Tirrell. Number of members, 120. *Supt. of Sunday School,* John S. Fogg. 18 teachers, 160 scholars.

SECOND UNIVERSALIST SOCIETY (South Weymouth). Organized March, 1850 *Pastor*, Rev. Jacob Baker, settled Feb., 1869; *Deacons*, Joseph Harding, Isaac N. Hollis; *Clerk of Society*, John Blanchard; *Clerk of Church*, Jason Farrington; *Treasurer*, Joseph Harding; *Parish Committee*, Joseph B. Howe, Timothy A. Stetson, Elon Sherman. Number of members, 75. *Supt. of Sunday School*, David S. Murray. 27 teachers, 132 scholars.

PILGRIM CONGREGATIONAL CHURCH AND SOCIETY, North Weymouth (Orthodox). Organized March 11, 1852. — *Pastor*, Rev. George Dodson, settled Nov. 23, 1876; *Deacons*, David Pratt, James Torrey; *Clerk of Society*, Henry A. Newton; *Clerk of Church*, Thomas B. Seabury; *Treasurer*, John A. Holbrook; *Parish Committee*, James Torrey, John E. Stoddard, Edward Blanchard. Number of members, 161. *Supt. of Sunday School*, Francis A. Bicknell. 16 teachers, 152 scholars.

THIRD UNIVERSALIST SOCIETY (North Weymouth). Organized 1853. — *Pastor*, Rev. George W. Whitney, settled April 1, 1872; *Deacons*, Wilmot Cleverly, Daniel Cram; *Clerk of Society and Church*, Augustus Beals; *Treasurer*. Elias S. Beals; *Parish Committee*, Thomas F. Cleverly, John W. Bartlett, Daniel Cram. Number of members, 29. *Supt. of Sunday School*, Wilmot Cleverly. 10 teachers, 75 scholars.

FIRST BAPTIST CHURCH (East Weymouth). Organized Feb. 7, 1854. *Pastor*, Rev. William C. Wright, settled Sept. 1, 1874; *Deacons*, John Dizer, Wm. D. Farren, of East Weymouth, Elias Vining, of South Weymouth; *Clerk of Society and Church*, W. P. Sanborn; *Treasurer*, M. C. Dizer; *Parish Committee*, M. C. Dizer, Joshua Binney. Number of members, 166. *Supt. of Sunday School*, Wm. D. Farren. 13 teachers, 110 scholars.

CHURCH OF THE SACRED HEART OF JESUS (Roman Catholic). Organized 1859. *Pastor*, Rev. Hugh P. Smythe, settled July 17, 1869; *Sexton*, P. Whalen. Number of members, 700. *Supts. of Sunday School*, P. Whalen, —— Reynolds. 20 teachers, 250 scholars.

EAST WEYMOUTH CONGREGATIONAL CHURCH (Trinitarian). Organized June 13, 1860. — *Pastor*, Rev. John A. Cruzan supplies; *Deacons*, Alvah Raymond, Jairus Sprague, David W. Bates, Edwin Howard; *Clerk of Society*, Martin E. Hawes; *Clerk of Church*, Charles B. Cushing; *Treasurer of Society*, Nathan Canterbury; *Treasurer of Church*, E. B. Powers; *Parish Committee*, Nathan D. Canterbury, John P. Lovell, Alvah Raymond. Number of members, 243. *Supt. of Sunday School*, Edwin Howard. 24 teachers, 257 scholars.

TRINITY CHURCH, Weymouth (Episcopal). Organized July 7, 1867. — *Rector*, Rev. Samuel R. Slack, settled Nov. 1, 1874; *Wardens*, Edward Avery, William Sprague Wallace; *Vestrymen*, Lewis M. Pratt, John M. Walsh, Charles A. Chessman, Cranmore N. Wallace, F. Jackson; *Clerk and Treasurer*, Lewis M. Pratt. Communicants, 70. *Supt. of Sunday School*, Charles A. Chessman. 8 teachers, 65 scholars.

CHURCH OF ST. FRANCIS XAVIER, South Weymouth (Roman Catholic). — Organized 1870; *Pastor*, Rev. Hugh P. Smythe, settled July 17, 1870; *Sexton*, Daniel O'Connor. Number of members, 400. *Supts. of Sunday School*, Michael Loguò, Peter Burke. 12 teachers, 93 scholars.

LOVELL'S CORNER CHRISTIAN UNION. Organized Nov. 1, 1872. — No settled pastor. *Deacon*, Asa P. Whitman; *Clerk of Society*, Bradford Hawes; *Clerk of Church and Treasurer*, Asa P. Whitman; *Parish Committee*, Asa P. Whitman. Number of members, 34. *Supt. of Sunday School*, Bradford Hawes. 7 teachers, 52 scholars.

CHURCH OF THE IMMACULATE CONCEPTION (Roman Catholic), East Weymouth. Organized 1872. — *Pastor*, Rev. Hugh P. Smythe, settled 1872; *Sexton*,

Robert Mackintosh. Number of members, 550. *Supt. of Sunday School,* John Hughes. 17 teachers, 144 scholars.

WRENTHAM.

ORIGINAL CONGREGATIONAL CHURCH (Trinitarian). Organized April 13, 1692. — *Pastor,* Rev. William R. Tompkins, settled Oct. 15, 1866; *Deacons,* William E. Pond, William S. Ide, Benjamin N. Shepard, George E. Blake; *Clerk of Society,* Nathan Fales; *Clerk of Church,* William M. Proctor; *Treasurer of Society,* David T. Stone; *Treasurer of Church,* William S. Ide; *Parish Committee,* The Pastor, Deacons, Clerk, and Artemas Aldrich, Edson W. George, Charles P. Kendall. Number of members, 185. *Supt. of Sunday School,* William E. Pond. 18 teachers, 140 scholars.
SHELDONVILLE BAPTIST SOCIETY. Organized 1769. — No settled pastor; *Deacons,* Jesse Miller, A. Fenner Hawkins, Daniel M. Hancock, Jr.; *Clerk of Society and Treasurer,* George S. Hancock; *Clerk of Church,* Joshua L. Grant; *Parish Committee,* Daniel M. Hancock, Jr., Warren Rhodes, Allen R. Ray. Number of members, 108. *Supt. of Sunday School,* Albert Follett. 8 teachers, 50 scholars.
TRINITY CHURCH (Episcopal). Organized June 6, 1864. — No settled rector; *Wardens,* David Newland Fales, Elijah Pond; *Vestrymen,* C. S. Doggett, William B. Nolan, James E. Pollard, David T. Stone, Thomas A. George; *Clerk,* Charles J. Randall; *Treasurer,* David T. Stone. Communicants, 30. *Supt. of Sunday School,* The rector supplying. 5 teachers, 30 scholars.
ST. MARY'S ROMAN CATHOLIC CHURCH. Organized 1872. — *Pastor,* Rev. Francis Gouesse, settled Nov. 17, 1872. Number of members, 90. *Supt. and Teacher of Sunday School,* Mary Hopkins. Number of scholars, 15.

PUBLIC LIBRARIES.

THAYER PUBLIC LIBRARY, BRAINTREE.

Founded by Gen. Sylvanus Thayer. Library building, of brick, will be finished in 1877.

Trustees, Asa French, Chairman; Francis A. Hobart, Henry A. Johnson, N. H. Hunt, N. F. T. Hayden; *Librarian,* Miss Abby L. Arnold. Present number of volumes in library, 3,000.

BROOKLINE PUBLIC LIBRARY.

Established 1857.

President, Thomas Parsons; *Secretary,* George M. Towle; *Treasurer,* Charles D. Head; *Trustees,* Thomas Parsons, Robert Amory, R. G. F. Candago, Alfred Chandler, Augustine Shurtleff, Charles H. Drew, Clement K. Fay, H. N. Brown, Henry V. Poor, Charles D. Head, George M. Towle, James M. Codman; *Librarian,* Miss Mary A. Bean; *Assistant Librarians,* Miss Amelia A. Woods, Miss Clara A. Woods. Number of volumes, 20,000.

DEDHAM PUBLIC LIBRARY.
Incorporated 1872.

(This is a private corporation, but giving the free use of books and reading-room to the citizens of the town, receiving therefor $850 a year from the town.)

President, Alfred Hewins; *Clerk*, Henry O. Hildreth; *Treasurer*, Henry W. Richards; *Trustees*, Alfred Hewins, Carlos Slafter, Edward Stimson, Thomas L. Wakefield, Henry O. Hildreth, Royal O. Storrs, Henry W. Richards, A. W. Lamson, Daniel Goodwin; *Librarian*, Miss Frances M. Mann; *Assistant*, Miss Mary W. Haskell. Permanent invested fund, $8,275. Number of volumes, 5,600.

BOYDEN LIBRARY, FOXBOROUGH.
Established 1870.

Trustees, William Carpenter, President; W. E. Horton, Secretary; Benj. B. Shepard, A. Thomas Starkey, David Carpenter, Carmi Richmond; *Librarian*, Miss Sarah A. Doolittle. Number of volumes, 2,390.

FRANKLIN LIBRARY ASSOCIATION.
Established 1858. Incorporated 1872.

Directors, Henry M. Greene, President; Joseph G. Ray, Vice-President; A. A. Russegue, Clerk; Waldo Daniels, Librarian; George King, Monroe Morse, William Rockwood, S. W. Squire, William M. Thayer, George W. Wiggin, A. St. John Chambre, H. C. Crane. Number of volumes, 2,700.

HOLBROOK PUBLIC LIBRARY.
Established 1874.

Trustees, John Underhay, George N. Spear, J. B. Kingsbury; *Librarian*, Z. A. French. Number of volumes, 2,500.

HYDE PARK FREE PUBLIC LIBRARY.
Established March 4, 1874.

Trustees, Theodore D. Weld, Chairman; Gordon H. Nott, Secretary and Treasurer; Perley B. Davis, Francis C. Williams, Isaac H. Gilbert, William J. Corcoran, Edward M. Lancaster, Edwin C. Aldrich, Charles W. W. Wellington; *Librarian*, Mrs. H. N. Thompson. Number of volumes, 5,300.

MEDFIELD PUBLIC LIBRARY.
Organized 1812.

Trustees, George Cummings, Isaac Fiske, John H. Richardson; *Librarian*, Miss Mary A. Sewall. Number of volumes, 1,600.

DEAN LIBRARY ASSOCIATION, MEDWAY.
Founded by Dr. Oliver Dean. Incorporated 1860.

President, Milton M. Fisher; *Clerk and Treasurer*, Orion A. Mason; *Directors*, Rufus K. Harlow, Clark Partridge, Edward Eaton, Wm. H. Cary, A. L. B. Monroe, H. E. Mason, A. S. Harding; *Librarian*, L. H..Metcalf. Number of volumes, 2,000.

MILTON PUBLIC LIBRARY.
Organized 1871.

Trustees, James M. Robbins, Chairman; Amor L. Hollingsworth, Secretary; George Vose, Treasurer; John H. Morison, Albert K. Teele, Edward L. Pierce, George K.

Gannett, Edwin D. Wadsworth, William B. Weston; *Librarian*, Miss Jennie E. Emerson. Number of volumes, 6,500.

NORWOOD PUBLIC LIBRARY.

Organized 1873.

Trustees, Ward L. Gay, Chairman; Rev. George Hill, Secretary; Francis Tinker, Treasurer and Librarian; Rev. Edwin Bromley, Herbert F. Morse, Rev. Joseph P. Bixby. Number of volumes, 2,300.

QUINCY PUBLIC LIBRARY.

Organized 1871.

Trustees, Charles F. Adams, Jr., President; H. A. Keith, Secretary; Henry Barker, Treasurer; Charles A. Foster, L. W. Anderson, Edward Whicher; *Acting Librarian*, Miss A. L. Bumpus. Number of volumes, 10,000.

TURNER LIBRARY, RANDOLPH.

Founded by heirs of Royal Turner, 1875.

President, Seth Turner; *Vice-President*, J. White Belcher; *Treasurer*, Royal W. Turner; *Secretary*, Gilbert A. Tolman; *Trustees*, Rev. John C. Labaree, Rev. John C. Foster, Rev. James E. O'Brien, Daniel Howard, John T. Flood, Benjamin Dickerman, John V. Beal, John L. French, Seth Mann, 2d, Sidney French, Nath'l Howard; *Librarian*, Dr. Charles C. Farnham. Number of volumes, 3,000.

STOUGHTON PUBLIC LIBRARY.

Organized March 9, 1874.

Trustees, J. Freeman Ellis, Henry Fitzpatrick, Henry C. Kimball, Christopher Farrell, Wales French; *Librarian*, ——— ———. Number of volumes, 2,000.

WALPOLE PUBLIC LIBRARY.

Organized March, 1876.

Trustees, George A. Kendall, Miss Mary R. Bird, Henry E. Craig, Mrs. Melzar Allen, Silas E. Stone, Hugh Clinton; *Librarian*, Mr. F. O. Pillsbury. Number of volumes, 1,200.

SAVINGS BANKS.

BRAINTREE SAVINGS BANK.

Incorporated March 21, 1870.

President, E. A. Hollingsworth; *Vice-Presidents*, B. F. Dyer, D. H. Bates, Norton Pratt; *Trustees*, D. H. Bates, F. A. Hobart, N. H. Hunt, S. S. French, P. D. Holbrook, Asa French, B. F. Dyer, N. Eugene Hollis, Jos. Dyer, Jr.; *Secretary and Treasurer*, C. H. Hobart. Number of depositors, Oct. 31, 1876, 356. Amount of deposits, $75,604.24.

70   NORFOLK COUNTY MANUAL.

BROOKLINE SAVINGS BANK.
Incorporated Feb. 24, 1871.

President, Edward Atkinson; *Vice-Presidents*, Charles D. Head, Alfred Kenrick, Jr., William A. Wellman; *Trustees*, John C. Abbott, Austin W. Benton, Philip Duffey, Horace James, Charles H. Stearns, Benjamin F. Baker, James Driscoll, J. Anson Guild, Martin Kingman, James M. Seamans, Moses Williams, Jr.; *Secretary and Treasurer*, Frederick W. Prescott. Number of depositors, Oct. 31, 1876, 1,050. Amount of deposits, Oct. 31, 1876, $163,710.84.

CANTON INSTITUTION FOR SAVINGS.
Incorporated 1835.

President, Charles H. French; *Vice-Presidents*, Oliver S. Chapman, Charles Endicott; *Trustees*, Ellis Ames, V. J. Messinger, Geo. E. Downes, James S. Shepard, Nath'l Dunbar, J. Mason Everett, Wm. Mansfield, Nath'l Bent, F. G. Webster, all of Canton; *Secretary and Treasurer*, Francis W. Deane. Number of depositors, Oct. 31, 1876, 1,225. Amount of deposits, Oct. 31, 1876, $323,735.76.

COHASSET SAVINGS BANK.
Incorporated Feb. 28, 1845.

President, Martin Lincoln; *Trustees*, Thomas N. Tower, Newcomb Bates, J. Q. A. Lothrop, A. H. Tower, Jr., Edward E. Tower, Charles H. Willard, Zaccheus Rich, John W. Bates, Morgan B. Stetson, Thomas M. Smith, Louis N. Lincoln, Philander Bates, all of Cohasset; *Secretary and Treasurer*, Levi N. Bates. Number of depositors, Oct. 31, 1876, 960. Amount of deposits, Oct. 31, 1876, $387,110.95.

DEDHAM INSTITUTION FOR SAVINGS.
Incorporated May, 1831.

President, Thomas Barrows; *Vice-Presidents*, William Bullard, Waldo Colburn; *Trustees*, Francis Guild, Erastus Worthington, Henry W. Richards, Eliphalet Stone, Augustus B. Endicott, Ezra W. Taft, Joseph Fisher, Josephus G. Taft, Chauncey C. Churchill, William Ames, 2d, Edward Stimson, Royal O. Storrs, all of Dedham; *Clerk and Treasurer*, Calvin Guild. Number of depositors, Oct. 31, 1876, 3,596. Amount of deposits, Oct. 31, 1876, $1,184,247.70.

FOXBOROUGH SAVINGS BANK.
Incorporated 1855.

President, Otis Cary; *Trustees*, Carmi Richmond, Charles W. Hodges, C. Clark Sumner, Elisha White, Eli Phelps, Albert Fisher, James Capen, L. B. Wilbur, W. P. Turner, C. Calvin Sumner, W. H. Cobb, A. H. Messenger, Charles Capen, M. Ryan, Lewis Pond, W. B. Crocker, Albert L. Pond, William H. Young, Isaac P. Carpenter, Henry C. Williams, all of Foxborough; *Secretary and Treasurer*, James F. Leonard. Number of depositors, Oct. 31, 1876, 882. Amount of deposits, Oct. 31, 1876, $229,130.89.

BENJAMIN FRANKLIN SAVINGS BANK, FRANKLIN.
Incorporated 1871.

President, Davis Thayer, Jr.; *Vice-Presidents*, Henry M. Greene, James M. Freeman, James P. Ray, Albert E. Daniels, Daniel A. Cook, A. H. Morse; *Trustees*, Joseph G. Ray, A. A. Fletcher, E. H. Sherman, Waldo Daniels, J. L. Fitzpatrick, Erastus L. Metcalf, Joseph Harrod, Wm. B. Nolen, William E. Whiting, C. W. Stewart, Hugh McParland,

John P. Farmer, F. L. Metcalf, Henry R. Jenks, George W. Wiggin, E. P. Chapman, of Franklin; Calvin Fairbanks, C. H. Cutler, of Bellingham; George Sheldon, of Wrentham; Josiah Ware of Norfolk; *Secretary and Treasurer*, C. W. Stewart. Number of depositors, Oct. 31, 1876, 1,113. Amount of deposits, Oct. 31, 1876, $222,852.84.

HYDE PARK SAVINGS BANK.
Incorporated March 8, 1871.

President, Charles F. Gerry; *Vice-Presidents,* Henry Grew, J. E. Piper, Rev. Amos Webster, D.D., A. H. Brainard; *Trustees,* Henry Blasdale, Robert Bleakie, Orin T. Gray, Ezra G. Perkins, Rinaldo Williams, Alfred Downing, Wilbert J.Case, William J. Stuart, J. J. Brown, Jairus Pratt, John M. Twichell, Nathaniel Shepard, Edward S. Hathaway, George C. Silsbury, Levi A. Runnells; *Secretary and Treasurer,* Henry S. Bunton. Number of depositors, Oct. 31, 1876, 432. Amount of deposits, Oct. 31, 1876, $60,004.41.

MEDWAY SAVINGS BANK.
Incorporated Feb. 20, 1871.

President, Milton M. Fisher; *Trustees,* Clark Partridge, Edward Eaton, Wales Kimball, James O'Donnell, A. P. Phillips, A. M. B. Fuller, D. J. Hastings, Wm. H. Cary, M. M. Fisher, James Lacroix, Charles F. Daniels, Willard P. Clark, Charles H. Deans, of Medway; Charles Hamant, of Medfield, S. W. Richardson, of Franklin; Henry Trowbridge, of Norfolk; *Secretary,* Charles H. Deans; *Treasurer,* Orion A. Mason. Number of depositors, Oct. 31, 1876, 770. Amount of deposits, Oct. 31, 1876, $160,161.72

NEEDHAM SAVINGS BANK.
Incorporated 1874.

President, Galen Orr; *Vice-Presidents,* George White, Charles E. Keith, Ephraim Wilson, Henry Billings, Enos H. Tucker, Joseph E. Fiske; *Trustees,* Matthias Mills, Levi Ladd, Dexter Kingsbury, Charles E. Keith, Alexander Lynes, Bradford Curtis, Charles C. Greenwood, George White, Henry Billings, Enos H. Tucker, Solomon Flagg, Joseph E. Fiske, William R. Mills, James Mackintosh, of Needham; Ephraim Wilson, Josiah Whiting, of Dover; *Secretary and Treasurer,* Emory Grover. Number of depositors, Oct. 31, 1876, 237. Amount of deposits, Oct. 31, 1876, $28,017.34.

QUINCY SAVINGS BANK.
Incorporated 1845.

President, Edward Turner; *Vice-President,* Israel W. Munroe; *Trustees,* Daniel Baxter, Noah Cummings, Whitcomb Porter, George A. Brackett, Charles A. Howland, Horace B. Spear, John D. Whicher, John Quincy Adams, Daniel H. Bills, George B. Wendell, all of Quincy; *Secretary and Treasurer,* George L. Gill. Number of depositors, Oct. 31, 1876, 3,526. Amount of deposits, Oct. 31, 1876, $1,287,671.31.

RANDOLPH SAVINGS BANK.
Incorporated April, 1851.

President, J. White Belcher; *Vice-Presidents,* Royal W. Turner, of Randolph, Thomas White, of Boston; *Trustees,* Alfred W. Whitcomb, Richard Stevens, Daniel Howard, John L. French, J. Winsor Pratt, Charles Harris, Nathaniel Howard, Sidney French, Benjamin Dickerman, all of Randolph; *Secretary and Treasurer,* Seth Turner. Number of depositors, Oct. 31, 1876, 2,156. Amount of deposits, Oct. 31, 1876, $821,617.77.

WEYMOUTH SAVINGS BANK.
Incorporated 1833.

President, James Humphrey; *Vice-Presidents,* James Jones, Elias Richards, of Weymouth; Jonathan French, Naaman L. White, of Braintree; *Directors,* Albert Humphrey, James Torrey, Benjamin T. Dowse, John P. Lovell, Francis Ambler, Levi W. Hobart, Stephen W. Nash, E. Atherton Hunt, Francis P. Forsaith, John J. Loud, all of Weymouth; *Clerk and Treasurer,* A. S. White. Number of depositors, Oct. 31, 1876, 2,460. Amount of deposits, Oct. 31, 1876, $899,281.07.

SOUTH WEYMOUTH SAVINGS BANK.
Incorporated March, 1868.

President, Albert Tirrell; *Vice-President,* Oran White; *Trustees,* Albert Tirrell, Oran White, John S. Cobb, Jacob Loud, Thomas J. Nash, Joseph Dyer, Eri T. Joy, B. F. White, D. S. Murray, C. C. Tower, Jason Holbrook, William Dyer, Elon Sherman, C. C. Blanchard, all of South Weymouth; *Secretary and Treasurer,* B. F. White. Number of depositors, Oct. 31, 1876, 905. Amount of deposits, Oct. 31, 1876, $373,326.34.

EAST WEYMOUTH FIVE CENTS SAVINGS BANK.
Incorporated Feb. 14, 1872.

President, John P. Lovell; *Trustees,* John P. Lovell, Joseph Totman, Z. L. Bicknell, Cyrus Washburn, Alvah Raymond, David Tucker, George W. Fay, Peter W. French, II, F. Bicknell, Joseph Rogers, Bela French, Isaac Reed, Jr., J. H. Clapp, Elnathan Bates, Nathan D. Canterbury, C. H. Pratt, M. C. Dizer, all of Weymouth; *Secretary and Treasurer,* N. Canterbury. Number of depositors, Oct. 31, 1876, 384. Amount of deposits, Oct. 31, 1876, $69,739.50.

NATIONAL BANKS.

NEPONSET NATIONAL BANK, CANTON.
Incorporated as a State Bank, 1836. Reorganized as a National Bank, 1865.

President, Charles H. French (since 1851); *Cashier,* Francis W. Deane (since 1845); *Directors,* Charles H. French, Oliver S. Chapman, V. J. Messenger, George E. Downes, Charles Endicott, of Canton; H. Augustus Lothrop, of Sharon; J. Freeman Ellis, of Stoughton. Capital, $250,000. Paid during the year two dividends of five per cent. each.

DEDHAM NATIONAL BANK, DEDHAM.
Incorporated as a State Bank, 1814. Reorganized as a National Bank, 1865.

President, Ezra W. Taft; *Cashier,* Lewis H. Kingsbury; *Directors,* Ezra W. Taft, Ira Cleveland, Joseph Day, Joseph Fisher, Lewis H. Kingsbury, Waldo Colburn, William Bullard. Capital, $300,000. Paid during the year two dividends: one of four per cent., and one of three per cent.

FRANKLIN NATIONAL BANK, FRANKLIN.

Incorporated at Blackstone, Mass., as the Worcester County Bank, in 1850. Reorganized as a National Bank in 1864, and removed to Franklin in 1871.

President, James P. Ray; *Cashier*, Moses Farnum; *Directors*, James P. Ray, Henry M. Greene, J. P. Daniels, Davis Thayer, Jr., A. H. Morse, A. A. Russegue, Joseph G. Ray, all of Franklin. Capital, $200,000. Paid two dividends of five and four per cent. during the year.

NATIONAL GRANITE BANK, QUINCY.

Incorporated as a State Bank, 1836. Reorganized as a National Bank, 1864.

President, Charles Marsh; *Cashier*, R. F. Claflin; *Directors*, Charles Marsh, John Faxon, Charles R. Mitchell, John D. Whicher, of Quincy; Jesse Bunton, of Milton; James Torrey, Alexis Torrey, of Weymouth. Capital, $150,000. Paid two dividends of four per cent. each during the year.

NATIONAL MOUNT WOLLASTON BANK OF QUINCY.

Incorporated as a State Bank, 1853. Reorganized as a National Bank, 1864.

President, Joseph W. Robertson; *Cashier*, Horace B. Spear; *Directors*, Joseph W. Robertson, Edward Turner, Eleazer Frederick, Lemuel Baxter, Israel W. Munroe, A. W. Russell, of Quincy; Elias S. Beals, of Weymouth. Capital, $150,000. Paid two dividends of six and five per cent. during the year.

RANDOLPH NATIONAL BANK, RANDOLPH.

Incorporated as a State Bank, 1836. Reorganized as a National Bank, 1864.

President, Royal W. Turner; *Vice-President*, Seth Turner; *Cashier*, C. G. Hathaway; *Directors*, Royal W. Turner, Seth Turner, Ebenezer Alden, Abiel Howard, David Burrill, J. Winsor Pratt. Capital, $200,000. Paid two dividends of six per cent. each during the year.

UNION NATIONAL BANK OF WEYMOUTH.

Originally the Union Bank of Weymouth and Braintree, and incorporated March 17, 1832. Reorganized as a National Bank under its present name, Sept. 6, 1864.

President, Albert Humphrey; *Cashier*, John J. Loud; *Directors*, Albert Humphrey, James Jones, Thomas Humphrey, M. C. Dizer, John P. Lovell, Minot Tirrell, Amos L. White, Edwin P. Worster, of Weymouth; Jonathan French, of Braintree. Capital, $100,000. Paid during the year two dividends: one of three and one-half per cent., and one of three per cent.

FIRST NATIONAL BANK OF SOUTH WEYMOUTH.

Organized Nov., 1864.

President, John S. Fogg; *Vice-President*, Josiah Reed; *Cashier*, Benjamin F. White; *Assistant Cashier*, J. H. Stetson; *Directors*, John S. Fogg, Josiah Reed, Loring Tirrell, Alfred Tirrell, James Tirrell, C. C. Blanchard, B. F. White, all of Weymouth. Capital, $150,000. Paid during the year two dividends of four per cent., each.

THE NATIONAL BANK OF WRENTHAM.

Incorporated 1833. Reorganized as a National Bank, 1865.

President, Daniel A. Cook; *Cashier*, F. N. Plympton; *Directors*, Daniel A. Cook, Thomas Proctor, of Wrentham; Otis Cary, Foxboro; Davis Thayer, Franklin; S. Richardson, Attleborough. Capital, $105,000, in 1,500 shares; par value, $70 per share. Paid during the year, two dividends: one of three dollars a share, and one of three per cent. on par value.

INSURANCE COMPANIES.

COHASSET MUTUAL FIRE INSURANCE COMPANY. Incorporated March 18, 1845. — *President,* Martin Lincoln; *Secretary,* J. Q. A. Lothrop; *Treasurer,* Abraham H. Tower; *Directors,* Martin Lincoln, Loring Bates, Isaac Kent, Warren Willcutt, Thomas Smith, James Creed, Zaccheus Rich, Ephraim Snow, Louis N. Lincoln, all of Cohasset.

NORFOLK MUTUAL FIRE INSURANCE COMPANY. Located at Dedham. Incorporated 1825. — *President and Treasurer,* Ira Cleveland; *Secretary,* George D. Gordon; *Directors,* Ira Cleveland, Joseph Fisher, William Ames, 2d, Dedham; Luther Metcalf, Medway; Eleazer J. Bispham, Dorchester; William Mansfield, Canton; Lyman Smith, Norwood; George B. Faunce, Roxbury; J. White Belcher, Randolph.

WEYMOUTH AND BRAINTREE MUTUAL FIRE INSURANCE COMPANY. Incorporated Feb. 20, 1833. — *President,* Naaman L. White; *Secretary,* Elias Richards; *Directors,* Naaman L. White, Joseph R. Frasier, Braintree; Elias S. Beals, Richard A. Hunt, Thomas B. Porter, Elias Richards, Z. L. Bicknell, Jacob Loud, Weymouth; F. P. Howland, Abington.

DEDHAM MUTUAL FIRE INSURANCE COMPANY. Incorporated 1837. — *President and Treasurer,* Ira Cleveland; *Secretary,* George D. Gordon; *Directors,* Ira Cleveland, Waldo Colburn, Ezra W. Taft, Lewis H. Kingsbury, Dedham; Eleazer J. Bispham, Dorchester; William Mansfield, Canton; George B. Faunce, Roxbury.

QUINCY MUTUAL FIRE INSURANCE COMPANY. Incorporated March 22, 1851. — *President and Treasurer,* Israel W. Munroe; *Secretary,* Charles A. Howland; *Directors,* Israel W. Munroe, Whitcomb Porter, William B. Duggan, Thomas Curtis, Charles A. Howland, John Hardwick, Quincy; Alfred Loring, Hingham; George Marston, New Bedford; H. W. Blanchard, Dorchester; Sumner A. Hayward, Brockton; Royal W. Turner, Randolph; Solomon J. Beal, Cohasset; Charles Breck, Milton; J. Alba Davis, West Roxbury; J. F. C. Hyde, Newton; John Gates, Worcester.

GAS COMPANIES.

BROOKLINE GAS COMPANY. Incorporated 1853. — *President,* John C. Abbott; *Clerk,* George F. Homer; *Treasurer,* D. W. Salisbury; *Directors,* John C. Abbott, William A. Wellman, Edward S. Philbrick, D. W. Salisbury, Austin W. Benton, Robert Amory, B. F. Ricker. Capital, $350,000. Paid two dividends during the year amounting to six and a half per cent.

DEDHAM AND HYDE PARK GAS COMPANY. Dedham Gas Company incorporated 1853. Name changed, as above, 1871. — *President,* Joseph W. Clark; *Clerk and Treasurer,* C. A. Taft; *Directors,* Joseph W. Clark, Henry W. Richards, Charles Van Brunt. Capital, $125,000.

CITIZENS' GAS LIGHT COMPANY OF QUINCY. Incorporated 1860. — *President and Treasurer,* Edward H. Dewson; *Directors,* Edward H. Dewson, Stedman Williams, John S. Williams. Capital, $12,500.

COLLEGES, ACADEMIES, ETC.

WELLESLEY COLLEGE, NEEDHAM.

Incorporated March 17, 1870, as Wellesley Female Seminary, for the purpose of giving to young women opportunities for education equivalent to those usually provided in colleges for young men. Name changed, March 7, 1873.

BOARD OF TRUSTEES.

Rev. Noah Porter, D.D., President of Yale College, *President;* Rev. Howard Crosby, D.D., Chancellor of the University of the City of New York, *Vice-President;* Rev. John Hall, D.D., New York; Rev. Alexander H. Vinton, D.D., Boston; Rev. William F. Warren, D D., President of Boston University; Rev. Joseph Cummings, D.D., of Wesleyan University, Middletown, Conn.; Rev. Galusha Anderson, D.D., Chicago; Rev. Austin Phelps, D.D., of Andover Theological Seminary; Rev. Nathaniel G. Clark, D.D; Abner Kingman, Elisha S. Converse, Boston; Hon. William Claflin, Mrs. William Claflin, Newton; M. H. Simpson, Mrs. M. H. Simpson, Boston; Hon. Rufus S. Frost, Chelsea; Mrs. Arthur Wilkinson, Cambridge; Henry F. Durant, Mrs. Henry F. Durant, Boston.

BOARD OF INSTRUCTION.

Ada L. Howard, *President;* Mary E. Horton, Prof. of Greek; Frances E. Lord, Prof. of Latin; Susan M. Hallowell, Prof. of Natural History; Sarah F. Whiting, Prof. of Physics; Maria S. Eaton, Prof. of Chemistry; Mary D. Sheldon, Prof of Literature; Sarah P. Eastman, Teacher of History; Anna C. Cantrell, Teacher of English Composition; Sarah W. Bigelow and Frances V. Emerson, Teachers of Mathematics; Esther E. Thompson, Catherine E. Worcester and Lucia F. Clark, Teachers of Latin; Elizabeth H. Denio and Caroline A. Farley, Teachers of German; Lucy C. Hall and Jenny Nelson, Teachers of French; Sophia B. Horr, Teacher of Penmanship and Drawing; Grace Carter, Teacher of Painting; Charles H. Morse, Prof. of Music; A. Louise Gage, Teacher of Vocal Music; Gertrude E. Randall, Teacher of Piano; Ida F. Parker, Teacher of Gymnastics; Emelie H. Jones, Physician; Annie R. Godfrey, Librarian; Rosamond Pentecost, Assistant Librarian; Emily J. Hurd, Supt. of Domestic Department; Caroline M. Torrey, House Matron; Harriot A. Walker, Curator of Herbarium.

Number of students, 320.

DEAN ACADEMY, FRANKLIN.

Incorporated 1865.

BOARD OF TRUSTEES.

Rev. A. St. John Chambré, Franklin, *President;* Henry D. Williams, Boston, *Vice-President;* J. C. Wellington, Cambridge, *Treasurer;* Rev. Henry I. Cushman, Providence, R. I., *Secretary;* John D. W. Joy, Boston; Augustus Harrington, Peabody; Rev. T. E. St. John, Worcester; Thomas H. Frothingham, Salem; Rev. A. J. Patterson, D.D., Roxbury; Hon. Joseph Day, Norwood; Albert Dickerman, Boston; Hon. Joseph G. Ray, Franklin; Hon. Josiah G. Peabody, Lowell; Rev. E. H. Capen, President of Tufts College; Hon. L. W. Ballou, Woonsocket, R. I.; D. C. Gateley, Newton, Conn.; Rev. E. C. Bolles, Salem; Seth M. Vose, Providence, R. I.; Charles Whittier, Roxbury; Rev. J. D. Pierce, N. Attleboro'; Albert Metcalf, Boston; Hon. Amasa Whiting, Boston; Rev. J. K. Mason, Stamford, Conn.; Gen. Olney Arnold, Pawtucket, R. I.; B. F. Spinney, Lynn.

EXECUTIVE COMMITTEE.

Rev. E. H. Capen, Charles Whittier, J. C. Wellington, Rev. A. St. John Chambré, Rev. A. J. Patterson, D.D., Hon. Joseph G. Ray, Gen. Olney Arnold.

BOARD OF INSTRUCTION.

Rev. J. P. Weston, D.D., *Principal*, Goddard Professor of Mental and Moral Science; Charles C. Bates, A.M., Chase Classical Professor; Leslie A. Lee, A.M., and J. Clarance Lee, Teachers of Natural Sciences; Miss Harriet B. Stetson, Preceptress, Teacher of French and German; Misses Annie W. Stiles and N. Mariah Stevens, Assistant Teachers of Higher English; Miss Emma E. Teulon, Assistant Teacher; Louis H. Isenbeck, Professor of Music; Miss Mary E. Weston, Teacher of Painting and Drawing; Mrs. M. Little, Teacher of Vocal Music; Miss C. C. Ballou, Librarian and Book-keeper; Mr. A. A. Fletcher, Steward. Number of students: ladies, 63; gentlemen, 69; total, 132.

ADAMS ACADEMY, QUINCY.

Founded by Ex-President John Adams. Opened September, 1872.

BOARD OF MANAGERS.

Hon. Charles Francis Adams, *Chairman;* Luther W. Anderson, Josiah P. Quincy, Henry Barker, James E. Tirrell; Charles H. Porter, *Secretary.*

BOARD OF INSTRUCTION.

Master, William Reynolds Dimmock, LL.D.; *Sub-Master*, William Royall Tyler, A.B.; Assistant Teachers, Jesse Peck Worden, A.B., Louis Eugene Robson, A.B., Henry Preble, A.B.; Instructor in French, Armand Guys; Instructor in German, Eugène Thoré; Instructor in Drawing, Leslie Miller; Instructor in Elocution, Henry Wilson Smith, A.M. Number of scholars, first class, 28; second class, 19; third class, 25; fourth class, 43; preparatory class, 16; total, 131.

STOUGHTONHAM INSTITUTE, SHARON.

Principal, Sanford Waters Billings; and

REV. CALVIN S. LOCKE'S SCHOOL, WEST DEDHAM.

At both of which young men are fitted for college or for business pursuits.

GRAND ARMY OF THE REPUBLIC.

BRAINTREE.

GEN. S. THAYER POST 87. — *Com.*, E. L. Curtis; *S.V.C.*, William L. Gage; *J.V.C.*, Royal Belcher; *Adj.*, Henry A. Monk, *Q.M.*, M. A. Perkins; *Surg.*, L. A. Dyer; *Chap.*, J. M. Cutting; *O.D.*, Solon David; *O.G.*, Thos. Fallon; *S.M.*, J. V. Hunt; *Q.M.S.*, T. B. Stoddard.

BROOKLINE.

CHARLES L. CHANDLER POST 143. — *Com.*, Charles H. Drew; *S.V.C.*, William B. Sears; *J.V.C.*, Horace A. Allen; *Adj.*, George E. Everett; *Q.M.*, George F. Dearborn; *Surg.*, Dr. J. B. Cushing; *Chap.*, Edmund Russell, *O.D.*, James Sinclair; *O.G.*, John Sweeney; *S.M.*, William Pree; *Q.M.S.*, Phillip Daniels.

CANTON.

REVERE POST 94. Organized 1869. — *Com.*, F. G. Webster; *S.V.C.*, Adam Kinsley; *J.V.C.*, S. L. Smith; *Adj.*, R. L. Weston; *Q.M.*, E. A. Morse; *Surg.*, A. R. Holmes; *Chap.*, H. A. Freeman; *O.D.*, A. A. Harrington; *O.G.*, E. S. Champney; *S.M.*, H. D. Seavey, *Q.M.S.*, J. C. Breslyn.

DEDHAM.

CHARLES W. CARROLL POST 144. — *Com.*, Henry C. Bonney; *S.V.C.*, John II. Nichols; *J.V.C.*, Henry Hitchings; *Adj.*, Amasa Guild; *Q.M.*, David L. Hodges; *Surg.*, John W. Chase; *Chap.*, Joseph Guild; *O.D.*, John B. Fisher; *O.G.*, Horace E. Towle; *S.M.*, Edward Sherwin; *Q.M.S.*, F. C. Field.

FOXBOROUGH.

E. P. CARPENTER POST 91. — *Com.*, J. S. Carver; *S.V.C.*, C. B. Morse; *J.V.C.*, J. Ferguson; *Adj.*, A. L. Bundy; *Q.M.*, W. H. Kempton; *Surg.*, Dr. J. G. S. Hitchcock; *Chap*, A. M. Morse; *O.D.*, L. C. Winn; *O.G.*, William Fales; *S.M.*, S. D. Robinson; *Q.M.S.*, J. B. Davidson.

HYDE PARK.

H. A. DARLING POST 121. — Organized March 24, 1870. — *Com.*, Henry A. Darling; *S.V.C.*, Richard F. Boynton; *J.V.C.*, Elisha E. Rollins; *Adj.*, Henry S. Dunton; *Q.M.*, Silas P. Blodgett; *Surg.*, Charles C. Hayes, M.D.; *Chap.*, Rev. Francis C. Williams; *O.D.*, William O'Connell; *O.G.*, Sylvanus Cobb, Jr.; *S.M.*, Fergus A. Easton; *Q.M.S.*, G. Henry Perkins.

MEDFIELD.

MOSES ELLIS POST 117. — *Com.*, P. C. Grover; *S.V.C.*, Francis Rhoades; *J.V.C.*, James Griffin; *Adj.*, William F. Guild; *Q.M.*, Joseph Clark; *Surg.*, J. H. Richardson, M.D.; *Chap.*, Lowell Babcock; *O.D.*, H. S. Richardson; *O.G.*, A. H. Wiley; *S.M.*, Wm. Crane; *Q.M.S.*, N. F. Harding.

MEDWAY (WEST).

WILDER DWIGHT POST 105. — *Com.*, S. J. Clark; *S.V.C.*, Lewis Goulding; *J.V.C.*, George Andrews; *Adj*, David A. Partridge; *Q.M.*, Geo. R. Drake; *Surg.*, Charles A. Grant; *Chap.*, George Bullard; *O.D.*, D. S Woodman; *O.G.*, Charles Williams; *S.M.*, William Rawson; *Q.M.S.*, Amos Morse.

QUINCY.

PAUL REVERE POST 88. — *Com.*, William Emerson; *S.V.C.*, C. A. Follett; *J.V.C.*, A. A. Holt; *Adj.*, J. M. Holt; *Q.M.*, W. W. Penniman; *Chap.*, Henry Chubbuck; *O.D.*, S. B. Turner; *O.G.*, George Phillips; *S.M.*, E. A. Spear, 2d; *Q.M.S.*, John Faircloth.

RANDOLPH.

CAPT. HORACE NILES POST 110. Organized Oct. 29, 1869. — *Com.*, Galen Hollis; *S.V.C.*, Peter Mahon; *J.V.C.*, Moses N. Hunt; *Adj.*, William A. Croak; *Q.M.*, Samuel White; *Surg.*, Joseph W. Thayer; *Chap.*, Royal W. Thayer; *O. D.*, —— Deuch; *S.M.*, Marcus M. Poole; *Q.M.S.*, Hiram C. Alden; *Treas. Charity Fund*, Hiram C. Alden.

STOUGHTON.

A. ST. JOHN CHAMBRÉ POST 72. — *Com.*, George W. Dutton; *S.V.C.*, E. A. Lunt; *J.V.C.*, A. J. Keene; *Adj.*, Leonard A. Thayer; *Q.M.*, Charles T. Drake; *Chap.*, David Ward; *O.D.*, William O. Jones; *O.G.*, Robert Barlow; *S.M.*, S. Parker; *Q.M.S.*, John Mills.

WEYMOUTH.

REYNOLDS POST 58. — *Com.*, Benj. S. Lovell; *S.V.C.*, Edward H. Davis; *J.V.C.*, Samuel Pray; *Adj.*, Charles W. Hastings; *Q.M.*, Elbridge Nash; *Surg.*, Moses R. Greeley; *Chap.*, Samuel L. Gracey; *O.D.*, John H. Whelan; *O.G.*, Thomas B. Loud; *S.M.*, Geo. F. Cushing; *Q.M.S.*, Walter H. Joy.

MASONIC SOCIETIES.

BROOKLINE.

BETH-HORAN. Organized 1870. — *W.M.*, James W. Edgerley; *S.W.*, C. K. Kirby; *J.W.*, Benj. W. Hackett; *Treas.*, David Damon; *Sec.*, Francis H. Bacon; *Chap.*, Rev. Howard N. Brown; *Marshal*, R. G. F. Candage; *S.D.*, John E. Hoar; *J.D.*, Manning Seamans; *S.S.*, A. E. Kenrick; *J.S.*, Albert Haven; *I.S.*, Francis J. Nash; *Tyler*, John S. G. Aspinwall.

CANTON.

BLUE HILL. Organized 1864. — *W.M.*, F. J. Sawyer; *S.W.*, J. W. Cushman; *J.W.*, A. A. Harrington; *Treas.*, E. S. Brewster; *Sec.*, N. W. Dunbar; *Chap.*, Rev. Edwin Davis; *Marshal*, Frank G. Webster; *S.D.*, J. B. Robinson; *J.D.*, S. H. Capen; *S.S.*, F. L. Gates; *J.S.*, Jonathan Linfield; *Tyler*, R. L. Weston.

COHASSET.

KONOHASSETT. — *W.M.*, Andrew W. Williams; *S.W.*, David Bates; *J.W.*, Morgan B. Stetson; *Treas.*, Henry W. Beal; *Sec.*, James H. Bouvé; *Marshal*, Charles P. Seaverns; *S.D.*, Alfred A. Seaverns; *J.D.*, Edward E. Ellms; *S.S.*, Edwin A. Olmsted; *J.S.*, Frank Studley; *Tyler*, Joseph J. Bates.

DEDHAM.

CONSTELLATION. Organized 1872. — *W.M.*, David L. Hodges; *S.W.*, Chas. C. Nichols; *J.W.*, Henry A. Hutchinson; *Treas.*, Sanford Carroll; *Sec.*, Edwin A. Brooks; *Chap.*, Rev. Edw. Crowninshield; *Marshal*, Henry White; *S.D.*, George F. Wight; *J.D.*, Theron B. Ames; *S.S.*, George P. Goding; *J.S.*, George F. Richards; *I.S.*, Edward F. Clark; *Or.*, Frederick Bradley; *Ch.*, F. F. Favor; *Tyler*, David S. Hill.

FOXBOROUGH.

ST. ALBANS. Organized 1818. — *W.M.*, Isaac R. Carpenter; *S.W.*, Junius B. Mowrey; *J.W.*, Geo. S. Wheeler; *Treas.*, Albert L. Pond; *Sec.*, W. W. Turner; *S.D.*, Wm. B. Crocker; *J.D.*, George Foster; *S.S.*, James W. Leonard; *J.S.*, Fred S. Lane; *Tyler*, A. A. Wilmarth.

KEY-STONE ROYAL ARCH CHAPTER. — *M.E.H.P.*, Herbert W. Mason; *M.E.K.*, George S. Wheeler; *M.E.S.*, George C. Forrest; *C.C.H.*, M. Ryan; *P.S.*, Junius B. Mowrey; *R.A.C.*, William H. Young; *M. 3d V.*, W. W. Turner; *M. 2d V.*, Edward A. Boyden; *M. 1st V.*, Warren B. Mason; *Treas.*, Albert L. Pond; *Sec.*, R. W. Folsom; *Tyler*, A. A. Wilmarth.

FRANKLIN.

EXCELSIOR. Organized 1867. — *W.M.*, George W. Wiggin; *S.W.*, Joseph H. Partridge; *J.W.*, Daniel O. Corbin; *Treas.*, James M. Freeman; *Sec.*, William A. Wyckoff; *Chap.*, Hamilton P. Stewart;. *Marshal*, William A. Stanley; *S.D.*, Henry R. Jenks; *J.D.*, Edgar Thayer; *S.S.*, Zachary T. Colvin; *J.S.*, Thomas C. Taft; *Tyler*, S. C. Taft.

MILLER ROYAL ARCH CHAPTER. Chartered 1872. — *H.P.*, A. St. John Chambré; *E.K.*, J. T. Stetson; *E.S.*, E. Copleston; *C. of H.*, F. A. B. King; *P.S.*, J. Pickens; *R.A.C.*, C. B. Craig; *M. 3d V.*, L. R. Whitaker; *M. 2d V.*, C. A. Frazer; *M. 1st V.*, W. B. Nolen; *Treas.*, J. M. Freeman; *Sec.*, E. R. Maynard; *S.S.*, J. W. Heaton; *J.S.*, James Hood; *Sen.*, S. C. Taft.

HYDE PARK.

HYDE PARK. Instituted Feb. 1, 1866. — *W.M.*, William H. Ingersoll; *S.W.*, Daniel J. Goss; *J.W.*, Clark C. Gregg; *Treas.*, William J. Stuart; *Sec.*, Henry S. Bunton; *Chap.*, John M. Williams; *Marshal*, G. Henry Perkins; *S.D.*, John F. Ross; *J.D.*, Philander Harlow; *S.S.*, Francis L. Gerald; *J.S.*, Samuel J. Denham; *Sen.*, Samuel Blee; *Tyler*, David A. McDonald.

NORFOLK ROYAL ARCH CHAPTER. Instituted May 18, 1870. — *M.E.H.P.*, Henry S. Bunton; *E.K.*, Fergus A. Easton; *E.S.*, William H. Ingersoll; *C. of H.*, Charles C. Nichols; *P.S.*, G. Henry Perkins; *R.A.C.*, Hobart M. Cable; *M. of 3d V.*, Philander Harlow; *M. of 2d V.*, Daniel J. Goss; *M. of 1st V.*, John F. Ross; *Treas.*, William J. Stuart; *Sec.*, Augustus M. Fisher; *Chap.*, John M. Williams; *S.S.*, James L. Vialle; *J.S.*, Henry S. Holtham; *Tyler*, David A. McDonald.

HYDE PARK COUNCIL SELECT AND ROYAL MASTERS. Instituted Dec. 21, 1872. — *T.I.M.*, Henry S. Bunton; *D.M.*, William H. Ingersoll; *P.C. of W.*, Augustus M. Fisher; *Treas.*, Hobart M. Cable; *Rec.*, G. Henry Perkins; *C. of G.*, John F. Ross; *C. of C.*, Philander Harlow; *M. of C.*, Henry C. Chamberlain; *Chap*, John M. Williams; *Stew.*, John Beatey; *Sen.*, Joel F. Goodwin.

CYPRUS COMMANDERY KNIGHTS TEMPLARS. Instituted Oct. 31, 1873. — *E.C.*, Henry C. Chamberlain; *G.*, Henry S. Bunton; *C.G.*, George F. Lincoln; *Prel.*, Sylvanus Cobb, Jr.; *S.W.*, G. Henry Perkins; *J.W.*, John F. Ross; *Treas.*, Daniel J. Goss; *Rec.*, Geo. H. Butler; *S.B.*, Chas. L. Farnsworth; *S.B.*, Clark C. Gregg; *War.*, William H. Ingersoll; *Guards*, Hobart M. Cable, Edwin C. Aldrich, Francis L. Gerald; *Arm.*, David A. McDonald; *Sen.*, Joel F. Goodwin.

MEDWAY (WEST).

CHARLES RIVER LODGE. Organized April 11, 1871. — *W.M.*, R. K. Colcord; *S.W.*, C. W. Seavey; *J.W.*, G. H. Daniels; *Treas.*, L. S. Daniels; *Sec.*, H. C. Austin; *Chap.*, V. Y. A. Boardman; *Marshal*, J. V. Huntress; *S.D.*, C. P. Harding; *J.D.*, G. M. Farrington; *S.S.*, R. B. McElroy; *J.S.*, G. R. Temple; *I.S.*, M. A. Fuller; *Tyler*, C. F. Cook; *Relief Com.*, D. A. Partridge, C. H. Cutler, F. W. Cummings.

NORWOOD.

ORIENT. Organized 1862. — *W.M.*, James A. Rhoades; *S.W.*, Lewis Smith, Jr.; *J.W.*, Walter C. Shapleigh; *Treas.*, Joseph Day; *Sec.*, Newman N. Sumner; *Chap.*, Rev. George Hill; *S.D.*, Albert G. Webb; *J.D.*, Ward L. Hartshorn; *Tyler*, Warren E. Rhoades.

NEEDHAM.

NORFOLK. — *W.M.*, James E. Chapman; *S.W.*, Edward A. Mills; *J.W.*, Edward Dorsey; *Treas.*, Elbridge G. Leach; *Sec.*, Charles S. Dupee; *Chap.*, Rev. Stephen G. Abbott; *Marshal*, Aaron Twigg.

QUINCY.

RURAL. — *W.M.*, E. W. H. Bass; *S.W.*, Wm. G. Sheen; *J.W.*, F. L. Jones; *Treas.*, Levi Stearns; *Sec.*, Charles H. Porter; *Chap.*, Rev. Samuel Kelly; *Marshal*, A. Glines; *S.D.*, W. L. Braddock; *J.D.*, J. W. Hersey; *S.S.*, F. A. Massey; *J.S.*, J. D. Nutting; *Tyler*, S. B. Colby.

RANDOLPH.

NORFOLK UNION. Incorporated 1819. — *W.M.*, Frank Morton; *S.W.*, John T. Southworth; *J.W.*, Hiram C. Alden; *Treas.*, Ralph Houghton; *Sec.*, John H. Field; *Chap.*, Ezra S. Conant; *Asst. Chap.*, George H. Wilkins; *Marshal*, N.

Everett Buck; *S.D.*, William H. Alden; *J.D.*, John W. Chessman; *S.S.*, Eugene Snell; *J.S.*, Geo. H. Thayer; *I.S.*, Andrew J. Gove; *Tyler*, Hiram Alden.

STOUGHTON.

RISING STAR. Instituted in 1799. — *W.M.*, Elmer Walker; *S.W.*, D. S. Hall; *Treas.*, George Talbot; *Sec.*, L. A. Thayer; *Chap.*, C. Southworth; *Marshal*, George F. Walker; *S.D.*, Charles H. Drake; *J.D.*, Robert Jackson; *S.S.*, Geo. O. Wentworth; *J.S.*, E. Bryden, Jr.; *Tyler*, James W. Richardson.

MOUNT ZION R. A. CHAPTER. — *H.P.*, George F. Walker; *K.*, Joshua Britton; *S.*, Jonathan R. Gay; *C. of H.*, George Talbot; *P.S.*, Elmer W. Walker; *R.A.C.*, James May; *M. 3d V.*, ———; *M. 2d V.*, Frank M. Elms; *M. 1st V.*, Guerdon Southworth; *Treas.*, ———; *Sec.*, Henry Britton.

WEYMOUTH.

DELTA. — *W.M.*, William S. Wallace; *S.W.*, John M. Walsh; *J.W.*, Lewis M. Pratt; *Treas.*, Amos S. White; *Sec.*, Charles G. Thompson; *Chap.*, Joseph W. Armington; *Marshal*, James T. Pease; *S.D.*, Joseph W. White; *J.D.*, John E. Hunt; *S.S.*, Charles W. Smith; *J.S.*, Edward E. Richards; *Or.*, Richard A. Hunt; *Sen.*, Edward G. Stoddard; *Tyler*, Reuben Tirrell.

WEYMOUTH (EAST).

ORPHAN'S HOPE. — *W.M.*, Leavitt Bates; *S.W.*, T. H. Humphrey; *J.W.*, G. W. Bates; *Treas.*, James Torrey; *Sec.*, T. J. Evans; *Chap.*, Alvah Raymond; *Marshal*, B. F. Thomas; *S.D.*, F. A. Bicknell; *J.D.*, W. H. Bartlett; *S.S.*, H. A. Newton; *J.S.*, John Nelson; *Or.*, Alpheus Bates; *Sen.*, G. C. Drew; *Tyler*, H. B. Raymond; *Trus.*, Z. L. Bicknell, A. J. Richards, John Blanchard.

PENTALPHA R. A. CHAPTER. — *H.P.*, Samuel A. Bates; *K.*, William Cushing; *S.*, Thomas H. Humphrey; *C. of H.*, J. Warren Hardwick; *P.S.*, John M. Walsh; *R.A.C.*, Joel F. Sheppard; *M. 3d V.*, Francis K. Slack; *M. 2d V.*, Alden Bowditch; *M. 1st V.*, Reuben Tirrell; *Treas.*, Amos S. White; *Sec.*, Charles G. Thompson; *Chap.*, William S. Wallace; *Or.*, Richard A. Hunt; *Tyler*, E. W. Richards, Jr.

SOUTH SHORE COMMANDERY. — *E.C.*, George W. Fay; *G.*, William Humphrey; *C.G.*, William S. Wallace; *P.*, Charles H. Pratt; *S.W.*, Andrew J. Garey; *J.W.*, Thomas H. Humphrey; *Treas.*, Edmund G. Bates; *Rec.*, Charles N. Marsh; *Sword Bearer*, Richard V. Merchant; *Standard Bearer*, F. J. Fuller; *W.*, William Fearing, 2d; *Guards*, Nathan A. Brickett, E. W. H. Bass, Hiram E. Raymond; *Or.*, Richard A. Hunt; *Sen. and Ar.*, John Nelson; *Trus.*, Z. L. Bicknell, E. Atherton Hunt, E. Waters Burr.

KNIGHTS OF PYTHIAS.

WEYMOUTH.

DELPHI LODGE NO. 15. — *C.C.*, J. K. Davidson; *V.C.*, F. M. Drown; *P.*, L. D. North; *K.R.S.*, Darius Smith; *M. of F.*, A. W. Tilden; *M.E.*, N. O. Smith; *M.A.*, Reuben Tirrell; *I.G.*, J. R. H. Wilkins; *O.G.*, C. C. Wilbor; *P.C.*, Joshua Binney; *Rep. to G.L.*, Darius Smith.

HYDE PARK.

NEW ERA LODGE NO. 36. — *C.C.*, H. M. Cable; *V.C.*, Geo. H. Adler; *P.*, T. C. Holmes; *P.C.*, John Beatey; *M.E.*, Louis Totman, Jr., *M. of F.*, E. B. Simpson;

K.R.S., Joel F. Goodwin; *M.A.*, E. F. Simpson; *I.G.*, David A. McDonald; *O.G.*, Merrill Underhill; *Rep. to G.L.*, Thomas C. Holmes.

QUINCY.

ST. PAUL'S LODGE NO. 37. — *C.C.*, James E. Maxim; *V.C.*, J. T. French; *P.*, W. S. Leavitt; *K.R.S.*, B. F. Billings; *M. of F.*, E. Richardson; *M. of E.*, E. S. Fellows, *M. at A.*, E. Cross; *I.G.*, J. A. Moore; *O.G.*, George Hayden; *P.C.*, E. B. Souther; *Rep. to G.L.*, William S. Leavitt.

ODD FELLOWS LODGES.

Officers elected for the term commencing July 1, 1876.

NO. 21. WILDEY, South Weymouth. — *N. G.*, Thaddeus M. Graves; *V.G.*, E. Faxon Shaw; *Sec.*, Geo. Hollis; *Treas.*, George R. Thayer; *P. Sec.*, J. Leonard Curtis.

NO. 58. ELLIOTT, Needham. — *N.G.*, Lewis Armstrong; *V.G.*, John Dixon; *Sec.*, Geo. E. Jones; *Treas.*, O. J. Upham; *P. Sec.*, A. A. Fisher.

NO. 72. STOUGHTON, Stoughton. — *N.G.*, M. O. Walker; *V.G.*, W. Holmes; *Sec.*, J. W. Richardson; *Treas.*, C. R. Seaver; *P. Sec.*, A. F. Lunt.

NO. 76. RISING STAR, Randolph. — *N.G.*, Andrew G. Dean; *V.G.*, S. Edgar Burrill; *Sec.*, R. Houghton; *Treas.*, Chas. E. Lyons.

NO. 82. CRESCENT, E. Weymouth. — *N.G.*, Jason Gardner; *V.G.*, E. R. Shackford; *Sec.*, Jacob R. Lovell; *Treas.*, Hiram E. Raymond; *P.Sec.*, S. S. Marden.

NO. 99. RISING SUN, West Medway. — *N.G.*, Joshua Scavey; *V.G.*, H. F. Metcalf; *Sec.*, W. E. Fairbanks; *Treas.*, Geo. McIntosh; *P. Sec.*, H. B. Woodman.

NO. 148. FOREST, Hyde Park. — *N.G.*, Henry Routley; *V.G.*, F. A. Easton; *Sec.*, E. B. Noyes; *Treas.*, Wm. Price.

NO. 163. MEDWAY, Medway. — *N.G.*, A. Barton; *V.G.*, J. W. Thompson; *Sec.*, S. G. Clark; *Treas.*, H. Partridge; *P. Sec.*, Geo. L. Boos.

NO. 173. SINCERITY, Wellesley, Needham. — *N.G.*, T. W. Willard; *Sec.*, William Jennings; *Treas.*, Charles E. Townsend; *P. Sec.*, E. A. Wood.

SONS OF TEMPERANCE.

Officers, Oct. 1, 1876.

DIVISION NO. 15. NEHOIDEN, Highlandville, Needham. — *W.P.*, C. Evons, Sr.; *R.S.*, R. J. Hardie.

DIVISION NO. 43. FAIRMOUNT, Hyde Park. — *W.P.*, Mary M. Williams; *R.S.*, Henry S. Bunton.

DIVISION NO. 45. VICTORIA, Quincy. — *W.P.*, Arthur C. Merritt; *R.S.*, Minnie E. Brown.

DIVISION NO. 69. MORNING STAR, Sheldonville, Wrentham. — *W.P.*, Clara Ware; *R.S.*, G. S. Hancock.

DIVISION NO. 83. INDIAN ROCK, Franklin. — *W.P.*, William E. Nason; *R.S.*, Addie M. Shaw.

DIVISION NO. 86. PIERCE, Brookline. — *W.P.*, Fannie A. Cooper; *R.S.*, Osavius Vernoy.

82   *NORFOLK COUNTY MANUAL.*

DIVISION NO. 107. WILLARD, West Quincy. — *W.P.*, George O. Shirley; *R.S.*, Benjamin R. Fuller.
DIVISION NO. 120. HOPE, West Medway. — *W.P.*, Sylvester A. Greenwood; *R.S.*, S. Newman Metcalf.

INDEPENDENT ORDER GOOD TEMPLARS.

Officers, Oct. 31, 1876.

LODGE NO. 9. UNION, Weymouth. Instituted March 6, 1859. — *W.C.T.*, C. W. Stevens; *W.V.T.*, Mary P. Crocker; *W. Sec.*, Francis Hayward.
LODGE NO. 16. MINOT'S LIGHT, Cohasset. Instituted April 11, 1876. — *W.C.T.*, Edwin G. Stewart; *W.V.T.*, Lottie C. Beal; *W. Sec.*, Arthur H. Thayer.
LODGE NO. 41. PURITAN, Randolph. Instituted Dec. 20, 1854. — *W.C.T.*, Hiram C. Alden; *W.V.T.*, Mary R. Beal; *W. Sec.*, Isabel C. Beal.
LODGE NO. 44. HOPE, East Stoughton. Instituted Dec. 5, 1864. — *W.C.T.*, Ellis A. Lothrop; *W.V.T.*, Annie S. Porter; *W. Sec.*, Mary E. Snell.
LODGE NO. 46. FAITH, East Braintree. Instituted July 17, 1876. — *W.C.T.*, Alverdo H. Mason; *W.V.T.*, Eliza J. Duguy; *W. Sec.*, Alonzo L. Mason.
LODGE NO. 47. HIGH ROCK, Needham. Instituted July 18, 1871. — *W.C.T.*, Lewis Riggs; *W.V.T.*, Ella Armstrong; *W. Sec.*, George Smith.
LODGE NO. 50. FRANKLIN, Holbrook. Instituted April 17, 1872. — *W.C.T.*, Henry S. Smith; *W.V.T.*, Martha Chandler; *W. Sec.*, Lizzie S. Belcher.
LODGE NO. 56. REYNOLDS, Quincy. Instituted March 13, 1876. — *W.C.T.*, Walter G. Gill; *W.V.T.*, Carrie Baxter; *W. Sec.*, William H. Hansom.
LODGE NO. 59. MORNING STAR, West Medway. Instituted Oct. 9, 1865. — *W.C.T.*, John Stone, Jr.; *W.V.T.*, Nettie M. Camp; *W. Sec.*, George S. Lesure.
LODGE NO. 72. CRYSTAL SPRING, Brookville, Holbrook. — Instituted Nov. 30, 1870. — *W.C.T.*, Amos M. Howard; *W.V.T.*, Clara J. Leonard; *W. Sec.*, Vicena R. White.
LODGE NO. 88. MONTANA, East Dedham. Instituted January 16, 1866. — *W.C.T.*, Andrew B. Ferguson; *W.V.T.*, Lizzie T. White; *W. Sec.*, Samuel Fiske.
LODGE NO. 114. UNITY, South Braintree. Instituted Nov. 18, 1871. — *W.C.T.*, John S. Henry; *W.V.T.*, Lydia Bishop; *W. Sec.*, Mehitable White.
LODGE NO. 119. MUTUAL, North Weymouth. Instituted, Nov. 28, 1871. — *W.C.T.*, Augustus Beal; *W.V.T.*, Sophia H. Lovell; *W. Sec.*, Frank H. Torrey.
LODGE NO. 158. WESSAGUSSETT, South Weymouth. Instituted, Jan. 1, 1875. — *W.C.T.*, Cornelius A. Pratt; *W.V.T.*, M. E. Hawes; *W. Sec.*, Miss E. S. Skilted.
LODGE NO. 163. OAKDALE, East Dedham. Instituted Feb. 27, 1874. — *W.C.T.*, Edwin Walker; *W.V.T.*, Sarah Hamilton; *W. Sec.*, Edwin C. Paul.
LODGE NO. 181. HIGHLAND LIGHT, South Weymouth. Instituted Feb. 4, 1876. — *W.C.T.*, Louis Alden; *W.V.T.*, Mary B. Tirrell; *W. Sec.*, Hattie C. Torrey.
LODGE NO. 191. FOXBOROUGH, Foxborough. Instituted Oct. 8, 1866. — *W.C.T.*, J. Frank Bayley; *W.V.T.*, Marie King; *W. Sec.*, Clara M. Crowley.
LODGE NO. 265. SOUTH WALPOLE, South Walpole. Instituted Sept 6, 1867; reorganized Jan. 14, 1876. — *W.C.T.*, Isaac H. Bullard; *W.V.T.*, R. K. Delano; *W. Sec.*, H. L. Boyden.

MECHANICS' TEMPLE OF HONOR NO. 25, ORDER OF TEMPERANCE, EAST WEYMOUTH. — *P.C.*, Robt. Mills; *W.C.*, N. H. Pratt; *W.V.*, Waldo Turner; *W. Rec.*, Joseph A. Cushing; *W. Asst. Rec.*, Abbott Bates; *W.F.R.*, John Nelson; *W.Treas.*, E. B. Tirrell; *W.U.*, Geo. Gardner; *W.A U.*, James T. Moran; *W.S.*, Chas. Burrell; *W.G.*, Geo. E. Gardner. Membership, 230.

DELPHI COUNCIL NO. 12, ORDER OF TEMPERANCE, EAST WEYMOUTH. — *Chief*, Geo. W. Dyer; *Sen.*, Wm. Sharpless; *Jun.*, W. T. Rice; *Rec.*, M. Collyer; *Treas.*, D. W. Bates; *Prot.*, Jacob Gardner; *Chap.*, Waldo Turner; *Man.*, Geo. Gardner; *D. Man.*, G. Damon. Membership, 68.

REFORM CLUBS.

BROOKLINE TEMPERANCE REFORM CLUB. Organized July 14, 1876. — *President*, Charles P. Ladd; *Vice-Presidents*, George F. Johnson, Eben Morse, A. Kenrick, Jr.; *Secretary*, Murray M. Wing; *Treasurer*, Osavius Verney; *Chaplain*, Enoch Doran.

THE GOOD SAMARITAN CLUB, DEDHAM. Organized May 13, 1876. — *President*, Rev. Carlos Slafter; *Vice-Presidents*, Sanford Carroll, Austin Lindley, William H. Ivers, Abby T. Crane; *Secretary*, Scott Morse; *Treasurer*, Melvin A. Galucia; *Executive Committee*, Charles T. Gray, Edwin Ramsdell, Nathaniel Morse. Number of members, 200.

FOXBOROUGH GOOD SAMARITAN CLUB. Organized by delegation from Stoughton Club, April 19th, 1876; now has 947 members. Officers elected quarterly. — First Board was as follows: *President*, J. E. Carpenter; *Vice-Presidents*, John S. Dill, Charles W. Hodges and Oliver C. Pettee; *Secretary*, R. Walter S. Blackwell; *Assistant Secretary*, E. W. Clarke; *Treasurer*, Ira B. Richmond. Present Board: *President*, R. W. S. Blackwell; *Vice-Presidents*, John E. Bonney, John S. Dill, and L. C. Winn; *Secretary*, R. W. Carpenter; *Assistant Secretary*, Fred. E. Butterworth; *Treasurer*, C. W. Hodges. Since the Club was organized, nearly one thousand dollars have been subscribed and contributed to carry on the work. A new hall, known as "Samaritan Hall," has been fitted up for the Club. In summer, meetings are held in a pavilion seating five hundred persons. Meetings have been held semi-weekly since the Club was formed. This Club has started clubs in South Walpole, Medfield, Wrentham and East Foxborough. Political and sectarian topics are excluded from meetings by the constitution. The Ladies' Aid Society, connected with this Club, numbers over fifty members, and has done much good in assisting the poor and furthering the interests of the Club.

HYDE PARK REFORM CLUB. Organized June, 1876. — *President*, Edmund Davis, *Vice-Presidents*, Henry A. Darling, George W. Chapman, N. H. Tucker; *Cor. Sec.*, Harry C. Pease; *Rec. Sec.*, William Hathaway; *Treasurer*, Merrill Underhill; *Managers*, E. H. Howard, E. S. Hathaway, J. G. Hamblin, Jr., H. C. Holt. Number of members, 500.

SCOTT TEMPERANCE REFORM CLUB, WEST MEDWAY. Organized March 28, 1876. — *President*, Nathan S. Hollis; *Vice-Presidents*, John Stone, James E. Lawrence, Horace Bishop; *Secretary*, E. W. Hill; *Financial Secretary*, George E. Hill; *Treasurer*, George S. Lesure; *Chaplain*, William L. Ripley; *Executive Committee*, E. G. French, H. S. Greenwood, J. Maginnis, J. Barry; *Steward*, H. J. Wilmarth; *Marshals*, Samuel Adams, Warren Nourse; *Sergeant at Arms*, Henry Ripley. Number of members, 270.

NEEDHAM REFORM CLUB. Organized June, 1876. — *President*, Thomas McAdams; *Vice-President*, Arthur G. Eaton; *Secretary*, Charles McNear; *Treasurer*, E. H. Greenwood.

NORWOOD REFORM CLUB. Organized 1876. — *President*, E. Fred Fletcher; *Secretary*, Hill Howard; *Treasurer*, Arthur Burdin. Number of members, 550.

WOMAN'S TEMPERANCE LEAGUE, Norwood. Organized 1876. — *President*, Maria E. Hartshorn; *Secretary*, Louisa Rhodes. Number of members, 100.

QUINCY REFORM CLUB. Organized Feb. 27, 1876. — *President*, Samuel T. Allen; *Vice-Presidents*, John Maxium, John Bent, James Dolan; *Secretary*, E. W. Underwood; *Treasurer*, John R. Graham; *Directors*, John P. Bigelow, William B. Wooster, John R. Graham. Present number of members, 325.

GOOD SAMARITAN TEMPERANCE REFORM CLUB, Randolph. Organized April, 1876. — *President*, Winslow Battles; *Vice-Presidents*, Charles E. Pratt, Ezra R. Paine, Albert Tabor; *Secretary*, Nelson Mann; *Treasurer*, Henry Beal.

SHARON REFORM CLUB. Organized May 28, 1876. — *President*, Charles S. Curtis; *Vice-Presidents*, Charles F. Davis, Davis L. White, George N. A. Dunakin; *Recording Secretary*, Fred. L. Holbrook; *Financial Secretary*, Adelbert Smith; *Treasurer*, John Wiswall; *Executive Committee*, Charles S. Curtis, George S. Cook, Charles E. Hall. Number of members, 65.

GOOD SAMARITAN CLUB, OF STOUGHTON. Organized January 13, 1876. — *President*, George H. Goward; *Vice-Presidents*, Sylvanus C. Phinney, Sumner Hackett; *Secretaries*, Ellery Clapp, Sumner Hackett; *Assistant Secretary*, Mary Alcorn; *Treasurer*, William Marriott. About 2,000 members.

WALPOLE REFORM CLUB. Organized March 4, 1876. — *President*, Lawson D. Gray; *Vice-Presidents*, Charles McPherson; A. F. Engley, J. Sanborn, Henry Pember, James A. Hartshorn; *Secretary and Treasurer*, Horace W. Mann; *Executive Committee*, Stephen Pember, Harvey F. Bird, N. B. Winslow, Mrs. Horace W. Mann, Annie Hutchinson, Mrs. Geo. H. Morse. Number of members, 239.

AGRICULTURAL SOCIETIES.

NORFOLK AGRICULTURAL SOCIETY. Organized 1849. — *President*, Henry S. Russell, Milton. *Honorary President*, Hon. Marshall P. Wilder, Dorchester. *Vice-Presidents*, Hon. Otis Cary, Foxborough; Alonzo W. Cheever, Wrentham; John Quincy Adams, Quincy; Theodore Lyman, Brookline; William R. Mann, Sharon; Hon. Henry L. Pierce, Dorchester. *Corresponding and Recording Secretary*, Henry O. Hildreth, Dedham. *Treasurer*, Chauncey C. Churchill, Dedham. *Executive Committee*, E. C. R. Walker, Dedham; Augustus P. Calder, West Roxbury; William T. Cook, Foxborough; Henry M. Mack, Dorchester; David W. Tucker, Milton; Atherton T. Brown, Brookline; Alfred W. Whitcomb, Randolph; Abel F. Stevens, Needham; J. Walter Bradlee, Milton. *Finance Committee and Auditors*, Eliphalet Stone, Dedham; William J. Stuart, Hyde Park; Augustus B. Endicott, Dedham. Delegate to the State Board of Agriculture, Eliphalet Stone, Dedham.

BOARD OF TRUSTEES.

Bellingham: George H. Crooks. *Braintree:* Alva Morrison, David H. Bates, George Wales, E. A. Hollingsworth. *Brookline:* William J. Hyde, George Griggs, Charles Stearns, William J. Griggs. *Canton:* Edmund Tucker, James T. Sumner, Adam McIntosh, Nathaniel S. White. *Cohasset:* Solomon J. Beal, Abraham H.

Tower. *Dedham:* Luther Eaton, Edward Sumner, Jeremiah W. Gay, Augustus B. Endicott. *Dorchester:* Lemuel Clapp, Samuel J. Capen, Aaron D. Capen, Joseph E. Hall, George Dorr, Manly W. Cain. *Dover:* Henry Goulding, Ephraim Wilson, Benjamin N. Sawin, Amos W. Shumway. *Foxborough:* James Capen, Francis D. Williams, Charles F. Howard, James F. Leonard. *Franklin:* Erastus L. Metcalf, John W. Richardson, Francis B. Ray, Davis Thayer. *Holbrook:* Everett E. Holbrook. *Hyde Park:* Henry A. Darling, William J. Stuart, Charles F. Gerry, C. L. Farnsworth. *Medfield:* Charles C. Sewall, Elijah Thayer, Alonzo B. Parker, William C. Allen. *Medway:* Willard P. Clark, Clark Partridge, William Daniels, Milton M. Fisher. *Milton:* Albert K. Teele, Lyman Davenport, Charles L. Copeland, Joshua W. Vose. *Needham:* Abel F. Stevens, Charles H. Mansfield, Henry Blackman, James Mackintosh. *Norfolk:* Walter H. Fisher, Erastus Dupee, Lucas Pond, George E. Holbrook. *Norwood:* James R. Fisher, Isaac Ellis, Josiah W. Talbot, Sidney E. Morse. *Quincy:* Joseph W. Robertson, Lemuel Billings, Charles A. Howland, William L. Faxon. *Randolph:* J. White Belcher, William Porter, Ephraim Mann, Seth Mann, 2d. *Roxbury:* Roland Worthington, J. Austin Rogers, Isaac Haydon, Joseph H. Chadwick, George Curtis, Samuel Little. *Sharon:* Asahel S. Drake, Lewis W. Morse, George R. Mann, Thomas Decatur. *Stoughton:* Lucius Clapp, Henry Bird, Robert Porter, Jr., Albert H. Drake. *Walpole:* Willard Lewis, Henry M. Plimpton, Edmund Polley, Naaman B. Wilmarth. *West Roxbury:* Alfred S. Brown, Joseph W. Page, Hamilton J. Farrar, George S. Curtis. *Weymouth:* Albert Tirrell, Erastus Nash. *Wrentham:* John F. Cowell, Ebenezer B. Parker, Chauncey G. Fuller, Robert P. Grant.

NORFOLK FARMER'S CLUB, Norfolk. Organized January, 1859. — *President,* Silas E. Fales; *Vice-Presidents,* Henry Southland, N. H. Rockwood; *Recording Secretary,* L. C. Keith; *Corresponding Secretary,* David Sharp; *Treasurer and Librarian,* Levi Blake.

WEYMOUTH AGRICULTURAL AND INDUSTRIAL SOCIETY. — *President,* Albert Tirrell; *Vice-Presidents,* Elias S. Beals, Erastus Nash, J. Murray Whitcomb; *Secretary,* William Dyer; *Treasurer,* Oran White; *Directors,* John S. Fogg, S. S. Spear, Charles Merritt, George Hollis, D. L. Sterling, William A. Shaw, Leonard B. Tirrell, Edward Nolan, Josiah Reed, Charles H. Newton, Thomas H. Humphrey, Joseph H. Clapp, Alexis Torrey, E. D. Raymond, J. T. Dizer, Joshua Binney, of Weymouth; B. L. Morrison, J. M. Cutting, Joshua Wilkins, Braintree; Bela Nash, Abington; Geo. B. Clapp, Rockland; *Supt. of Grounds,* Leonard B. Tirrell; *Supt. of Hall,* William H. Sargent.

MUSICAL SOCIETIES.

STOUGHTON MUSICAL SOCIETY. — *President,* Winslow Battles, Randolph. *Vice-Presidents,* Isaac Swan, Stoughton; Marcus A. Perkins, Braintree; George N. Spear, Holbrook; William R. Bowen, Brockton; J. Murray Whitcomb, Weymouth; J. Horace Willis, North Easton; Webster S. Wales, North Abington. *Chorister,* Hiram Wilde, Randolph. *Vice-Chorister,* John Berry Thayer, Randolph. *Treasurer,* A. W. Whitcomb, Randolph. *Secretary,* D. H. Huxford, Randolph.

The "Stoughton Musical Society," organized in 1786, by singers and players resident in Stoughton, Canton and Sharon, now having a membership of about 500, resident for the most part in Randolph, Holbrook, Braintree, Brockton, Weymouth, Abington, Easton, and the above-named original towns, has maintained this long existence without a break in its annual meetings, which have generally fallen on Christmas afternoon and evening, with a hot turkey supper. Of late years this annual meeting, or festival, has been held at Randolph, when not only classical choruses, songs and concerted pieces are sung, but those stirring old tunes of American composition, which our sires sang with such spirit and vigor, are given with a delight and accuracy second only to the rendering of the fathers.

A cherished object of this society is to keep alive and in esteem the music of the early American composers, unique and weird in its melody, irregular in its harmony, yet having a ring and gush that savor of the eternal songs.

RANDOLPH CHORAL SOCIETY. Organized about 1850. — *President*, Winslow Battles; *Vice-President*, Dr. C. C. Farnham; *Conductor*, John Berry Thayer; *Secretary and Treasurer*, Sanford W. Leach.

MISCELLANEOUS ASSOCIATIONS.

NORFOLK DISTRICT MEDICAL SOCIETY. Organized 1850. — *President*, Dr. John P. Maynard, Dedham. *Vice-President*, Dr. Robert Amory, Brookline. *Secretary and Librarian*, Dr. Arthur H. Nichols, Roxbury. *Treasurer*, Dr. George J. Arnold, Roxbury. *Commissioner of Trials*, Dr. Thomas H. Dearing, Braintree. *Councillors*, Drs. George J. Arnold, Roxbury; Henry Blanchard, Dorchester; B. E. Cotting, Roxbury; Robert T. Edes, Roxbury; D. S. Fogg, Norwood; F. F. Forsaith, Weymouth; Charles C. Hayes, Hyde Park; C. C. Holmes, Milton; George King, Franklin; James H. Morison, Quincy; Joel Seaverns, Roxbury; Joseph Stedman, Jamaica Plain; Charles C. Tower, Weymouth. *Censors*, Drs. John W. Chase, Dedham; George Faulkner, Jamaica Plain; Francis W. Goss, Roxbury; O. F. Rogers, Dorchester; W. B. Trull, Brookline.

NORFOLK CONFERENCE OF UNITARIAN AND OTHER CHRISTIAN CHURCHES. — This association which was organized at Dedham, Dec. 5, 1866, includes churches in Brookline, Canton, Dedham, Dorchester (4), Dover, Grantville, Hyde Park, Jamaica Plain, Medfield, Milton, Needham, Quincy, Randolph, Roxbury (2), Sharon, Sherborn, South Natick, Walpole, West Dedham, West Roxbury. *President*, J. Mason Everett, Canton; *Secretary*, Rev. Francis C. Williams, Hyde Park; *Treasurer*, Jonathan H. Cobb, Dedham.

NORFOLK COUNTY SUNDAY SCHOOL ASSOCIATION. Organized May 16, 1855. — *President*, John W. Porter, Dorchester. *Vice-Presidents*, Rev. Adams Ayer, Roxbury; Richard C. Humphreys, Dorchester; Mrs. Abijah W. Draper, West Roxbury. *Secretary and Treasurer*, Rev. S. W. Bush, Boston. *Directors*, Rev. Dr. John H. Morison, Milton; John Kneeland, Roxbury; Rev. Edward Crowninshield, West Dedham; Miss E. P. Channing, Milton; Mrs. George Morse, Medfield.

TEMPORARY ASYLUM FOR DISCHARGED FEMALE PRISONERS, DEDHAM. — *President*, Mrs. Horatio Chickering; *VicePresident*, Mrs. Henry V. Poor; *Secretary*, Mrs. Charles W. Dexter; *Treasurer*, Francis A. Peters; *Assistant Treasurer*, Mrs. Martin L. Bradford; *Board of Managers*, Mrs. Horatio Chickering, Boston; Mr. Henry V. Poor, Brookline; Miss H. B. Chickering, Dedham; Mrs. Henry A. Rice, Boston; Mrs. F. T. Gray, Boston; Mrs. Thomas Howe, Brookline; Miss S. D. Bar-

rett, Boston; Mrs. Micah Dyer, Jr., Dorchester; Mrs. H. F. Durant, Boston; Miss
Ellen C. Clark, Jamaica Plain; Mrs. James Cutler, Boston; Mrs. Thomas C. Stearns,
Boston; Mrs. M. L. Bradford, Dorchester; Mrs. Charles W. Dexter, Boston; Mrs.
Gertrude B. Pope, Boston; Mrs. Henry A. Clapp, Boston; Miss Abby R. Loring,
Boston; Mrs. Harrison Porter, Boston; Mrs. J. Wells, Longwood; Mrs. John E. Tyler,
Boston; Mrs. B. W. Field, Boston; Mrs. Edward P. Burgess, Dedham; Mrs. Waldo
Colburn, Dedham; Mrs. Henry B. McIntosh, Roxbury; *Advisory Board,* Messrs. Geo.
B. Emerson, Abner Kingman, E. G. Burgess, M.D., Henry A. Rice, Francis A. Peters,
John Ayres, John E. Tyler, M.D; *Executive Committee,* Mrs. John E. Tyler, Mrs.
James Cutler, Mrs. Horatio Chickering, Mr. Henry A. Rice; *Auditing Committee,*
Messrs. Stephen G. Deblois, Daniel Denny; *Finance Committee,* Messrs. Henry A.
Rice, John Ayres; *Purchasing Committee,* Messrs. Abner Kingman, John E. Tyler,
M.D., Mrs. Henry F. Durant, Miss A. R. Loring; *Matron,* Miss L. M. Tolman;
Sewing Matron, Miss C. E. Burnap; *Farmer,* Mr. R. R. Field; *Laundry Matron,*
Mrs. A. W. Cook; *Housekeeper,* Mrs. R. R. Field; *Nursery Matron,* Miss Alsina
Thompson.

SAILOR'S SNUG HARBOR, QUINCY. For seamen diseased and disabled in the U. S.
merchant service. Incorporated May 22, 1852. — *President,* Thomas Motley; *Sec-
retary,* J. Francis Tuckerman; *Treasurer,* William B. Storer; *Executive Committee,*
Thomas Motley, Eben Bacon, Jos. B. Glover, William B. Storer, Thomas Parsons;
Trustees, F. H. Bradlee, J. Q. Adams, W. W. Greenough, Thomas Motley, Thomas
Parsons, S. C. Thwing, Nath'l Emmons, J. Francis Tuckerman, J. B. Kettell, W. B.
Storer, David Whiton, W. A. Wellman, L. Saltonstall, J. P. Bayley, J. B. Glover,
W. C. Rogers, Eben Bacon, Geo. B. Upton, George A. Gardner, H. C. Brooks, Wm.
E. Perkins, J. G. Whitney, and Collector of the Port of Boston, *ex officio.*

NATIONAL SAILORS' HOME, QUINCY. A home for sailors, mariners, and others em-
ployed in the naval service of the United States, disabled by wounds, sickness, and
old age. Incorporated March 14, 1865. Home dedicated Aug. 1, 1866. — *Trustees,*
Hon. Alexander H. Rice, President; James L. Little, Treasurer; William Perkins,
Samuel C. Cobb, Gen. Charles G. Loring, Peter Butler, Charles J. Morrill, Admiral
Charles Steadman, U.S.N., Clerk and Auditor, Joshua Crane; Dr. William L. Faxon,
Superintendent and Physician; Mrs. W. L. Faxon, Matron.

DEDHAM HISTORICAL SOCIETY. Incorporated April 23, 1862. — *President,* Henry
O. Hildreth; *Vice-President,* Alfred Hewins; *Corresponding Secretary,* A. Ward
Lamson; *Recording Secretary, Treasurer and Librarian,* John D. Cobb; *Curators,*
Waldo Colburn, William Bullard, Erastus Worthington; *Auditors,* A. W. Lamson,
George F. Fisher.

DEDHAM UNION. Connected with the First Church, and organized 1875. — *President,*
Winslow Warren; *Vice-President,* Herbert Maynard; *Secretary,* Miss S. E. Weather-
bee, *Treasurer,* Miss M. L. Talbot; *Directors,* Miss S. E. Hodges, Eben Hewins, Henry
Smith.

ST. PAUL'S GUILD. Connected with St. Paul's Episcopal Parish, Dedham. Organized
1875. — *President,* Rev. Daniel Goodwin; *Vice-President,* Erastus Worthington;
Secretary, John F. Wakefield; *Treasurer,* Mrs. Cornelia S. Hildreth; *Counsellors,*
Frederick D. Ely, Miss Sarah S. Haskell, Charles E. Conant.

JUSTICES OF THE PEACE AND QUORUM.

THROUGHOUT THE COMMONWEALTH.

Braintree.

Edward Avery, Asa French, Naaman L. White.

Brookline.

Seth Ames, William Aspinwall. Clement K. Fay, Thomas Parsons, Frederick A. Searle, Augustine Shurtleff, Ginery Twitchell, Thomas H. Talbot, James S. Whitney, Moses Williams, Jr.

Canton.

Ellis Ames. Charles Endicott, Charles H. French, Samuel B. Noyes, Rufus C. Wood.

Cohasset.

Aaron Pratt.

Dedham.

Franklin Copeland, Henry O. Hildreth, Charles A. Mackintosh, Ezra Wilkinson, Erastus Worthington.

Medway.

Milton M. Fisher.

Milton.

Joseph McKean Churchill, Robert B. Forbes, Edward L. Pierce, Henry S. Russell, Nathaniel F. Safford.

Needham.

Charles A. Phelps, George White.

Quincy.

John Quincy Adams, William B. Duggan.

Randolph.

J. White Belcher, John V. Beal, Seth Turner.

Sharon.

Sanford Waters Billings.

Walpole.

Francis W. Bird.

Weymouth.

Everett C. Bumpus, James Humphrey.

FOR THE COUNTY OF NORFOLK.

Dedham.

Jonathan H. Cobb, Chauncey C. Churchill, Ira Cleveland, Waldo Colburn, Charles C. Sanderson.

Foxborough.

James E. Carpenter.

Hyde Park.

W. H. H. Andrews, Orin T. Gray.

Weymouth.

Alvah Raymond.

JUSTICES OF THE PEACE FOR THE COUNTY OF NORFOLK.

BELLINGHAM.

Andrew A. Bates, Nathan A. Cook, David Lawrence, Savel Metcalf.

BRAINTREE.

David H. Bates, Phillip Curtis, Eben Denton, N. F. T. Hayden, Elias Hayward, Francis A. Hobart, Nathaniel H. Hunt, Arza B. Keith, John Kimball, William F. Locke, Amos W. Stetson, Elisha Thayer, E. F. E. Thayer, Noah Torrey, Cranmore N. Wallace, A. Judson Warren.

BROOKLINE.

H. Edward Abbott, Benjamin F. Baker, William I. Bowditch, Charles Burrill, Sumner C. Chandler, Horace D. Chapin, William D. Coolidge, Joshua Crane, David H. Daniels, Charles H. Drew, Gustavus M. Finotti, William B. Haseltine, Martin P. Kennard, Bradford Kingman, Francis W. Lawrence, Robert S. Littell, George A. Mudge, Charles F. Perkins, Peter W. Pierce, James M. Seamans, William B. Sears, Lewis Slack, Howard Stockton, Charles A. Williams, Moses Withington.

CANTON.

Frank M. Ames, Henry F. Buswell, John Cronin, George E. Downes, Nathaniel W. Dunbar, Thomas E. Grover, William Mansfield, Jacob Silloway, Jr., James T. Sumner.

COHASSET.

Solomon J. Beal, Louis T. Cushing, David S. G. Doane, Edward E. Ellms, Franklin D. Goodrich, Martin Lincoln, J. Q. A. Lothrop, Henry Tolman.

DEDHAM.

John H. Burdakin, Charles J. Capen, Jonathan Cobb, John D. Cobb, John Cox, Jr., Charles Dean, Merrill D. Ellis, Frederick D. Ely, Augustus B. Endicott, Charles H. Farrington, Calvin Guild, Alfred Hewins, Don Gleason Hill, Lewis H. Kingsbury, John N. McKery, Edward S. Rand, Jr., Henry W. Richards, Nathaniel Smith, Royal O. Storrs, Mirick P. Sumner, John W. Thomas, Ezra W. Taft, Alonzo B. Wentworth, Henry White, Philander S. Young.

DOVER.

Edwin C. Moulton, Amos W. Shumway, Ephraim Wilson.

FOXBOROUGH.

William Boyd, Edgar R. Butterworth, James Capen, Robert W. Carpenter, Otis Cary, Edwin W. Clarke, Alfred Fales, Alfred Hodges, Charles W. Hodges, James F. Leonard, Carmi Richmond, Isaac Smith, A. Thomas Starkey, Charles W. Sumner.

FRANKLIN.

Paul B. Clark, Adams Daniels, Henry M. Greene, William E. Nason, James E. Pollard, Stephen W. Richardson, William Rockwood, Alpheus A. Russegue, Adin D. Sargeant, Charles W. Stewart, George W. Wiggin.

HOLBROOK.

John Adams, David Blanchard, Elisha W. Thayer, Jacob Whitcomb, John Underhay.

HYDE PARK.

Joseph C. Bates, Albion P. Bickmore, Wilmot E. Broad, Isaac J. Brown, Henry S. Bunton, Charles M. Chapin, Charles G. Chick, William J. Corcoran, Henry H. Curtice, Edmund Davis, Enoch P. Davis, Willard F. Estey, Charles Sturtevant, Henry B. Terry, Benjamin C. Vose.

MEDFIELD.

George H. Ellis, Jeremiah B. Hale, Charles Hamant, James Hewins, Charles C. Sewall.

MEDWAY.

Willard P. Clark, Charles H. Deans, Asa M. B. Fuller, Joel E. Hunt, Orion A. Mason, Addison P. Thayer, Israel P. Quimby, Jr., Erastus H. Tyler.

MILTON.

Samuel Babcock, Gideon Beck, Charles Breck, J. Walter Bradlee, Jesse Bunton, C. M. S. Churchill, George Penniman, James Sumner, James Tucker, George Vose, Edwin D. Wadsworth, Horace E. Ware, James C. White, Henry A. Whitney, Seth D. Whitney.

NEEDHAM.

Thomas E. Barry, Charles Blaisdell, Edgar H. Bowers, Richard Boynton, Albion R. Clapp, William H. Crocker, George K. Daniell, Henry F. Durant, George E. Eaton, Joseph E. Fiske, Solomon Flagg, Joshua J. Gould, Charles C. Greenwood, Emery Grover, Abel Jennings, William Jennings, Mark Lee, Charles H. Mansfield, Clough R. Miles, William R. Mills, Enoch L. Pope, Francis H. Stevens.

NORFOLK.

Charles J. Bryant, Daniel J. Holbrook, Lewis. D. Metcalf, Saul B. Scott, Henry Trowbridge.

NORWOOD.

Willard Gay, Samuel E. Pond, Francis Tinker, Francis O. Winslow.

QUINCY.

Brooks Adams, Henry Barker, Lewis Bass, Ebenezer Bent, D. Howard Bills, Charles W. Carter, Noah Cummings, Benjamin Dodge, R. Augustus Duggan, William L. Faxon, Ensign S. Fellows, Washington M. French, George L. Gill, John Hardwick, Lewis F. Hobbs, Charles A. Howland, Jediah P. Jordan, George H. Locke, Joseph W. Lombard, Lucius W. Lovell, Henry Lunt, Charles Marsh, Albert G. Olney, William S. Pattee, Whitcomb Porter, E. Granville Pratt, Josiah P. Quincy, Joseph W. Robertson, Horace B. Spear, Edmund B. Taylor, James E. Tirrell, Edward Turner, John T. White, Isaiah G. Whiton.

RANDOLPH.

Hiram C. Alden, Horatio B. Allen, Eleazer Beal, Ezra S. Conant, Benjamin Dickinson, John T. Flood, Charles G. Hathaway, Daniel Howard, Nathaniel Howard, Seth Mann, 2d, James E. O'Brien, John G. Poole, J. Winsor Pratt, John B. Thayer, James A. Tower, Royal W. Turner, George W. Wales, Jonathan Wales, Thomas West, Oramel White.

SHARON.

Thomas Decatur, Charles T. Howard, Josiah Johnson, Otis Johnson, William R. Mann, Lewis W. Morse, William B. Wickes.

STOUGHTON.

John A. Bowdlear, J. Merrill Browne, Lucius Clapp, Christopher Dyer, Jr., John C. Galvin, Jesse Holmes, Clifford Keith, James Keith, Henry C. Kimball, Abram C. Paul, Bradford Raymond, John H. Simmons, George Talbot, Jabez Talbot, Jr.

WALPOLE.

Charles Bird, Nathaniel Bird, Henry S. Clarke, Joshua B. Hanners, James G. Hartshorn, George A. Kendall, James H. Leland, Isaac N. Lewis, William Moore, George P. Morey, Henry A. Perkins, Charles H. Prescott, James G. Scott, Hubbard W. Tilton.

WEYMOUTH.

Elias S. Beals, Zeeberiah L. Bicknell, Nathan Canterbury, Joseph Dyer, George W. Fay, E. Atherton Hunt, Ebenezer W. Hunt, John W. Hunt, Frank W. Lewis, Jacob Loud, John J. Loud, Henry Newton, George E. Porter, Thomas B. Porter, Nathan H. Pratt, Quincy L. Reed, Augustus J. Richards, Elias Richards, Norton Q. Tirrell, James Torrey, Noah Vining, Samuel Webb, Benjamin F. White, George W. White, Jr., Oran White.

WRENTHAM.

John J. Archer, William W. Cowell, Nathan Ely, Abraham W. Harris, Silas Metcalf, Samuel Warner, George M. Warren.

NOTARIES PUBLIC.

Canton.
Francis W. Deane, Charles Endicott, Thomas E. Grover, Jacob Silloway, Jr.

Dedham.
Chauncey C. Churchill, Lewis H. Kingsbury, Royal O. Storrs.

Franklin.
Alpheus A. Russegue.

Hyde Park.
Henry S. Bunton, Willard F. Estey.

Medway.
Milton M. Fisher.

Milton.
Horace E. Ware.

Needham.
Emery Grover.

Quincy.
Henry F. Barker, Rupert F. Claflin.

Randolph.
Royal W. Turner.

Weymouth.
John J. Loud, Quincy L. Reed.

Wrentham.
Samuel Warner.

ATTORNEYS.

Braintree.
Edward Avery, Asa French, Henry A. Johnson, Naaman L. White.

Brookline.
William Aspinwall, William I. Bowditch, J. B. Braman, Alfred D. Chandler, Sumner C. Chandler, Charles H. Drew, Clement K. Fay, George Griggs, Frank R. Hall, Bradford Kingman, Arthur Lincoln, Albert Mason, Moorfield Storey, Thomas H. Talbot, E. W. E. Tompson, Samuel Tompson, Charles A. Williams, Moses Williams, Jr.

Canton.
Ellis Ames, Henry F. Buswell, Charles Endicott, Thomas E. Grover, Samuel B. Noyes.

Cohasset.
Louis T. Cushing.

Dedham.
John R. Bullard, John D. Cobb, Jonathan H. Cobb, Frederick D. Ely, Don Gleason Hill, A. Ward Lamson, Charles A. Mackintosh, F. W. Pelton, Arnold A. Rand, Edward S. Rand, Jr., John F. Wakefield, Thomas L. Wakefield, Winslow Warren, Alonzo B. Wentworth, Samuel S. Willson, Erastus Worthington.

Foxborough.
James E. Carpenter, Robert W. Carpenter.

Franklin.
George W. Wiggin.

Hyde Park.
W. H. H. Andrews, Z. S. Arnold, C. G. Chick, J. E. Cotter, Edmund Davis, Willard F. Estey, Alfred E. Giles, Orin T. Gray, Henry H. Smith, Henry B. Terry.

Medfield.
James Hewins.

Medway.
George W. Deans.

Milton.
Charles M. S. Churchill, Edward L. Pierce, Nathaniel F. Safford, Nathaniel Morton Safford, Horace E. Ware.

Needham.
Thomas E. Barry, Samuel G. Clarke, Emery Grover, C. R. Miles.

Norfolk.
Daniel J. Holbrook,

Quincy.
John Q. Adams, E. Granville Pratt, James E. Tirrell.

Randolph.
John V. Beal, John F. Kilton, James A. Tower, Jonathan Wales.

Sharon.
Bushrod Morse.

Stoughton.
J. Merrill Browne.

Weymouth.
E. C. Bumpus, James Humphrey, Frank W. Lewis.

Wrentham.
Charles J. Randall, Samuel Warner.

PHYSICIANS.

Bellingham.
Roland Hammond.

Braintree.
Thomas H. Dearing, William O. Faxon, Noah Torrey.

Brookline.
Robert Amory, Ira B. Cushing, C. Irving Fisher, Tappan E. Francis, George K. Sabine, Augustine Shurtleff, N. C. Towle, Washington B. Trull, D. B. VanSlyck, Geo. P. Wesselhœft.

Canton.
Alexander R. Holmes, Rufus S. Parker, C. S. Young.

Cohasset.
Gustavus P. Pratt.

Dedham.
Ebenezer G. Burgess, John W. Chase, John P. Maynard, George A. Southgate, William G. Ware, Charles H. Witham.

Foxborough.
Lemuel Dickerman, William A. Dickerman, J. G. S. Hitchcock, Isaac Smith.

Franklin.
Shadrack Atwood, George King, William B. Nolen, Jacob Blake.

Holbrook.
J. B. Kingsbury.

Hyde Park.
Charles L. Edwards, Willard S. Everett, Francis L. Gerald, Freeman Hatch, Charles C. Hayes, Charles Sturtevant, Thomas F. Sumner.

Milton.
C. C. Holmes, Jonathan Ware.

Medfield.
J. H. Richardson.

Medway.
C. A. Bemis, James A. Galo, J. C. Gallison, A. Le Baron Monroe.

Norwood.
Francis M. Cragin, David S. Fogg.

Needham.
Albert D. Kingsbury, Henry T. Mansfield, G. H. Hackett, Isaac H. Hazelton, Albert E. Miller, W. O. B. Wingate.

Quincy.
Alvah M. Dam, Miss M. K. Galo, John H. Gilbert, J. A. Gordon, James F. Harlow, A. W. Keene, James Morison, William S. Pattee, James A. Stetson, Joseph Underwood.

Randolph.
Ebenezer Alden, Emery A. Allen, Warren M. Babbitt, Augustus L. Chase, Thadeus T. Cushman, Charles C. Farnham, Bradford L. Wales.

Sharon.
Amasa D. Bacon.

Stoughton.
S. S. Gifford, — Harvey, W. E. C. Swan, Simeon Tucker.

Walpole.
Silas Emleyn Stone, Andrew J. Runnells.

Weymouth.
Roscoe E. Brown, G. W. Fay, — Fitzgerald, F. F. Forsaith, — Fraser, Moses R. Gredy, W. A. Hathaway, Granville C. Pinkham, N. Q. Tirrell, C. C. Tower.

Wrentham.
George F. Butman.

JURORS.

GRAND JURORS FOR THE YEAR 1870.

William H. Hitchcock, *Foreman,*	Sharon.
John M. Whitcomb, *Clerk,*	Weymouth.
Asa W. Adams,	Medway.
George E. Allen,	Medfield.
Zenas Allen,	Hyde Park.
Charles Bailey,	Dedham.
William N. Eaton,	Quincy.
Charles L. Fales,	Foxborough.
William F. Haley,	Canton.
Davis L. Hartshorn,	Walpole.
Alexander W. Hayden,	Cohasset.
Jeremiah Horgan,	Norwood.
Edward D. Howard,	Needham.
William A. Howe,	Dover.
Charles W. Mansfield,	Braintree.
Richardson Metcalf,	Franklin.
Ellis T. Norcross,	Bellingham.
Martin P. Pike,	Randolph.
Caleb Thayer,	Holbrook.
Thomas P. Toomey,	Stoughton.
Hiram Ware.	Wrentham.
Amos L. Wood,	Brookline.

JURORS SUPREME JUDICIAL COURT.

FEBRUARY TERM, 1876.

WILLIAM C. ENDICOTT, of Salem, Presiding Judge.

First Jury.		Second Jury.	
Edwin C. Aldrich, *Foreman*,	Hyde Park.	Charles Gowen, *Foreman*,	Franklin.
Warren W. Adams,	Quincy.	Henry H. Dimon,	Holbrook.
Daniel J. Bates,	Cohasset.	Robert Draper,	Canton.
Charles G. Blake,	Dover.	Robert S. Gray,	Walpole.
Henry Blaney,	Brookline.	Francis A. Jewett,	Brookline.
William Fales,	Dedham.	Isaac Littlefield,	Stoughton.
Thomas Farrell,	Stoughton.	Edson A. Morse,	Foxborough.
Azel R. French,	Braintree.	Amasa S. Niles,	Randolph.
Isaac F. French,	Weymouth.	Richard Oldham,	Norwood.
Ansel O. Clarke,	Braintree.	Elijah Partridge, 2d,	Medway.
Oliver Clifford,	Medfield.	Willard Richards,	Sharon.
Joseph Colburn,	Dedham.	Jesse K. Snow,	Franklin.

SUPERNUMERARIES.

William A. McKean,	Bellingham.	George Veazie,	Quincy.
Walter F. Partridge,	Wrentham.	Edwin D. Wadsworth,	Milton.
Saul B. Scott,	Norfolk.	Daniel Warren,	Needham.
Warren Thayer,	Weymouth.		

PETIT JURORS FOR SUPERIOR COURT.

APRIL CRIMINAL TERM, 1876.

JOHN P. PUTNAM, of Boston, Presiding Judge.

First Jury.		Second Jury.	
William P. Hewins, *Foreman*,	Medfield.	George Scott, *Foreman*,	Dover.
Charles Badger,	Franklin.	Thomas W. Lincoln,	Quincy.
Stephen D. Bennett,	Brookline.	Cyrus Littlefield,	Stoughton.
Elijah Clark,	Medway.	Benj. Lyman Morrison,	Braintree.
Arthur Cunningham,	Milton.	James O'Donovan,	Weymouth.
Charles H. Dowing,	Needham.	Lewis B. Paine,	Randolph.
Geo. W. Dunakin,	Sharon.	George C. Park,	Walpole.
William C. Fisher,	Norwood.	Joseph W. Porter,	Holbrook.
Alonzo Forsaith,	Stoughton.	Josephus Shaw,	Braintree.
George H. Haggett,	Dedham.	Joseph H. Smith,	Cohasset.
Henry P. Horne,	Quincy.	William H. Stratton,	Foxborough.
Benj. R. Kennison,	Weymouth.	Horatio G. Turner,	Dedham.

SUPERNUMERARIES.

Joseph Day,	Franklin.	Henry H. Watson,	Norfolk.
Hobart M. Cable,	Hyde Park.	Nath'l S. White,	Canton.
Francis Redman,	Brookline.	Addison L. Wight,	Bellingham.
George M. Warren,	Wrentham.		

APRIL CIVIL TERM, 1876.

WILLIAM ALLEN, of Northampton, Presiding Judge.

First Jury.		Second Jury.	
Samuel A. Vining, *Foreman*,	Holbrook.	Oliver B. Shaw, *Foreman*,	Weymouth.
Samuel Allen,	Walpole.	Cornelius McMahon,	Randolph.
F. D. J. Barney,	Bellingham.	Willard Miller,	Franklin.
William M. Comey,	Norfolk.	Elbert S. Moses,	Franklin.
Timothy Corey,	Brookline.	George W. Nickerson,	Milton.
Seth Dewing, Jr.,	Quincy.	George K. Nickerson,	Cohasset.
James W. Edgerley,	Brookline.	Willard K. Poole,	Sharon.
William Geary,	Stoughton.	Jonathan Prescott,	Canton.
Joel H. Goodwin,	Hyde Park.	John A. Quincy,	Medfield.
Thomas H. Humphrey,	Weymouth.	Amasa S. Thayer,	Braintree.
Benjamin G. Kimball,	Needham.	Ansel K. Tisdale,	Dover.
William G. Kimball,	Quincy.	William R. Wild,	Braintree.

SUPERNUMERARIES.

Allen C. Doolittle,	Foxborough.	Nathaniel M. Warren,	Stoughton.
T. Francis Guy,	Norwood.	Benjamin Weatherbee,	Dedham.
Samuel D. Northrup,	Wrentham.	John E. Weatherbee,	Dedham.
Augustus L. Ware,	Medway.		

SEPTEMBER CRIMINAL TERM, 1876.

P. EMORY ALDRICH, of Worcester, Presiding Judge.

First Jury.		*Second Jury.*	
Timothy F. Clary, *Foreman,*	Milton.	John N. Smith, *Foreman,*	Walpole.
Eustis Baker,	Dedham.	Francis P. Loud,	Quincy.
Philander Bates,	Cohasset.	Francis A. Massey,	Quincy.
Bradford A. Bennett,	Wrentham.	Anson Morse,	Norwood.
John Blanchard,	Weymouth.	Clarence C. Porter,	Stoughton.
Samuel Bowditch,	Braintree.	George Richards,	Sharon.
Edwin Clarke,	Brookline.	Asa Sargent,	Franklin.
Martin V. Cook,	Bellingham.	Joshua Seavey,	Medway.
Andrew A. Harrington.	Canton.	Charles H. Spaulding,	Medfield.
Daniel J. Holbrook,	Norfolk.	J. Isaac Spear,	Stoughton.
Henry Martin Hollis,	Braintree.	Nathaniel P. Sprague,	Holbrook.
John Humphrey,	Dover.	Charles Calvin Sumner,	Foxborough.

SUPERNUMERARIES.

Rufus A. Thayer,	Randolph.	Benjamin C. Vose,	Hyde Park.
James P. Ingalls,	Needham.	George E. Whiting,	Dedham.
Charles M. Newell,	Brookline.	Willard C. Whiting,	Franklin.
Walter P. Tirrell,	Weymouth.		

SEPTEMBER CIVIL TERM, 1876.

EZRA WILKINSON, of Dedham, Presiding Judge.

First Jury.		*Second Jury.*	
Louis T. Cushing, *Foreman,*	Cohasset.	John Panter, *Foreman,*	Brookline.
Charles L. Badger,	Quincy.	Mark Lee,	Needham.
J. B. Baker, Jr.,	Dedham.	Sidney E. Morse,	Norwood.
Berthier R. Ballou,	Stoughton.	Stephen Partridge,	Medway.
William Bowditch,	Braintree.	James T. Penniman,	Quincy.
George W. Bruce,	Medfield.	Benj. F. Richards,	Weymouth.
Waldo C. French,	Weymouth.	David B. Robinson,	Foxborough.
Geo. H. Gilmore,	Franklin.	George W. Saunders,	Canton.
Lewis Gomez,	Braintree.	Charles Smith,	Dedham.
David J. Harmon,	Brookline.	Jona Whiting,	Dover.
Andrew R. Jones,	Norfolk.	Theophilus W. Whiting,	Holbrook.
R. Warren Jones,	Sharon.	Elbridge G. Whitney,	Bellingham.

SUPERNUMERARIES.

Charles W. Clarke,	Franklin.	John M. Forbes,	Milton.
Joseph L. Ellis,	Walpole.	William Henstis,	Hyde Park.
Benj. R. Follett,	Wrentham,	John Riley,	Stoughton.

DECEMBER CRIMINAL TERM, 1876.

JOHN P. PUTNAM, of Boston, Presiding Judge.

First Jury.		*Second Jury.*	
Douglass A. Brooks, *Foreman,*	Braintree.	John H. Kingsbury, *Foreman,*	Norfolk.
Jeremiah Allen,	Dover.	Benjamin Hobart,	Quincy.
Andrew J. Bates,	Braintree.	Daniel F. Kendall,	Hyde Park.
Walter S. Beal,	Cohasset.	James La Croix,	Medway.
Sylvester S. Burleigh,	Brookline.	George H. Morse,	Norwood.
Philip Carver,	Quincy.	Willard M. Nottage,	Foxborough.
Irving Curtis,	Medfield.	William Pierce,	Needham.
John B. Fisher,	Dedham.	William T. Rice,	Weymouth.
Josiah K. Foster,	Canton.	John Spear,	Holbrook.
John J. Giles,	Dedham.	Robt. S. Sumner,	Stoughton.
Elbridge Grant,	Bellingham.	Leonard A. Thayer,	Stoughton.
Frederick Guild,	Walpole.	Thomas Decatur,	Sharon.

SUPERNUMERARIES.

Charles A. Deane,	Franklin.	Geo. W. Porter,	Wrentham.
Joseph W. Heaton,	Franklin.	Lemuel Torrey,	Weymouth.
Artemas S. Jones,	Brookline.	Alfred Tucker,	Randolph.
O. W. Peabody,	Milton.		

DECEMBER CIVIL TERM, 1876.

JOHN P. PUTNAM, of Boston, Presiding Judge.

First Jury.		Second Jury.	
Sanford Carroll, *Foreman,*	Dedham.	John Littlefield, *Foreman,*	Milton.
Horrett Adams,	Dedham.	John Mann,	Walpole.
E. W. H. Bass,	Quincy.	John McCormack,	Brookline.
S., Warren Bullard,	Sharon.	William M. McNamara,	Stoughton.
Seneca Burr,	Bellingham.	Matthew O'Dea,	Stoughton.
Charles B. Dexter,	Norwood.	James O'Donnell,	Medway.
Herman C. Farrington,	Wrentham.	William L. Perry,	Foxborough.
John L. Fisher,	Norfolk.	Loring Tirrell,	Weymouth.
Samuel W. Hollis,	Braintree.	Peter B. Turner,	Quincy.
Nathl. Howard,	Randolph.	Emery A. Wheeler,	Medfield.
Frank M. Howes,	Canton.	John S. Whitaker,	Braintree.
Eri T. Joy,	Weymouth.	Peter Adams,	Franklin.

SUPERNUMERARIES.

Lewis J. Bird,	Hyde Park.	George I. Partridge,	Franklin.
Washington Brown,	Cohasset.	Henry J. Winchenback,	Dover.
Luther A. Hayden, Jr.,	Holbrook.	William Heckle,	Needham.
Thacher Loring,	Brookline.		

POST OFFICES AND POSTMASTERS.

Bellingham.

Bellingham. — R. F. Thayer.
Caryville. — Calvin Fairbanks.
North Bellingham. — Stephen B. Smith.

Braintree.

Braintree. — Charles W. Proctor.
South Braintree. — Elias Hayward.

Brookline.

Brookline. — Cyrus W. Ruggles.

Canton.

Canton. — Rufus C. Wood.
Ponkapoag. — George M. Davenport.

Cohasset.

Cohasset. — Charles A. Gross.
Beechwoods. — Ezra Brown.
Nantasket. — Welcome Beal.

Dedham.

Dedham. — Ambrose B. Galucia.
Spring Vale. — Alonzo B. Wentworth.
West Dedham. — Theodore Gay.

Dover.

Dover. — George L. Howe.

Foxborough.

Foxborough. — Charles H. Briggs.
East Foxborough. — David Wyman.
West Foxborough. — Miss Fanny Everett.

Franklin.

Franklin. — Joseph A. Woodward.
South Franklin. — Joseph H. Wadsworth.

Holbrook.

Holbrook. — J. T. Southworth.
Brookville. — Frederick Merrill.

Hyde Park.

Hyde Park. — Silas P. Blodgett.
Readville Station. — Enoch P. Davis.

Milton.

Milton. — Henry Pope.
Blue Hill. — Stillman L. Tucker.
East Milton. — J. W. Babcock.

Medfield.

Medfield. — Isaac Fiske.

Medway.

Medway. — Henry E. Mason.
East Medway. — Mrs. Milton Daniels.
West Medway. — Mrs. Tourtellotte.
Rockville. — Frederic Swarman.

Needham.

Needham. — Charles C. Greenwood.
Charles River Village. — Marshall Newell.
Grantville. — Alvin Fuller.
Highlandville. — Mark Lee.
Wellesley. — William H. Flagg.

Norfolk.

Norfolk. — Henry Trowbridge.
Franklin City. — John F. Torrey.

Norwood.

Norwood. — Willard Gay.

Quincy.

Quincy. — John B. Bass.
Quincy Point. — Edward H. Starbuck.
West Quincy. — E. H. Doble.
Wollaston. — Joseph C. Russell.
Atlantic. — Thomas Gurney.

Randolph.

Randolph. — John G. Poole.

Sharon.

Sharon. — Charles F. Bryant.
East Sharon. — Warren Cobb.

Stoughton.

Stoughton. — Jesse Holmes.
East Stoughton. — James Keith.
North Stoughton. — Emery Hawes.

Walpole.

Walpole. — Sylvanus W. Hartshorn.
East Walpole. — Henry A. Perkins.
South Walpole. — Harvey L. Boyden.

Weymouth.

Weymouth. — George W. White.
East Weymouth. — Henry Loud.
North Weymouth. — John W. Bartlett.
South Weymouth. — Alfred H. Wright.

Wrentham.

Wrentham. — Almira S. Farrington.
Plainville. — Harland G. Bacon.
Sheldonville. — George Sheldon.
West Wrentham. — Philander P. Cook.

NEWSPAPERS.

Brookline Chronicle, Brookline. C. M. Vincent, publisher.
Dedham Transcript, Dedham. S. H. Cox, publisher.
Foxborough Journal, Foxborough. James M. Stewart, publisher.
Foxborough Times, Foxborough. E. W. Clarke, publisher.
Franklin Register, Franklin. James M. Stewart, publisher.
Medway Journal, Medway. James M. Stewart, publisher.
Needham Chronicle, Needham. George W. Southworth, publisher.
Norfolk County Gazette, Hyde Park. S. R. Moseley, publisher.
Norfolk County Register, Randolph. Daniel H. Huxford, publisher.
Quincy Patriot, Quincy. Greene & Prescott, publishers.
Stoughton Sentinel, Stoughton. D. S. Hasty, publisher.
Walpole Standard, Walpole. James M. Stewart, publisher.
Weymouth Courier, East Weymouth. S. G. Jones, publisher.
Weymouth Gazette, Weymouth. C. G. Easterbrook, publisher.
Wrentham Recorder, Wrentham. James M. Stewart, publisher.

POLITICAL ORGANIZATIONS.

NORFOLK COUNTY COMMITTEES.

Republican. — Henry O. Hildreth, Dedham, *Chairman;* Charles C. Greenwood, Needham; John Q. A Lothrop, Cohasset; E. A. Hunt, Weymouth; William E. Nason, Franklin; Bradford Lewis, Walpole.

Democratic. — William Aspinwall, Brookline, *Chairman;* Charles H. Farrington, Bellingham; N. H. Hunt, Braintree; E. V. Kingsley, Canton; Louis N. Lincoln, Cohasset; John R. Bullard, Dedham; Eli Phelps, Foxborough; William B. Nolen, Franklin; J. E. Cotter, Hyde Park; Henry Newcomb, Holbrook; William Q. Fisher, Medfield; Dr. C. A. Bemis, Medway; James Sumner, Milton; L. D. Metcalf, Norwood; George T. Barnes, Needham; L. W. Lowell, Quincy; T. T. Cushman, Randolph; Bushrod Morse, Sharon; J. Freeman Ellis, Stoughton; James G. Hartshorne, Walpole; Z. L. Bicknell, Weymouth; C. J. Randall, Wrentham.

SECOND CONGRESSIONAL DISTRICT COMMITTEES.

Republican. — Dr. J. C. Gleason, Rockland, *Chairman;* Jediah P. Jordan, Quincy; Ezra Davol, Taunton.

Democratic — William S. Pattee, Quincy, *Chairman;* Charles Albro, Taunton; William Moore, Walpole; Henry Hobart, Braintree; Samuel Thaxter, Abington; Jonathan Jones, Dighton; Edwin V. Kingsley, Canton; S. H. Loud, Weymouth; J. T. Hart, South Scituate.

EIGHTH CONGRESSIONAL DISTRICT COMMITTEES.

Republican. — Adin B. Underwood, Newton, *Chairman;* Aaron C. Mayhew, Milford; Samuel C. Knights, Cambridge; George W. Merritt, Brookline; Joseph G. Ray, Franklin; Eliphalet Stone, Dedham; E. P. Butler, West Roxbury; Henry O. Hildreth, Dedham, *Secretary.*

Democratic. — George E. Brydges, Newton, *Chairman;* J. H. Wells, Cambridge; Orison Underwood, Milford; P. F. Griffin, Boston; George Wilson, Brighton; James M. Freeman, Franklin; H. C. Derby, Watertown; William Everett, Medway; H. P. Wells, Boston; Jeremiah W. Coveney, Cambridge.

SECOND COUNCILLOR DISTRICT COMMITTEES.

Republican. — Theodore Dean, Taunton, *Chairman;* Dr. E. B. Harvey, Westborough; Joseph Bennett, Brighton; Dr. W. E. C. Swan, Stoughton; E. H. Tucker, Needham.

Democratic. — James A. Tower, Randolph, *Chairman;* Jeremiah Gatchell, Blackstone; Charles A. Mackintosh, Dedham; E. B. O'Connor, Taunton, J. Duncklee, Brighton.

FIRST NORFOLK SENATORIAL DISTRICT COMMITTEES.

Republican. — David W. Tucker, Milton, *Chairman;* J. M. Whitcomb, Weymouth; E. C. Monk, Stoughton.

Democratic. — William G. A. Pattee, Quincy, *Chairman;* A. C. Drinkwater, Braintree, *Secretary;* Gideon Howard, Holbrook; David T. Hagan, Canton; O. E. Sheldon, Milton; John T. Flood, Randolph; Henry Fitzpatrick, Stoughton; Alanson A. Holbrook, Weymouth.

SECOND NORFOLK SENATORIAL DISTRICT COMMITTEES.

Republican. — James F. Leonard, Foxborough, *Chairman;* Enos H. Tucker, Needham; Warren E. Locke, Norwood.

Democratic. — Don Gleason Hill, Dedham, *Chairman;* C. J. Randall, Wrentham; Saul B. Scott, Norfolk; James M. Freeman, Franklin; Joseph T. Massey, Bellingham; Charles A. Bemis, Medway; Charles Hamant, Medfield; F. W. Bird, Walpole; George F. Howard, Sharon; J. B. Neal, Hyde Park; Samuel Howard, Norwood; S. G. Clarke, Needham; A. M. Shumway, Dover; D. D. Brodhead, Brookline.

BELLINGHAM.

Republican. — Daniel J. Pickering, *Chairman;* Nathan A. Cook, H. A. Whitney.
Democratic. — Alanson Bates, *Chairman;* J. J. Gerstle, Jr., John C. Rich.

BRAINTREE.

Republican. — Francis A. Hobart, *Chairman;* N. F. T. Hayden, B. L. Morrison, Geo. D. Willis, Horace Abercrombie.
Democratic. — Elisha Thayer, *Chairman;* C. N. Wallace, C. W. Mansfield, A. J. Bates, John Cavanaugh, A. C. Drinkwater.

BROOKLINE.

Republican. — R. G. F. Candage, *Chairman;* Edward I. Thomas, *Secretary;* F. Hunnewell, W. Y. Gross, W. G. Train.
Democratic. — William Aspinwall, *Chairman;* Justin Jones, *Secretary and Treasurer;* William D. Coolidge, A. J. Harrington, Oliver Cousens, John Taylor, Terence Gallaher.

CANTON.

Republican. — Charles Endicott, *Chairman;* George E. Downes, F. G. Webster; N. William Dunbar, *Secretary.*
Democratic. — William W. Brooks, *Chairman;* Edwin V. Kinsley, Thomas Lonergan, John B. Robinson, John McArdle, Zadoc C. Howes.

COHASSET.

Republican. — J. Q. A. Lothrop, *Chairman;* Charles A. Gross, Edward E. Ellms.
Democratic. — Louis N. Lincoln, *Chairman;* Caleb F. Nichols, Philip Fox.

DEDHAM.

Republican. — Franklin Copeland, *Chairman;* F. D. Ely, Henry N. Hooper, F. C. Field, Thomas Murphy.
Democratic. — Alonzo B. Wentworth, *Chairman;* D. G. Hill, *Secretary and Treasurer;* Howard Colburn, F. F. Favor, W. F. Fisher, F. M. Bailey, James H. Prince, A. C. Stone, Daniel F. Lynch.

DOVER.

Republican. — Ansel K. Tisdale, *Chairman;* Chas. H. Smith, *Secretary;* George Scott.
Democratic. — Amos W. Shumway, *Chairman;* Frank Smith.

FOXBOROUGH.

Republican. — James F. Leonard, *Chairman;* Francis D. Williams, E. O. Nichols.
Democratic. — Eli Phelps, *Chairman;* William H. Torrey, *Secretary;* Henry G. Warren.

FRANKLIN.

Republican. — George W. Wiggin, *Chairman;* Joseph G. Ray, William E. Nason.
Democratic. — William B. Nolen, *Chairman;* Erastus L. Metcalf, *Secretary;* Edmund Hartshorne, J. L. Fitzpatrick, W. W. Warren.

HOLBROOK.

Republican. — J. Tisdale Southworth, *Chairman;* Z. Aaron French, *Secretary;* Richmond T. Pratt.
Democratic. — Francis Gardner, *Chairman;* L. F. Wilde, John O'Neill, M. B. Faxon, Henry Newcomb, L. S. Whitcomb, John F. Porter.

HYDE PARK.

Republican. — William J. Stuart, *Chairman;* Richard L. Gay, *Secretary;* D. W. C. Rogers, *Treasurer;* Edward S. Hathaway, Benjamin C. Vose.
Democratic. — Edwin R. Walker, *Chairman;* J. E. Cotter, *Secretary;* Levi B. Runnells, J. D. McAvoy.

MEDFIELD.

Republican. — Isaac Fisko, *Chairman;* Jacob R. Cushman, James Hewins.
Democratic. — Charles Hamant, *Chairman;* William Q. Fisher, Daniel D. Hamant.

MEDWAY.

Republican. — M. M. Fisher, *Chairman;* A. M. B. Fuller, E. B. Daniell.
Democratic. — William Everett, *Chairman;* James O'Donnell, *Secretary;* Henry S. Partridge, C. A. Bemis, Patrick Kerry, Isaac Follansbee, J. E. Tyler.

MILTON.

Republican. — J. McKean Churchill, *Chairman;* John D. Bradlee, David W. Tucker.
Democratic. — Samuel Cook, *Chairman;* E. V. R. Reed, *Secretary.*

NEEDHAM.

Republican. — L. K. Putney, *Chairman;* Emery Grover, George K. Daniell, Charles C. Greenwood, Daniel S. Pratt.
Democratic. — Samuel G. Clarke, *Chairman;* T. E. Barry, Walter Bowen, 2d, Charles Rice, Daniel Warren.

NORFOLK.

Republican. — Asa B. Ware, *Chairman;* S. E. Fales, *Secretary.*
Democratic. — None.

NORWOOD.

Republican. — Warren E. Locke, *Chairman;* Charles T. Wheelock, *Secretary;* Lewis Day, Marcus M. Alden, Charles S. Mackenzie.
Democratic. — Samuel E. Pond, *Chairman;* George E. Draper, *Secretary;* Joseph W. Roby, George H. Morse, Isaiah Merrifield.

QUINCY.

Republican. — William B. Wooster, *Chairman;* John P. Bigelow, *Secretary;* John Q. A. Field, *Treasurer;* Henry H. Faxon, Charles Marsh, Geo. F. Pinkham,, J. P. Jordan, E. A. Perkins, H. M. Federhen, Geo. B. Pray, Samuel Ames, Jonas Shackley, Noah A. Glover, W. W. Adams, Edmund B. Taylor.
Democratic. — William A. Hodges, *Chairman;* William G. A. Pattee, *Secretary;* Eleazer Frederick, A. B. Packard, Ensign S. Fellows, John Arnold, George Shepard, John A. Duggan, Geo. W. B. Taylor, Henry A. Jones, John Chamberlain, Wm. S. Pattee, Wm. Parker, Geo. H. Hobart, Seth Dewing, Jr., William Barry, and 19 others.

RANDOLPH.

Republican. — J. White Belcher, *Chairman;* Jonathan Wales, *Secretary;* J. Winsor Pratt, Alfred W. Whitcomb, Benjamin Dickerman.
Democratic. — James A. Tower, *Chairman;* John T. Flood, *Secretary;* Daniel Howard, James Frizzell, John Dooley, John Mahoney, Franklin Porter.

SHARON.

Republican. — Sanford Waters Billings, *Chairman;* John M. Bullard, Lewis W. Morse.
Democratic. — George H. Hixon, *Chairman;* Asahel S. Drake, Esrom Morse.

STOUGHTON.

Republican. — W. E. C. Swan, *Chairman;* Elisha Hawes, Calvin Howland, Henry Standish, Wales French, Christopher Farrell.
Democratic. — J. Freeman Ellis, *Chairman;* Warren P. Bird, Matthew O'Don, Ezra Stearns, Henry Fitzpatrick.

WALPOLE.

Republican. — George P. Morey, *Chairman;* Henry S. Clarke, Henry L. Perkins.
Democratic. — David E. Metcalf, *Chairman;* Samuel Allen, Daniel E. Everett.

WEYMOUTH.

Republican. — James Humphrey, *Chairman;* William S. Wallace, *Secretary;* Geo. L. Newton, Henry Stoddard, Martin E. Hawes, Nathan D. Canterbury, Peter W. French, Augustus J. Richards, Edgar C. Porter, William Nash, Geo. Hayden, F. Dexter Pratt, Noah B. Thayer, J. Murry Whitcomb, Josiah Martin.
Democratic. — Frank W. Lewis, *Chairman;* Herbert A. Newton, *Secretary;* Z. L. Bicknell, *Treasurer;* Alanson A. Holbrook, Alvah Raymond, Jr.

WRENTHAM.

Republican. — B. H. Hoyt, *Chairman.*
Democratic. — Charles J. Randall, *Chairman;* James C. Whiting, *Secretary;* Orrin Sheldon, Oliver B. Cook, Thomas Proctor.

OFFICIAL STATEMENT OF VOTES CAST AT THE STATE ELECTION, NOV. 7, 1876.

Governor and Presidential Electors at Large.

COUNTIES.	GOVERNOR.				PRESIDENTIAL ELECTORS.				
	Alexander H. Rice, of Boston. *Republican.*	Charles Francis Adams, of Quincy. *Democrat.*	John I. Baker, of Beverly. *Prohibition.*	All others.	Thomas Talbot, of Billerica. *Republican.*	Stephen Salisbury, of Worcester. *Republican.*	William Gaston, of Boston. *Democrat.*	Edward Avery, of Braintree. *Democrat.*	All others.
Suffolk	21,270	24,090	1,622	23	22,837	22,832	25,101	25,100	141
Essex	19,422	13,980	2,843	50	21,685	21,689	14,895	14,890	165
Middlesex	25,575	18,893	1,965	19	27,301	27,304	19,561	19,562	193
Worcester	20,519	14,106	1,401	5	22,051	22,054	14,319	13,834	123
Hampshire	4,552	2,846	118	2	5,018	5,020	2,507	2,507	2
Hampden	7,379	6,839	296	5	7,963	7,963	6,605	6,605	46
Franklin	3,760	2,300	216	1	4,072	4,072	2,257	2,257	20
Berkshire	5,875	5,547	49	. .	6,015	6,015	5,478	5,478	4
Norfolk	8,069	6,225	818	19	8,963	8,956	6,685	6,682	22
Plymouth	7,272	4,480	1,039	9	8,310	8,310	4,518	4,518	19
Bristol	9,973	5,490	1,618	2	11,576	11,578	5,814	5,814	38
Barnstable	3,281	809	195	. .	3,494	3,493	785	785	6
Dukes	363	138	48	. .	399	399	149	149	. .
Nantucket	355	107	16	. .	379	379	103	103	. .
Total	137,065	106,850	12,274	115	150,063	150,064	108,777	108,284	779

Presidential Electors.

Towns.	Thomas Talbot, of Billerica, Rep.	Stephen Salisbury, of Worcester, Rep.	William Gaston, of Boston, Dem.	Edward Avery, of Braintree, Dem.	Scattering.
Bellingham	122	122	87	87	..
Braintree	395	395	403	403	..
Brookline	658	658	465	465	..
Canton	344	344	373	373	..
Cohasset	218	218	121	121	..
Dedham	518	518	504	504	10
Dover	53	53	38	38	..
Foxborough	395	330	127	124	..
Franklin	292	292	183	184	..
Holbrook	293	233	106	106	..
Hyde Park	635	635	344	344	..
Medfield	157	157	77	77	..
Medway	433	433	289	289	..
Milton	310	310	188	188	..
Needham	456	456	214	214	4
Norfolk	80	80	55	55	..
Norwood	240	240	169	169	..
Quincy	867	867	852	852	..
Randolph	323	323	527	527	..
Sharon	153	153	115	115	4
Stoughton	523	523	457	457	..
Walpole	227	227	165	165	..
Weymouth	1,078	1,079	715	714	4
Wrentham	258	255	111	111	..
	8,963	8,956	6,685	6,682	22

State Officers.

Towns.	GOVERNOR.			LT. GOV.			SEC. STATE.			TREAS.		AUDITOR.			ATT'Y GEN.		
	Alexander H. Rice, of Boston, Rep.	Charles F. Adams, of Quincy, Dem.	John I. Baker, of Beverly, Pro.	Horatio G. Knight, of Easthampton, R.	Wm. R. Plunkett, of Pittsfield, D.	Daniel C. Eddy, of Boston, P.	Henry B. Peirce, of Abington, R.	Weston Howland, of Fairhaven, D.	David R. Gurney, of Abington, P.	Charles Endicott, of Canton, R.	David N. Skillings, of Winchester, D.	Julius L. Clarke, of Newton, R.	John E. Fitzgerald, of Boston, D.	Jonathan H. Orne, of Marblehead, P.	Charles R. Train, of Boston, R.	Richard Olney, of Boston, D.	Orin T. Gray, of Hyde Park, P.
Bellingham	119	87	..	122	87	..	122	87	..	122	87	122	87	..	122	87	..
Braintree	347	386	57	360	398	43	370	400	29	370	429	368	398	32	367	400	32
Brookline	636	471	14	642	472	17	651	462	18	651	474	653	464	11	664	459	14
Canton	317	374	23	335	372	7	340	369	5	363	345	340	358	5	341	359	5
Cohasset	210	121	10	212	120	9	212	120	9	212	121	212	120	9	211	121	9
Dedham	486	499	31	481	506	8	487	505	35	491	538	490	500	35	489	502	36
Dover	52	36	2	51	37	2	53	38	..	53	39	53	38	..	53	38	..
Foxborough	358	126	22	363	122	19	372	122	11	372	135	372	122	11	367	122	13
Franklin	251	177	41	284	183	8	288	183	6	250	188	288	183	6	288	183	6
Holbrook	194	111	5	207	114	24	210	116	1	229	117	229	115	1	229	116	1
Hyde Park	599	338	33	605	336	30	617	339	26	617	364	614	336	26	601	330	49
Medfield	153	76	5	156	76	2	156	75	3	156	77	157	74	3	157	75	2
Medway	374	287	54	381	291	30	386	290	41	386	331	386	290	41	386	290	40
Milton	295	292	1	357	191	..	205	190	..	303	189	310	186	..	300	188	..
Needham	409	230	40	443	216	41	422	213	38	422	240	422	213	38	422	213	33
Norfolk	73	55	8	73	55	8	73	55	8	73	63	73	55	8	73	55	8
Norwood	190	157	63	192	157	62	192	156	62	192	218	192	156	62	194	155	61
Quincy	811	871	31	828	849	30	842	849	26	842	872	842	849	26	843	849	26
Randolph	291	504	35	397	525	18	309	525	16	310	541	310	525	16	310	524	17
Sharon	144	116	8	143	115	8	149	114	3	155	114	149	114	3	149	115	6
Stoughton	443	443	92	452	443	83	454	449	80	455	529	454	449	81	454	449	81
Walpole	201	166	20	203	166	16	209	167	16	209	183	209	167	15	210	167	15
Weymouth	872	690	227	801	695	208	902	694	196	898	802	900	693	196	902	606	193
Wrentham	244	112	6	250	115	5	252	112	4	251	111	252	112	4	252	112	4
	8060	6625	818	8283	6646	687	8374	6630	630	8427	7196	8397	6604	623	8300	6605	656

SCATTERING. — For Governor, 19; Lieut. Governor, 1; Secretary of State, 3; Treasurer, 10; Auditor, 2; Attorney General, 5.

Representatives in Congress.

DISTRICT NO. 2.

TOWNS.	Benjamin W. Harris, of E. Bridgewater, *Rep.*	Edward Avery, of Braintree, *Dem.*	Scattering.	TOWNS.	Benjamin W. Harris, of E. Bridgewater, *Rep.*	Edward Avery, of Braintree, *Dem.*	Scattering.
Abington	494	225	....	Norfolk	74	55	....
Attleborough	913	423	....	Norton	191	87	....
Berkley	134	13	....	Quincy	865	849	....
Braintree	377	413	....	Randolph	325	524	1
Bridgewater	359	289	....	Raynham	217	58	....
Brockton	1,346	629	....	Rehoboth	234	76	....
Canton	344	371	....	Rockland	470	281	....
Cohasset	215	125	....	Scituate	298	211	....
Dighton	252	66	....	Seekonk	120	88	....
Easton	356	224	....	Sharon	152	116	....
East Bridgewater	348	257	....	South Abington	299	192	....
Foxborough	378	129	....	South Scituate	257	121	1
Hanover	209	98	....	Stoughton	628	455	....
Hanson	166	70	....	Taunton	2,010	1,130	4
Hingham	583	283	1	Walpole	218	167	1
Holbrook	226	116	....	West Bridgewater	185	98	....
Hyde Park	635	342	....	Weymouth	1,073	712	....
Hull	31	25	....	Wrentham	250	113	....
Mansfield	239	136	....				
Milton	309	187	....		15,550	9,757	8

DISTRICT NO. 8.

TOWNS.	William Claflin, of Newton, *Rep.*	William W. Warren, of Boston, *Dem.*	Scattering.	TOWNS.	William Claflin, of Newton, *Rep.*	William W. Warren, of Boston, *Dem.*	Scattering.
Ashland	253	146	....	Medfield	157	75	....
Boston, Ward 22, Rox. and Dor.	399	738	....	Medway	424	292	....
Boston, Ward 23, W. Roxbury	960	1,058	2	Milford	838	742	....
Boston, Ward 25, Brighton	435	668	2	Natick	684	800	....
Brookline	628	486	3	Needham	437	231	....
Cambridge	3,559	3,585	6	Newton	1,745	848	2
Dedham	508	518	....	Norwood	239	171	....
Dover	53	38	....	Sherborn	124	76	....
Framingham	660	541	....	Southborough	197	84	....
Franklin	294	183	....	Watertown	504	381	....
Holliston	358	283	....	Wayland	239	143	....
Hopkinton	374	339	....	Weston	176	68	....
					14,245	12,497	15

Councillor.

SECOND COUNCILLOR DISTRICT.	Harrison Tweed, of Taunton, Rep.	Wm. Aspinwall, of Brookline, Dem.	Ezra S. Conant, of Randolph, Pro.	Henry D. Cushing, of Boston, Pro.	S. B. Phinney, of Barnstable, Dem.	Scattering.	SECOND COUNCILLOR DISTRICT.	Harrison Tweed, of Taunton, Rep.	Wm. Aspinwall, of Brookline, Dem.	Ezra S. Conant, of Randolph, Pro.	Henry D. Cushing, of Boston, Pro.	S. B. Phinney, of Barnstable, Dem.	Scattering.
Attleborough	844	...	52	..	425	.	Medway ..	389	288	38	..	..	..
Bellingham .	122	87	..	..	..	.	Mendon ...	127	73	4	..	..	..
Blackstone .	268	384	..	..	..	.	Milford ...	769	711	94	..	..	..
Boston, Ward 22, Rox. and Dor.....	394	717	21	..	..	.	Milton ...	309	189	..	..	..	..
							Needham ..	422	213	38	..	..	..
Boston, Ward 23, W. Rox.	1,015	983	37	..	..	1	Norfolk ...	80	45	..	..	..	..
							Northborough	174	75	25	..	..	..
Boston, Ward 24, Dor...	1,287	890	..	78	..	1	Northbridge .	346	247	..	..	..	..
							Norton ...	143	87	8	..	..	..
Boston, Ward 25, Bri. ..	438	619	55	..	..	.	Norwood ..	192	156	62	..	..	..
Boylston ...	41	21	..	..	..	82	Quincy ...	844	859	25	..	..	..
Braintree ..	365	398	33	..	..	.	Randolph ..	308	525	17	..	..	..
Brookline ..	667	436	..	..	..	17	Raynham ..	167	58	51	..	..	..
Canton ...	340	372	5	..	..	.	Seekonk ..	119	88	..	..	..	..
Dedham ..	483	508	35	..	..	.	Sharon ...	155	115	2	..	..	..
Douglas ..	167	219	..	..	..	.	Shrewsbury .	227	91	..	..	..	..
Dover	53	38	..	..	..	.	Southborough	184	81	21	..	..	..
Easton ...	357	221	1	..	..	.	Stoughton ..	453	451	81	..	..	..
Foxborough .	367	121	13	..	..	5	Taunton ..	1,906	1,056	159	..	..	1
Franklin ..	288	183	6	..	..	.	Upton ..	249	123	10	..	..	..
Grafton ...	365	198	3	..	..	.	Uxbridge ..	275	216	..	..	..	..
Holbrook ..	229	116	1	..	..	.	Walpole ..	209	166	16	..	..	..
Hyde Park .	564	340	26	..	..	.	Westborough	514	269	22	..	..	..
Mansfield ..	224	136	35	..	..	.	Weymouth .	893	697	193	..	..	..
Medfield ..	156	75	..	..	..	.	Wrentham .	252	112	4	..	..	..
								18,789	14,045	1,202	78	428	107

In Ward 24, City of Boston, the entire Prohibition vote (78) was cast for Henry D. Cushing, the Prohibition candidate in Councillor District No. 3.

In the Town of Attleborough, the entire Democratic vote (428) was cast for S. B. Phinney, the Democratic candidate in District No. 1.

County Treasurer (for three years).

TOWNS.	Churchill.	Allen.	Allen.	Scattering.	TOWNS.	Churchill.	Allen.	Allen.	Scattering.
Bellingham ...	122	87	..	..	Milton	308	189	..	..
Braintree	400	399	..	..	Needham ...	400	210	..	..
Brookline	678	451	..	..	Norfolk	81	55	..	..
Canton	353	361	..	..	Norwood ...	254	156	..	..
Cohasset	214	120	..	6	Quincy	870	776	73	..
Dedham	584	444	..	..	Randolph ...	324	525	..	..
Dover	52	40	..	..	Sharon	154	114	..	..
Foxborough ...	383	122	..	..	S oughton ...	553	450	..	..
Franklin	290	184	..	..	Walpole	162	227	..	..
Holbrook	230	116	..	..	Weymouth ...	1,086	660	46	..
Hyde Park ...	607	341	..	..	Wrentham ...	255	113	..	..
Medfield	157	75	..	..		8,062	6,514	119	6
Medway	425	290	..	..					

Chauncey C. Churchill, of Dedham, Republican, elected. Samuel Allen, of Walpole, was the Democratic candidate. In Quincy 73 votes and in Weymouth 46 votes thrown for Stephen Allen, of Walpole, were evidently intended for the Democratic candidate.

County Commissioner (for three years), Commissioner of Insolvency, and Clerk of Courts.

TOWNS.	COUNTY COMMISSIONER (for three years).				COMMISSIONER OF INSOLVENCY.		CLERK OF COURTS.		
	Galen Orr, of Needham.	James M. Freeman, of Franklin.	John M. Freeman, of Franklin.	Scattering.	George W. Wiggin, of Franklin. *Rep.*	John R. Bullard, of Dedham. *Dem.*	Erastus Worthington, of Dedham. *Rep.*	Charles G. Chick, of Hyde Park. *Dem.*	Scattering.
Bellingham .	78	13	. . . .	. . . .	122	87	122	87	. .
Braintree . .	400	399	. . . .	. . . .	399	370	386	399	. .
Brookline . .	664	465	. . . .	. . . .	659	458	667	448	. .
Canton	343	. .	373	. . . .	342	370	360	351	. .
Cohasset . . .	214	120	. . . .	6	214	120	215	121	6
Dedham . . .	501	519	. . . .	. . . .	484	507	583	442	. .
Dover	52	39	. . . .	. . . .	53	39	53	38	. .
Foxborough .	378	120	. . . .	. . . .	383	124	383	124	. .
Franklin . . .	240	237	. . . .	. . . .	288	184	293	183	. .
Holbrook . .	230	116	. . . .	. . . .	230	116	230	116	. .
Hyde Park . .	638	342	. . . .	. . . .	631	339	646	331	1
Medfield . . .	158	75	. . . .	. . . .	158	75	159	74	. .
Medway . . .	425	290	. . . .	. . . .	426	291	426	283	. .
Milton	308	189	. . . .	. . . .	309	188	310	185	1
Needham . .	458	202	. . . .	7	458	213	462	211	. .
Norfolk . . .	81	55	. . . .	. . . .	80	55	81	55	. .
Norwood . .	253	156	. . . .	. . . .	192	160	251	158	. .
Quincy . . .	861	853	. . . .	2	872	852	876	845	. .
Randolph . .	322	529	. . . .	. . . .	322	525	491	348	. .
Sharon	156	117	. . . .	. . . .	152	116	161	109	. .
Stoughton . .	534	451	. . . .	. . . .	534	430	535	449	. .
Walpole . . .	218	169	. . . .	. . . .	223	163	227	164	. .
Weymouth . .	1,081	712	. . . .	. . . .	1,082	713	1,083	709	. .
Wrentham . .	212	155	. . . .	. . . .	254	113	255	113	. .
Total	8,805	6,450	373	15	8,867	6,633	9,255*	6,848	8

For County Commissioner, Galen Orr, of Needham, Republican, was re-elected. James M. Freeman, of Franklin, was the Democratic candidate. In Canton the entire Democratic vote was thrown for John M. Freeman, of Franklin. In Needham, four votes were thrown for Galen Orr (not stating the residence), and three for Galen Orr of Franklin.

* Including the vote of Sharon, which was not returned to the Secretary of State, but which has been obtained from the Town Clerk.

Register of Deeds (for three years).

TOWNS.	Burdakin.	Farrington.	Scattering.	TOWNS.	Burdakin.	Farrington.	Scattering.
Bellingham	158	51	. . . .	Milton	275	222	. . . .
Braintree	424	375	. . . .	Needham	321	349	. . . .
Brookline	805	323	. . .,	Norfolk	112	17	. . . .
Canton	396	318	1	Norwood	189	184	2
Cohasset	205	120	6	Quincy	1,097	627	. . . .
Dedham	516	495	. . . .	Randolph	408	415	2
Dover	74	18	. . . .	Sharon	165	103	. . . .
Foxborough	205	302	. . . .	Stoughton	463	516	. . . .
Franklin	201	276	. . . .	Walpole	269	123	1
Holbrook	276	75	. . . .	Weymouth	767	1 025	. . . .
Hyde Park	300	585	. . . .	Wrentham	209	159	. . . .
Medfield	219	14	. . . .		8,635	6,919	12
Medway	431	215	. . . .				

John H. Burdakin, of Dedham, Democrat, elected. Charles H. Farrington, of Dedham, was the Republican candidate.

Senators.

FIRST NORFOLK DIST.	John D. Wheeler, of Quincy.	Wm. A. Hodges, of Quincy.	Bushrod Morse, of Sharon.	Scattering.	SECOND NORFOLK DIST.	Joseph E. Fiske, of Needham.	Bushrod Morse, of Sharon.	Scattering.	SECOND NORFOLK DIST.	Joseph E. Fiske, of Needham.	Bushrod Morse, of Sharon.	Scattering.
Braintree . .	4(0	390	..	.	Bellingham	122	87	.	Medway .	427	291	.
Canton . . .	343	352	13	.	Brookline .	667	462	.	Needham .	444	214	1
Holbrook . .	223	116	..	.	Dedham .	516	505	.	Norfolk . .	81	54	.
Milton . . .	309	178	10	.	Dover . . .	52	38	.	Norwood .	253	156	.
Quincy . . .	949	775	..	3	Foxborough	380	123	.	Sharon . .	143	127	.
Randolph . .	327	521	..	.	Franklin .	203	184	.	Walpole .	225	166	.
Stoughton . .	531	451	..	.	Hyde Park	640	349	.	Wrentham	256	112	.
Weymouth .	1,074	748	..	2	Medfield .	156	75	1				
	4,165	3,543	23	5						4,655	2,937	2

In the First Norfolk District, John D. Wheeler, of Quincy, Republican, was elected. William A. Hodges, of Quincy, was the Democratic candidate. The votes thrown for Bushrod Morse were intended for the Democratic candidate, but Mr. Morse was the regular Democratic candidate in the Second District.

In the Second Norfolk District, Joseph E. Fiske, of Needham, Republican, was re-elected. Bushrod Morse, of Sharon, was the Democratic candidate.

Representatives.

DISTRICT No. 1.

	Cobb.	Warren.	Smith.	Scattering.
Dedham,	508	489	27	1
Norwood,	193	152	64	..
	701	641	91	1

John D. Cobb, of Dedham, Republican, was elected.
Winslow Warren, of Dedham, was the Democratic candidate, and Charles L. Smith, of Norwood, the candidate of the Prohibitionists.

DISTRICT No. 2.

	Thomas.	Whitney.	Scattering.
Brookline,	604	511	5

Edward I. Thomas, of Brookline, Republican, was elected.
Henry M. Whitney, of Brookline, was the Democratic candidate.

DISTRICT No. 3.

	Gerry.	Walker.	Stuart.
Hyde Park,	405	359	203

Charles F. Gerry, of Hyde Park, the regular Republican candidate, was elected.
Edwin R. Walker was the Democratic candidate, and William J. Stuart was an Independent Republican candidate.

DISTRICT No. 4.

	Morse.	Lonergan.	Huntoon.
Canton,	309	2.96	100
Milton,	131	155	199
	440	451	299

Thomas Lonergan, of Canton, Democrat, elected.
Elijah A. Morse, of Canton, was the regular Republican candidate, and D. T. V. Huntoon, of Canton, was an Independent Republican candidate.

DISTRICT No. 5.

	Barker.	Lovell.	Hayden.	Packard.	Bicknell.	Sherman.	Brown.	Stevens.	Murray.	Scattering.
Quincy,	857	839	840	834	846	840	24	26	26	1
Weymouth,	908	879	891	667	722	677	154	177	160	117
	1,765	1,718	1,731	1,501	1,568	1,517	178	203	186	118

Henry F. Barker, of Quincy, and Benjamin S. Lovell and George F. Hayden, of Weymouth, Republicans, were elected.
Abner B. Packard, of Quincy, and Z. L. Bicknell and Cyrus Sherman, of Weymouth, were the Democratic candidates. William R. Brown, of Quincy, and Joseph Stevens and David S. Murray, of Weymouth, were the Prohibition candidates.
Of the scattering votes, which were rejected for non-compliance with the law, Z. L. Bicknell received 30; Cyrus Sherman, 29; Abner B. Packard, 32; Henry F. Barker, 17; and there were 10 for other candidates.

DISTRICT No. 6.

	Shaw.	Gardner.	Scattering.
Braintree,	397	391	1
Holbrook,	212	123	1
Total,	609	514	2

Josephus Shaw, of Braintree, Republican, was elected.
Francis Gardner, of Holbrook, was the Democratic candidate.

DISTRICT No. 7.

	Mann.	Morey.	Bird.	Robbins.	Southworth.	Scattering.
Randolph,	344	312	509	492	13	4
Stoughton,	531	419	450	453	90	5
Sharon,	151	147	117	115	2	1
Walpole,	211	186	187	156	23	..
Total,	1,237	1,064	1,263	1,216	128	10

Seth Mann, 2d, of Randolph, Republican and Prohibition, and Francis W. Bird, of Walpole, Democrat, were elected.
George P. Morey, of Walpole, was the regular Republican candidate, and George W. Robbins, of Stoughton, the regular Democratic candidate.
Consider Southworth, of Stoughton, was on the Prohibition ticket.

DISTRICT No. 8.

	Ray.	Tompkins.	Proctor.	Atwood.	Crowell.	Ryan.	Scattering.
Bellingham,	125	121	86	86	..	..	..
Foxborough,	367	385	127	122	12	..	..
Franklin,	300	291	167	183	..	..	4
Medway,	389	390	289	288	40	36	..
Wrentham,	215	260	121	100	..	..	1
Total,	1,426	1,447	790	779	52	36	5

James P. Ray, of Franklin, and William R. Tompkins, of Wrentham, Republicans, were elected.

Thomas Proctor, of Wrentham, and Dr. Shadrach Atwood, of Franklin, were the Democratic candidates. L. Crowell, of Medway, and George W. Ryan, of Franklin, were on the Prohibition ticket.

DISTRICT No. 9.

	Mackintosh.	Shumway.	Scattering.
Dover,	41	46	2
Medfield,	147	85	..
Needham,	392	257	19
Norfolk,	65	66	..
Total,	645	454	21

James Mackintosh, of Needham, Republican, was elected.
Amos W. Shumway, of Dover, was the Democratic candidate.

DISTRICTS.

County, Senatorial, Congressional and Councillor.

Bellingham	2d Norfolk Senatorial . . .	9th Congressional	2 1 Councillor.
Braintree	1st " " . . .	2d "	2d "
Brookline	2d " " . . .	8th "	2d "
Canton	1st " " . . .	2d "	2d "
Cohasset	2d Plymouth " . . .	2d "	1st "
Dedham	2d Norfolk " . . .	8th "	2d "
Dover	2d " " . . .	8th "	2d "
Foxborough	2d " " . . .	2d "	2d "
Franklin	2d " " . . .	8th "	2 1 "
Holbrook	1st " " . . .	2d "	2d "
Hyde Park	2d " " . . .	2d "	2d "
Medfield	2d " " . . .	8th "	2d "
Medway	2d " " . . .	8th "	2 1 "
Milton	1st " " . . .	2d "	2d "
Needham	2d " " . . .	8th "	2d "
Norfolk	2d " " . . .	2d "	2 1 "
Norwood	2d " " . . .	8th "	2d "
Quincy	1st " " . . .	2d "	2d "
Randolph	1st " " . . .	2d "	2 1 "
Sharon	2d " " . . .	2d "	2d "
Stoughton	1st " " . . .	2d "	2d "
Walpole	2d " " . . .	2d "	2d "
Weymouth	1st " " . . .	2d "	2d "
Wrentham	2d " " . . .	2d "	2d "

Representative.

DISTRICT No. 1. — Dedham, Norwood . . . . 1 Representative.
"   "   2. — Brookline 1   "
"   "   3. — Hyde Park 1   "
"   "   4. — Canton, Milton .1   "
"   "   5. — Quincy, Weymouth 3   "
"   "   6. — Braintree, Holbrook 1   "
"   "   7. — Randolph, Sharon, Stoughton, Walpole 2   "
"   "   8. — Bellingham, Foxborough, Franklin, Medway, Wrentham .2   "
"   "   9. — Dover, Medfield, Needham, Norfolk 1   "

Total 13   "

VITAL STATISTICS FOR 1876.

Towns.	Births.	Mar-riages.	Deaths.	Towns.	Births.	Mar-riages.	Deaths.
Bellingham .	22	16	22	Milton . . .	71	27	38
Braintree . .	96	45	77	Needham .	128	56	67
Brookline . .	203	53	138	Norfolk . .	22	9	23
Canton . . .	96	23	51	Norwood .	59	11	39
Cohasset . . .	52	17	43	Quincy . . .	212	76	160
Dedham . . .	138	33	110	Randolph .	79	36	71
Dover	5	9	8	Sharon . . .	15	9	26
Foxborough .	57	14	43	Stoughton .	100	41	76
Franklin . . .	81	17	59	Walpole . .	47	25	33
Holbrook . .	40	23	28	Weymouth	251	93	149
Hyde Park .	105	39	137	Wrentham .	35	14	39
Medfield . . .	20	17	19				
Medway . . .	79	34	77	Total . . .	2,059	737	1,543

HISTORICAL.

NORFOLK COUNTY, as first incorporated, included all the original territory of Suffolk, except the towns of Boston and Chelsea. May 10, 1643, the Colony of Massachusetts Bay was divided into four counties, viz. : Essex, Middlesex, Suffolk and Norfolk, the latter comprising the towns of Haverhill, Salisbury, Hampton, Exeter, Dover and Portsmouth. The four last-named towns having been set off to New Hampshire on its separation from Massachusetts in 1680, the others were set back to Essex, Feb. 4, 1680, and the original County of Norfolk ceased to exist.

For many years previous to the organization of the present County of Norfolk, great dissatisfaction had existed among the more remote towns, and several attempts were made for a division of the County of Suffolk, but it was not until the first session of the Legislature of 1793 that the long-continued movement for a new county prevailed. No copy of the original petitions upon which the act was passed have been preserved.

The following is the Act of Incorporation : —

Commonwealth of Massachusetts.

In the year of our Lord one thousand seven hundred and ninety-three.

AN ACT

For Dividing the County of Suffolk, and Establishing a new County by the name of Norfolk.

Be it enacted by the Senate and House of Representatives, in General Court assembled, and by the authority of the same, That all the territory of the county of Suffolk, not comprehended within the towns of *Boston* and *Chelsea,* from and after the twentieth day of *June* next, be, and hereby is formed and erected into an entire and distinct county, by the name of *Norfolk;* and *Dedham* shall be the shire town, till otherwise ordered by the General Court; and the inhabitants of said county of *Norfolk* shall have and possess and enjoy all the powers, rights and immunities, which, by the Constitution and Laws of this Commonwealth, the inhabitants of any county within the same, have, possess, exercise and enjoy, or are entitled to.

And be it further enacted, That there shall be held and kept within the said county of *Norfolk,* at the shire town thereof, a Court of General Sessions of the Peace, and a Court of Common Pleas, on the last Tuesdays of *April* and *September,* yearly; and a Supreme Judicial Court, on the Tuesday next preceding the last Tuesday in *August,* annually, to commence in the year one thousand seven hundred and ninety-four. And the Justices of said Courts of subordinate jurisdiction, when lawfully appointed and commissioned, shall have, hold, exercise and enjoy all the powers and authority which are given and granted to Justices of like Courts in any other county within this Commonwealth; and all the aforesaid Courts shall bear the same legal relation to each other, by process of every kind, as the like Courts do in the other counties of this Commonwealth.

And be it further enacted, That the methods and proceedings directed by law for choosing a County Treasurer and Register of Deeds, and the modes, forms and proceedings, known and practiced, in bringing forward and trying actions, causes, pleas or suits, and of originating and conducting legal process of every kind, whether civil or criminal, in the Judicial Courts established in the several counties in this Commonwealth, and for choosing Jurors to serve at said Courts, shall be observed, and put in practice within the said county of *Norfolk:* Provided that the choice of County Treasurer and Register of Deeds for said county of *Norfolk,* shall for the first time originate in the same manner as prescribed by law, where vacancies happen in said offices by death or resignation.

And be it further enacted, That all writs, suits, and process, of every kind, which may, before the said twentieth day of *June,* be depending in any Court, including Probate Courts, within the county of *Suffolk,* shall be heard and tried, proceeded and determined upon in the county of Suffolk, in the same manner as they would have been if this Act had not been made.

And be it further enacted, That all deeds for the conveyance of real estates within the said county of *Norfolk,* which shall be executed prior to the establishment of a Registry of Deeds, and qualification of a Register within said county of *Norfolk,* may be recorded in the Office of the Register of Deeds for the county of *Suffolk,* and shall have the same legal effect and operation as though they were recorded in the Registry of Deeds for the said county of *Norfolk.*

And be it further enacted, That the several towns and districts within the said county of *Norfolk,* shall pay their proportion of all county taxes already granted and assessed, in the same manner as they would have done if this Act had not been made; and shall be holden to pay their proportion of all debts that shall be owing by the county of *Suffolk,* on the said twentieth of *June* next, after the appropriation of the present outstanding taxes, and be entitled also to their proportion of all property belonging to said county of *Suffolk,* except in the county Court-House, Goal and Goal-House, and the land belonging thereto: And said county of *Norfolk* shall be obliged to build and keep in repair all bridges within the said county of *Norfolk,* which at this time are chargeable upon the county of *Suffolk,* and perform all other duties and obligations within their limits which the county of *Suffolk* are now obliged to perform.

And be it further enacted, That if it shall so happen that any person or persons shall be liable to be committed to prison within the said county of *Norfolk,* within two years from the passing of this Act, it shall be lawful to commit such person or persons by due process, to the common goal within the county of *Suffolk;* and all processes of law, and the powers of all Officers within said county of *Norfolk,* shall be as legal and binding for that purpose, as though the same goal was within the said county of *Norfolk;* and the keeper for said goal shall be liable for the safe keeping of all prisoners, so committed, in the same manner as though committed by due course of legal proceedings within the county of *Suffolk;* and all prisoners, so committed, shall be entitled to the same benefits and indulgencies as though committed within the said county of *Norfolk;* and all necessary expenses which shall arise in consequence of the commitment of any prisoners from the county of *Norfolk,* shall be defrayed by the same County.

IN THE HOUSE OF REPRESENTATIVES, March 22d, 1793.

This bill having had three several readings, passed to be enacted.

DAVID COBB, *Speaker.*

IN SENATE, March 22d, 1793.

This bill having had two several readings, passed to be enacted.

SAMUEL PHILLIPS, *President.*

By the Governor,

Approved March 26, 1793.   JOHN HANCOCK.

The towns thus set off from Suffolk were Bellingham, Braintree, Brookline, Cohasset, Dedham, Dorchester, Dover (district), Foxborough, Franklin, Hingham, Hull, Medfield, Medway, Milton, Needham, Quincy, Randolph, Roxbury, Sharon, Stoughton, Walpole, Weymouth, Wrentham.

At the June session of the same year (1793, Chapter 9 of the Act passed June 20th), so much of the above Act of Incorporation " as it respects the towns of Hingham and Hull, is hereby repealed and made null and void."

At the same session, Chapter 12 of the Acts provides that, whereas, in the Act dividing the County of Suffolk and establishing the County of Norfolk, " no provision is made for the choice of Grand Jurors to serve at the Court of General Sessions of the Peace in the several Counties of Suffolk and Norfolk, the present year," " the Clerk of the Court of the General Sessions of the Peace, in the said counties, be, and hereby are authorized respectively to make out their warrants to the Constables of the several towns in their respective counties, or, to so many of them as the Court shall order, requiring them, severally, to assemble the freeholders and inhabitants of their respective towns, qualified to vote for Representatives, to choose, by ballot, one or more good and lawful man, or men, in each town, as the Court shall direct, of like qualifications and of good moral character, as is already required by ' An Act regulating the appointment and services of Grand Jurors,' to appear at the Court of General Sessions of the Peace, next to be holden within the said counties respectively, and there to serve on the Grand Jury at every Court of General Sessions of the Peace, throughout the remainder of the present year, and until another Grand Jury shall be chosen, impanelled and sworn in their room, and the Constables shall notify the persons so chosen four days before the sitting of the Court, and their duty shall be the same as is already declared and designated in the before-mentioned ' Act regulating the appointment and services of Grand Jurors.' "

June 29, 1798, an act was passed by the Legislature establishing an additional term of the Supreme Judicial Court for the County of Norfolk, on the 1st Tuesday of February, annually.

March 3, 1802, an act was passed by the Legislature establishing an additional term of the Court of Common Pleas for the County of Norfolk, on the 1st Tuesday of January, annually, in addition to the terms already established.

COURTS OF COMMON PLEAS AND OF GENERAL SESSIONS OF THE PEACE.

July 3, 1782 (Chap. 12), an act was passed by the Legislature establishing a Court of Common Pleas in each county of the State, to be held by four substantial, discreet and learned persons, each of whom should be an inhabitant of the county wherein he should be appointed, to be commissioned by the Governor, and to have cognizance of all civil actions of the value of more than forty shillings.

July 3, 1782 (Chap. 15), an act was also passed establishing a Court of General Sessions of the Peace, to be held by the Justices of each county, " who are hereby empowered to hear and determine all matters relative to the Conservation of the Peace and the punishment of such offences as are cognizable by them at Common Law."

Feb. 27, 1787 (Chap. 15), an act was passed, the provisions of which gave to the Court of General Sessions of the Peace similar powers with those now held and exercised by County Commissioners.

The first session of the *Court of General Sessions of the Peace* was held at Dedham, on the last Tuesday of September, 1793, at which Nathaniel Ames, of Dedham, was appointed Clerk. Deacon Isaac Bullard, of Dedham, was chosen Treasurer of the county for the remainder of the year, and, upon examining the votes returned to said court, it appeared that Capt. Eliphalet Pond, of Dedham, was elected Register of Deeds by a large majority. Hon. Ebenezer Thayer, Esq., of Braintree, who had been appointed Sheriff by the Governor, nominated his bondsmen, who were approved. At the end of the record of this meeting occurs this statement: "John Jones, Esq., of Dover, President of this session."

The next record is as follows : —

"Norfolk, *ss.* January 7, 1794. Court of General Sessions of the Peace for said County, held at Dedham by adjournment from the first Tuesday in November last. Opened first in the old meeting-house, but, by reason of coldness, immediately adjourned to the sign of the Law Book, and there opened again."

The business of this session seems to have been the apportionment of the county tax, decision upon road matters, the issuing of licenses to victuallers, and the trial of offenders charged with gaming, slander and larceny. Deacon Isaac Bullard was also in open court sworn into office as the Treasurer of the county.

By the records of the Executive Council it appears, that on July 2, 1793, Samuel Niles, Esq., of Braintree, Richard Cranch, Esq., of Quincy, William Heath, Esq., of Roxbury, and Stephen Metcalf. Esq., of Bellingham, were appointed Justices of the Court of Common Pleas for the County of Norfolk. No notice of the declination of either of these gentlemen appears on the records of either the Court or the Council, but on the 3d of September of the same year, Nathaniel Ames, Esq., of Dedham, John Read, Esq., of Roxbury, and Ebenezer Warren, Esq., of Foxborough, were appointed Justices. and Edward H. Robbins, Esq., of Milton, and Solomon Lovell, Esq., of Weymouth, Special Justices of the Court of Common Pleas. September 24th following, James Endicott, Esq., of Stoughton, was appointed Justice of the Court of Common Pleas.

The first session of this Court was held at Dedham, September 24th, 1793, at which were present Hon. Stephen Metcalf and Ebenezer Warren and James Endicott, Esquires, Nathaniel Ames being Clerk of the Court. Daniel Perry, of Medfield, was appointed Special Justice of the Court February 25, 1794.

May 27, 1799, Edward H. Robbins, of Milton, was appointed Chief Justice, and Oliver Everett, of Dorchester, and Horatio Townsend, of Medfield, Special Justices of the Court of Common Pleas; and September 26, 1800, Oliver Everett was recommissioned a Justice. July 5, 1802, Daniel Perry was reappointed as a Justice, and Samuel Haven, of Dedham, a Special Justice; and May 24, 1803, Moses Everett, of Dorchester, and Samuel Bass, of Randolph, were appointed Special Justices.

June 15, 1804, Samuel Haven, of Dedham, was appointed Chief Justice of the Court of Common Pleas. January 29, 1805, Moses Everett, of Dorchester, was reappointed Justice, and David S. Greenough, of Roxbury, was appointed Special Justice. February 6, 1806, Thomas Williams, of Roxbury, was appointed Special

Justice, and May 10th, of the same year, Thomas Greenleaf, of Quincy, was also appointed Special Justice.

June 19, 1807 (Chap. 11), the Legislature passed an act in addition to an act entitled " An Act establishing Courts of General Sessions of the Peace," passed the 3d day of July, 1782, the first section of which provided that from and after the first of September following, " the Courts of General Sessions of the Peace, in the several counties, shall be holden by one Chief or First Justice, and by so many associate justices as shall be hereafter mentioned, and no more, to be designated and appointed by the Governor, with the advice of the Council, who shall issue commissions to them for that purpose, accordingly, instead of the same being holden by the Justices of the Peace of each county; the justices so appointed to meet in their several counties at the several times and places that now are. or hereafter may be, established by law for the holding of the several Courts of the General Sessions of the Peace."

Section two provided for the number of Associate Justices — " for the County of Norfolk, four." Section three provided that Justices should " have all the powers and perform all the duties that the Courts of General Sessions of the Peace now have, or perform in and by the act to which this is an addition, provided, always, that the justices shall not be appointed, or serve on any committee for the laying out. altering or discontinuing any road or highway." Section four provided that Justices should receive $3 per day, each, for actual attendance, and $2 for every ten miles' travel, or in that proportion for longer or shorter travel, to be paid out of the county treasury.

In accordance with the provisions of this law, the Governor, on the 3d of July, 1807, appointed Ebenezer Seaver. of Roxbury, Chief Justice, and William Aspinwall, of Brookline, John Ellis, of Medway. Joseph Bemis, of Canton, and Samuel Day. of Wrentham, Justices of the Court of General Sessions of the Peace for the County of Norfolk. August 22, of the same year, William Aspinwall resigned and Nathaniel Ruggles, of Roxbury, was appointed in his place.

June 19, 1809 (Chap. 17). the Legislature passed an act transferring the powers and duties of the Court of Sessions of the Peace to the Court of Common Pleas.

June 21, 1811 (Chap. 33), an act was passed establishing Circuit Courts of Common Pleas within this Commonwealth, the first section of which divided the State (except Dukes and Nantucket) into six circuits — the counties of Norfolk, Plymouth, Bristol and Barnstable to be one circuit, and to be called the southern Circuit. Section two provided that courts should be held in the several circuits, at such times and places as " are now by law appointed for holding the Courts of Common Pleas; to consist of one Chief Justice and two Associate Justices, who shall have original and exclusive jurisdiction of all civil actions arising within their respective circuits (excepting only such actions wherein the Supreme Judicial Court, or where Justices of the Peace now have original jurisdiction), and shall also have jurisdiction of all such offences, crimes and misdemeanors, as before the passing of this act were cognizable by the respective Courts of Common Pleas, and also appellate jurisdiction of all civil actions and all crimes, etc., where an appeal may now, by law, be made from the decisions of Justices of the Peace." Of this new Court, Thomas Boylston Adams, of Quincy, was appointed Chief

Justice, and Jairus Ware, of Wrentham, and Nahum Mitchell, of Bridgewater, Associate Justices.

June 25, 1811 (Chap. 81), an act was passed re-establishing the Court of General Sessions of the Peace, section first of which provided that "from and after the first of September next an act passed June 19, 1809, is repealed, and all acts before in force relative to the Court of Sessions revived." Section 3 of the act provided for the appointment of one Chief Justice, and not exceeding four and not less than two other persons as Justices. September 3, 1811, the judges of the former Court, viz., Ebenezer Seaver, of Roxbury, Chief Justice, and John Ellis, of Medway, Joseph Bemis, of Canton, Samuel Day, of Wrentham, and Nathaniel Ruggles, of Roxbury, were reappointed.

Feb. 28, 1814 (Chap. 197), the Legislature passed an act transferring the powers and duties of the Court of Sessions to the Circuit Court of Common Pleas, section first of which provided "that from and after the first day of June next the act entitled ' An Act to establish the Court of Sessions,' passed June 25, 1811, be, and the same is hereby, repealed, except so far as it relates to the Counties of Suffolk, Nantucket and Dukes." Section 4 of the act provided that the Governor appoint "two discreet persons, being freeholders within each county, who shall be Session Justices of the Circuit Court of Common Pleas in their respective counties."

June 11, 1814, Ebenezer Warren, of Foxborough, and Samuel Bass, of Randolph, were appointed Session Justices. August 21, 1816, Joseph Heath, of Roxbury, and November 21 of the same year, Samuel Swett, of Dedham, were appointed Session Justices.

Feb. 20, 1819 (Chap. 120), an act was passed establishing Courts of Sessions, and repealing the act of Feb. 28, 1814. The act provided for one Justice and two Associate Justices. June 16, 1819, Jairus Ware, of Wrentham, was appointed Justice, and Ebenezer Warren, of Foxborough, and Samuel Swett, of Dedham, Associate Justices.

The act (Chap. 79) passed Feb. 15, 1821, establishing a Court of Common Pleas for the Commonwealth of Massachusetts, superseded and abolished the Circuit Court of Common Pleas for Norfolk County.

Feb. 26, 1822 (Chap. 51), an act was passed increasing the number and extending the powers of Justices of the Courts of Sessions, and providing for the appointment of two Special Justices for every Court of Sessions. April 16, 1822, Jairus Ware, of Wrentham, was appointed Chief Justice, and Daniel Adams, of Medfield, and Samuel P. Loud, of Dorchester, were appointed Associate Justices.

March 4, 1826 (Chap. 171), an act was passed in addition to " An act directing the method of laying out highways; " the Governor to appoint five Commissioners of Highways. July 12, 1826, Ebenezer Seaver, of Roxbury (Chairman), Christopher Webb, of Weymouth, John Endicott, of Dedham, Lewis Fisher, of Franklin, and Nathaniel Tucker, of Milton, were appointed Commissioners of Highways for Norfolk County.

Sept. 1, 1826, Jairus Ware, of Wrentham, having been elected Clerk of the Courts of Norfolk County, resigned his position as Chief Justice of the Court of Sessions for Norfolk County, and Daniel Adams, of Medfield, was promoted to that office; and William Ellis, of Dedham, was made Associate Justice, the other being Samuel P. Loud, of Dorchester.

Feb. 26, 1828 (Chap. 77), an act was passed establishing County Commissioners in the several counties, which repealed the following: Act to establish Courts of Sessions, passed February 20, 1819; Act in addition, passed February 21, 1820; Act increasing numbers and powers of Judges of Courts of Sessions, passed February 6, 1822; Act of March 4, 1826, relating to highways.

The following are the material sections of the Act of 1828: —

"Section 4 enacts that from and after its passage the County Commissioners in their respective counties shall have, exercise and perform, except so far as modified by the provisions of this act, all the powers, authorities and duties which, before and until the passing of the act, the Courts of Sessions or Commissioners of Highways have by law exercised and performed.

"Sect. 5. All petitions, recognizances, warrants, certificates, orders, reports and processes made to, pending in, taken for, or continued or returnable to the Courts of Sessions, shall be returnable to and proceeded in by the County Commissioners."

The act further provided that the Governor should appoint four Commissioners in Norfolk County.

COUNTY COMMISSIONERS.

April 14, 1828, Samuel P. Loud, of Dorchester (Chairman), William Ellis, of Dedham, Lewis Fisher, of Franklin, and Nathaniel Tucker, of Milton, were appointed County Commissioners. The first meeting of the Board was held on the following day, as appears by the record: "April 15, 1828. This day being the time on which the County Commissioners for this county are to hold their meeting, by law, in Dedham, in said county, the meeting was opened by Hon. William Ellis, one of said commissioners, and a majority thereof not appearing to make a quorum, the said meeting was by him adjourned, pursuant to law, to Tuesday, the 22d day of April instant, at ten o'clock, A.M., and the clerk directed to give notice thereof in the 'Village Register,' printed in Dedham."

Of the next meeting, the following is the record: "The County Commissioners met, according to adjournment, the 22d of April, A.D. 1828. Present: Samuel P. Loud, Esq., Chairman; William Ellis, Lewis Fisher, Nathaniel Tucker, Esqs."

April 8, 1835 (Chap. 152), an act was passed providing for the choice in each county of the Commonwealth of three County Commissioners and two Special Commissioners at an election, to be held on the first Monday of May, 1835, and on the same day in every third year thereafter; in case of non-election or vacancy, a new election to be held until the Board was filled; County and Special Commissioners then in office by appointment to remain in office until their successors were chosen and qualified.

May 22, 1835, the record is as follows: "The new Board of County Commissioners and Special Commissioners appeared, and were qualified by James Richardson and Jairus Ware, appointed to qualify civil officers in said county." Hon. Samuel P. Loud, of Dorchester, Chairman; Seth Mann, Randolph; Joseph Hawes, Walpole. Special Commissioners, Benjamin P. Williams, Roxbury; John C. Scammell, Bellingham.

March 17, 1841 (Chap. 107), an act was passed which provided that in case of failure on the second trial to elect Commissioners, the Governor should fill vacancies from among the candidates receiving the highest number of votes.

June 22, 1841. Nathan Jones, of Medway, took the place of John C. Scammell, of Bellingham, as Special Commissioner.

May 28, 1844. James C. Doane, of Cohasset, took the place of Seth Mann, of Randolph, as Commissioner; and Martin Torrey, of Foxborough, the place of Nathan Jones, of Medway, as Special Commissioner.

1845. Nathan Jones, of Medway, took the place of B. P. Williams, of Roxbury, as Special Commissioner.

1847. Nathan Jones, of Medway, took the place of Joseph Hawes, of Walpole, as Commissioner; and Abraham F. Howe, of Roxbury, and Timothy P. Whitney, of Wrentham, became Special Commissioners, in place of Martin Torrey, of Foxborough, and Nathan Jones, of Medway.

April 4, 1853, there was an election for County Commissioners, at which but one candidate was elected, viz., Nathan Jones, of Medway, by a majority of six votes. At the second trial, held May 2, James C. Doane, of Cohasset, was re-elected by a small majority; and Abraham F. Howe, of Roxbury, and John A. Gould, of Walpole, were elected Special Commissioners. For the third Commissioner there was no choice, Asaph Churchill, of Dorchester, the candidate of the Free Soil and Democratic parties, having a plurality of seven votes over Nathaniel F. Safford, of Dorchester, who had been nominated by the Whig party in place of Hon. Samuel P. Loud, of Dorchester, who declined a renomination. There having been no election at the two trials, Governor Clifford apppointed Mr. Safford to fill the vacancy, and at the first meeting of the new board, Mr. Safford was chosen Chairman.

March 11, 1854 (Chap. 77), an act was passed providing for classification of County Commissioners into three classes: the first to hold office until the next election for Governor; the second until the State election in 1855; and the third until the election in 1856; providing further, for the election, at each State election, of one County Commissioner, who should hold office for three years only; and providing further, that the Special Commissioners then in office should hold their offices until the annual election of Governor in 1856, and each third year thereafter, when two Special Commissioners should be chosen, a plurality of votes to elect.

At the annual election, November 11, 1854, Bradford S. Farrington, of Roxbury, was elected a Commissioner in place of Nathan Jones, of Medway, whose term had expired.

1855. Mr. Safford was re-elected Commissioner.

1856. Seth Mann, 2d, of Randolph, was elected Commissioner in place of James C. Doane, of Cohasset; and Samuel B. Noyes, of Canton, and George W. Gay, of Sharon, were elected Special Commissioners, in place of Abraham F. Howe, of Roxbury, and John A. Gould, of Walpole.

1857. Lucas Pond, of Wrentham, was elected Commissioner, in place of Bradford S. Farrington, of Wrentham.

1858. Nathaniel F. Safford, of Dorchester, was re-elected Commissioner.

1859. Charles Endicott, of Canton, was elected Commissioner, in place of

Seth Mann. 2d, of Randolph; George W. Gay, of Sharon, was re-elected, and Asa B. Wales, of Weymouth, elected Special Commissioner, the latter in place of Samuel B. Noyes, of Canton.

1860. Lucas Pond. of Wrentham, was re-elected Commissioner.

1861. Nathaniel F. Safford, of Dorchester, was re-elected Commissioner.

1862. Charles Endicott, of Canton, was re-elected Commissioner, and George W. Gay. of Sharon, and Asa B. Wales, of Weymouth, were re-elected Special Commissioners.

1863. Milton M. Fisher, of Medway, was elected Commissioner in place of Lucas Pond, of Wrentham.

1864. Nathaniel F. Safford, of Dorchester, was re-elected Commissioner.

1865. David H. Bates, of Braintree, was elected Commissioner in place of Charles Endicott, of Canton, and Otis Cary, of Foxborough, and Amos H. Holbrook, of Bellingham, Special Commissioners in place of George W. Gay, of Sharon, and Asa B. Wales, of Weymouth.

1866. Milton M Fisher, of Medway, was re-elected Commissioner.

1867. Joseph M. Churchill, of Milton, was elected Commissioner in place of Nathaniel F. Safford, of Dorchester; and at the organization of the Board, January 1, 1868, Milton M. Fisher, of Medway, was chosen Chairman.

1868. David H. Bates, of Braintree, was re-elected Commissioner, Amos H. Holbrook, of Bellingham, was re-elected Special Commissioner, and Galen Orr, of Needham, was elected Special Commissioner in place of Otis Cary, of Foxborough.

1869. Milton M. Fisher, of Medway, was re-elected Commissioner. At the organization of the Board in January. 1870, Mr. Fisher having declined re-election as Chairman, Joseph M. Churchill, of Milton, was chosen.

1870. Joseph M. Churchill, of Milton, was re-elected Commissioner.

1871. March 31, Mr. Churchill having resigned the office of Chairman of the Board, Milton M. Fisher, of Medway, was chosen Chairman. April 8th, Mr. Churchill, having been appointed Judge of the Municipal Court of the City of Boston, resigned the office of Commissioner. At the election in November, David H. Bates, of Braintree, was re-elected Commissioner, and Galen Orr, of Needham, was elected Commissioner for the remainder of the term of Mr. Churchill (two years). George P. Morey, of Walpole, and John Q. A. Field, of Quincy, were elected Special Commissioners.

1872. Nathaniel F. Safford, of Milton (to which town he had removed after the annexation of Dorchester to Boston), was elected Commissioner, and at the organization of the Board, in January, 1873, was elected Chairman.

1873. Galen Orr, of Needham, was re-elected Commissioner.

1874. James Humphrey, of Weymouth, was elected Commissioner in place of David H. Bates, of Braintree; and George P. Morey, of Walpole, and John Q. A. Field, of Quincy, were re-elected Special Commissioners.

1875. Nathaniel F. Safford, of Milton, was re-elected Commissioner.

1876. Galen Orr, of Needham, was re-elected Commissioner.

BIOGRAPHICAL.

The following brief sketches of the several Judges of the Courts of Common Pleas and of General Sessions, and of the members of the Board of County Commissioners, have been carefully prepared from the best available sources of information. Those who afterwards occupied other county offices will be found mentioned in their appropriate places.

JUDGES OF THE COUNTY COURTS.

SAMUEL NILES, son of the distinguished clergyman of the same name, was a native of Braintree, and for many years one of the most prominent men of that town. He was Representative and Executive Councillor, and filled many other important offices. In 1793 he was appointed Justice of the new Court of Common Pleas for Norfolk County.

RICHARD CRANCH was born in Kingsbridge, near Exeter, in Devonshire, England, in November, 1726. At the age of twenty, in 1746, he came to this country with General Joseph Palmer, who had married his sister Mary. Being of a literary turn of mind, he became a man of considerable learning, received an honorary degree of A.M. from Harvard College, and was elected a member of the American Academy of Arts and Sciences. He studied law, and was admitted to the bar, and was appointed one of the first judges of the Court of Common Pleas, after the organization of the County of Norfolk in 1793. He married Mary, the eldest daughter of the Rev. William Smith, of Weymouth, John Adams marrying Abigail, the second daughter. Mr. Cranch died on the 16th, and his wife on the 17th of October, 1811, and both were buried on the same day, the 19th, when Rev. Peter Whitney preached a sermon, which was afterwards printed. They left three children, Judge William Cranch, late Chief Justice of the United States District Court at Washington, D. C.; Elizabeth, who married Rev. Jacob Norton, of Weymouth; and Lucy, who married Mr. John Greenleaf of Quincy.

JOHN READ was born in Sudbury in 1728. When two years old he was carried to Roxbury, where he lived till he became of age, and learned the trade of a tanner. He afterwards became an agent for Gov. Bowdoin, who owned extensive estates near Cape Cod, among which was Naushon Island and its dependencies, known as the Elizabeth Islands. He afterwards returned to Roxbury, and was much in public life, being for some time land agent for Massachusetts, at that time an office of much importance. The town of Readfield, in Maine, was named in his honor, and he named the town of Bowdoinham in honor of Gov. Bowdoin, he being proprietor of both townships. His residence in Roxbury was in the Gov. Shirley house, which was afterwards owned by Gov. Eustis. He was known as Major Read, from his having acted as paymaster of militia before the Revolution. His brother James was the first brigadier-general appointed by the Provincial Congress. He was Representative to the General Court in 1794, and a Senator from Norfolk County in 1796, '97, '98 and '99, and a member of the Executive Council in 1801. He was also one of the first Justices of the Court of Common Pleas after the incorporation of the County of Norfolk, in 1793. He died June 3, 1813, aged 85 years.

EBENEZER WARREN was born in Roxbury, in the year 1749, and continued there until after the Revolutionary War began. When the British troops marched from Boston, he left home and joined in the battle of Lexington, on the 19th of April, and was one of three brothers who were in arms on that day; the others being Gen. Joseph Warren, afterwards killed at Bunker Hill, and the late Dr. John Warren of Boston. He afterwards removed to Foxborough, and was a member of the State Convention which adopted the Federal Constitution. In the year 1793 he was appointed Justice of the Court of Common Pleas, and filled the office until the abolition of the Court in 1811. June 11, 1814, he was appointed Session Justice of the Circuit Court of Common Pleas. June 16, 1819, he was appointed Associate Justice of the new Court of Sessions. He died in Foxborough, January 9, 1821, aged 75 years.

JAMES ENDICOTT was born in Canton (then Stoughton), in 1739, and was for many years a prominent citizen of the town. He was captain of one of the seven companies of minutemen who marched to Cambridge on the 19th of April, 1775, and on the 4th of March, 1776, marched with his company of forty-one men "to the assistance of the Continental troops, when they fortified on the heights of Dorchester." A little later in the same year, with eighty-two men, he marched to Ticonderoga, and on the 28th of March, 1778, to Roxbury, "agreeable to an Order of Council," with seventy-eight men. He was Selectman of the town for several years, and Representative to the General Court in 1784, '85, '86, and '90. In 1793 he was appointed one of the justices of the new Court of Common Pleas, which office he held till his death, April 4th, 1799, in the 61st year of his age.

OLIVER EVERETT, born in Dedham, June 11, 1752, was graduated at Harvard College in 1779; taught school in Dorchester in 1776; was ordained pastor of the New South Church in Boston, January 2, 1782. After a ministry of ten years he was dismissed on account of ill-health. In 1799 he was appointed a Judge of the Court of Common Pleas for Norfolk County, which office he held until his death in Dorchester, December 19, 1802, at the age of 52 years and 6 months. Edward and Alexander H. Everett were his sons.

MOSES EVERETT, brother of the preceding, born in Dedham, July 15, 1750, was graduated at Harvard College in 1771, and was settled over the church in Dorchester, September 28, 1774. After preaching for eighteen years he was compelled by ill health to resign his charge, and in 1793 he obtained a dismission, but continued to reside in the town. He was chosen Representative to the General Court in 1794 and 1795. In 1803 he was appointed Justice of the Court of Common Pleas of Norfolk County to fill the vacancy caused by the death of his brother Oliver. He died March 25, 1813, aged 63 years.

SAMUEL BASS was born in Randolph (then Braintree), May 15, 1757, and was for many years active in town affairs. He was Town Clerk and Selectman for many years, and also Representative to the General Court. In 1803 he was appointed Special Justice of the Court of Common Pleas for Norfolk County, and in 1814 Session Justice of the Circuit Court of Common Pleas.

DAVID STODDARD GREENOUGH was born at Jamaica Plain, Roxbury, March 23, 1787, and was graduated at Harvard College in 1805. Studied law, but afterwards became a merchant, and was at one time Special Justice of the Court of Common Pleas for Norfolk County. He died August 6, 1830, aged 43 years.

THOMAS WILLIAMS, for many years a prominent lawyer in Roxbury, was appointed Special Justice of the Court of Common Pleas in 1806. He died of angina pectoris, Sept. 26, 1823, aged 59 years.

THOMAS GREENLEAF, born in Boston, May 15, 1767, was graduated at Harvard College in 1784. He removed to Quincy early in the present century, and devoted most of his time to the service of the town and the State. He was for more than twenty-five years Moderator of the town meetings, and was Representative to the General Court from 1808 to 1820, inclusive. He was a member of the Executive Council in 1820, '21, '22. In 1806 he was appointed a Special Justice of the Court of Common Pleas for the County of Norfolk. He died January 5, 1854, aged 86 years and 7 months.

EBENEZER SEAVER, born in Roxbury, July 5, 1763, was graduated at Harvard College in 1784, and chose the calling of a farmer. He was a member of Congress for the Norfolk District from 1803 to 1813, and a member of the Constitutional Convention of 1820. For many years he was Moderator of the town meetings in Roxbury, long time a Selectman and Chairman of the Board, and from 1794 to 1802 a Representative to the General Court. In 1832 the town of Roxbury passed him a vote of thanks "for his long, faithful and unremitted services for nearly forty years past." July 7, 1807, he was appointed Chief Justice of the new Court of General Sessions of the Peace of Norfolk County, which office he held until 1809, when the duties of the Court were transferred to the Court of Common Pleas. On the re-establishment of the Court of Sessions in 1811, he was reappointed Chief Justice, which position he occupied until 1814, when the duties of that Court were transferred to the Circuit Court of Common Pleas. He died March 1, 1844, aged 80 years, 7 months, 26 days.

WILLIAM ASPINWALL, born in Brookline, in 1743, was graduated at Harvard College in 1760, and studied medicine with Dr. Gale, a distinguished physician in Connecticut, and after attending medical lectures at Philadelphia, returned home, where he commenced business at the age of twenty-six. He soon acquired a large practice, and during the Revolutionary War was a leading surgeon in the army. He was for many years one of the foremost men of the town. He was Representative to the General Court in 1794, '95, '96, '97, '98, '99, and was a Senator from Norfolk County in 1800, '01 and '02. He was also a member of the Executive Council in 1810. July 3, 1807, he was appointed one of the Judges of the new Court of Peace for Norfolk County, which position he soon after resigned. He died April 16, 1823, aged 80 years.

JOHN ELLIS was born in Medway, November 25, 1754. He was chosen a Representative to the General Court in 1803, and was Senator from Norfolk County in 1800, '01, '02,' 03, '04, '05, '06. July 3, 1807, he was appointed Justice of the new Court of General Sessions of the Peace for the County of Norfolk. He died Nov. 25, 1826, aged 72 years.

JOSEPH BEMIS was for many years active in all public affairs in Canton, serving as Town Clerk, Selectman, and in other capacities. He represented the town in the General Court in 1800, '01, '02, '03, 04, '05, '06, '07, '10, '11, and '13, and was a Senator from Norfolk County in 1812, '14, 15, '16, '17 and '18. On the reorganization of the new Court of General Sessions of the Peace in 1807, he was appointed one of the justices, a position which he continued to hold for several years. He died October 3, 1825.

SAMUEL DAY was born in Wrentham, February 3, 1752. He was one of the Selectmen, and represented the town in the General Court in 1805, '06, '07, '08, and again in 1820. He was Senator from Norfolk County in 1809, '10 and '11. In 1807 he was appointed Justice of the new Court of General Sessions of the Peace for Norfolk County. He was chosen as a delegate to the Constitutional Convention in 1820, but failing health prevented his attendance. He died January 22, 1821, in the 69th year of his age.

NATHANIEL RUGGLES was born in Roxbury, November 11, 1761, and was for many years prominent in town and county affairs. In 1807 he was appointed Associate Justice of the Court of General Sessions of the Peace. February 3, 1813, having been elected a member of Congress from the Roxbury district, he resigned the office of Judge. He remained in Congress until his death, which occurred from paralysis, Dec. 19, 1819, at the age of 59. The late Hon. David A. Simmons, and the late Hon. Benjamin F. Copeland, both of Roxbury, married daughters of Mr. Ruggles.

THOMAS BOYLSTON ADAMS, third son of President John Adams, was born in Quincy (then Braintree), Sept. 15, 1772; was graduated at Harvard College in 1790; entered upon the practice of the law; and upon the creation of the Circuit Court of Common Pleas in 1811 was made Chief Justice of the Southern Circuit. In 1805 he represented the town of Quincy in the General Court, and in 1811 was a member of the Executive Council. He died March 12, 1832, aged 59 years and 6 months.

JOSEPH HEATH, son of Gen. Heath, was born in Roxbury, April 2, 1766. Appointed Session Justice of the Court of Common Pleas in 1816. He died July 5, 1842, aged 76 years.

SAMUEL SWETT was born in Boston, and became prominent as a merchant. He early removed to Dedham, and in 1816 was appointed Session Justice of the Circuit Court of Common Pleas, and in 1819 was appointed Associate Justice of the Court of Sessions for Norfolk County. He died December 25th, 1853, aged 79 years and 4 months.

DANIEL ADAMS, born in Watertown, March 26th, 1779, was graduated at Harvard College 1799, and soon after commenced the practice of law at Medfield. Was Representative to the General Court in 1812, '13, '14, '16, '17, '19, '20 and '41. He was appointed Judge of the Court of Sessions of Norfolk County in 1822, and on the retirement of Judge Ware in 1826, was promoted to the office of Chief Justice. Died Sept. 2, 1852, aged 73 years, 5 months and 6 days.

CHRISTOPHER WEBB, of Weymouth, was graduated at Brown University in 1803, represented the town in the General Court in 1807, '08, '09, '10, '11, '12, '13, '14, '16, '17, '18, '20, '21, '22 and '24, and was member of the Senate from Norfolk County in 1827, '28, '29, '30, '31 and '34. He was for several years County Attorney for Norfolk, and in 1826 was appointed Commissioner of Highways of the County. He died in Baltimore in February, 1848, aged 67 years.

JOHN ENDICOTT was born in Canton, February 4, 1764, and removed to Dedham in 1787. He was for many years a man of great influence both in the town and county. He was Representative to the General Court in 1805, '06, '07, '08, '09, '10, '11, '12, '13 '14, '16, '35. He was a Senator from Norfolk County in 1817, '18, '19, and in 1831, '32, '33, and was a member of the Executive Council in 1827, '28, '30. In 1826 he was appointed Commissioner of Highways for Norfolk County, which position he held until the organization of the new Board of County Commissioners in 1828. He was for many years a deacon in the First Church. He died January 31, 1857, aged 93 years.

COUNTY COMMISSIONERS.

SAMUEL PRINCE LOUD was born in Weymouth, March, 1783; was graduated at Brown University in 1805; studied in the office of John Quincy Adams, and began the practice of law in Dorchester in 1809. He represented that town in the General Court in 1828, '29, '30, '31, '36, '38, '43 and '44. He was a member of the Senate from Norfolk County in 1832 and 1833; member of the Executive Council in 1841 and 1842, and represented the town in the Constitutional Convention of 1853. He was for six years a Justice of the Court of Sessions for the county; and from the establishment of the Board of County Commissioners in 1828 to 1853 (when he declined further service), a period of twenty-five years of continuous service, he was Chairman of that body. He died at Dorchester, July 11th, 1875, at the age of 92 years and 4 months.

WILLIAM ELLIS was born in Dedham in 1780, and was for many years the leading land surveyor in that part of the county. He was much occupied in public affairs, having been a Selectman, and represented the town in the General Court in 1816, '17, '18, '19, '20, '23, '21, '36, and was a member of the Senate in 1825, '26 and '27. He was two years Associate Justice of the Court of Sessions, and from 1828 to 1835 a member of the first Board of County Commissioners for Norfolk County. He died November 28, 1852, aged 72 years.

LEWIS FISHER was born in Franklin, in 1767. He was a Representative in the General Court in 1816, '18, '19, '20, '21, '23, '26 and '28, and Senator from Norfolk County in 1822. He was a member of the first Board of Commissioners for Norfolk County, holding the office from 1828 to 1835. He died November 28, 1844, aged 77 years.

NATHANIEL TUCKER was born in Milton in 1769. He was a member of the first Board of Commissioners for Norfolk County, holding the office from 1828 to 1835. He died in February, 1838, aged 69 years.

JOSEPH HAWES was born in Walpole, May 13, 1783. Represented the town in the General Court from 1827 to 1831, and again in 1835. He was Senator from Norfolk County in 1832 and 1833. He was County Commissioner for Norfolk County from 1835 to 1847, a period of twelve years. He died July 24, 1849, aged 66 years.

SETH MANN was born in Randolph, August 11, 1781, and at an early age removed, with his father's family, to Braintree, Vt., where he resided until he was of age, when he returned to Randolph, and soon entered into active and widely-extended business. He was much in public life, being for twelve years one of the Selectmen of the town, and Representative in the General Court in 1823, '21, '26, '27, '28, '20 and '31. He was elected County Commissioner of Norfolk County in 1835, and held the office until his death, October 21, 1843. He was 62 years of age.

BENJAMIN PAYSON WILLIAMS was born in Roxbury, October 17, 1787. Bred a farmer, he was called to various civil and military offices. He was Representative to the General Court in 1828, '29, '30 and '31, and Senator from Norfolk County in 1836 and 1837. He was also Special Commissioner of Norfolk County from 1835 till his death. He died suddenly, of angina pectoris, September 15, 1844, aged 57 years.

JOHN CORBET SCAMMELL was born in Milford, August 5, 1793, but passed most of his life as a farmer in Bellingham. He was a major in the militia, Representative to the General Court in 1827 and 1831, and from 1835 to 1841 was a Special Commissioner of the County of Norfolk. He died January 26, 1848, aged 54 years and 4 months.

NATHAN JONES was born in Medway in 1786. His business was that of a farmer, but he was early called into public life. He filled nearly all the various town offices in Medway, and was for more than twenty years a Deputy Sheriff of the county. In 1841 he was elected Special Commissioner, which position he held for five years, when he was chosen County Commissioner, remaining in that office for seven years, retiring in 1854. In 1858 he removed to Medfield, where he resided until his death, which occurred Dec. 8, 1870, at the age of 84 years.

JAMES CUTLER DOANE was born in Cohasset, September, 1788. Represented the town in the General Court in 1824, '27, '30, '32 and '46. He was a Senator from Norfolk County in 1848 and 1849; a member of the Constitutional Convention in 1853, and County Commissioner from 1844 to 1856, a period of twelve years.

MARTIN TORREY was born in Pembroke, June 28, 1780, but early removed to Foxborough, where he remained until his death. He was for several years one of the Selectmen, and was captain of the militia company. Representative to the General Court in 1849 and 1851, and Special Commissioner from 1844 to 1847. He died Nov. 2, 1864, aged 72 years and 5 months.

ABRAHAM FAY HOWE was born in Northborough in May, 1783. Early in life he came to Boston and engaged in business as a grocer. In 1817 he removed to West Roxbury, although still continuing business in Boston. In 1836 he removed to Roxbury, where he continued to reside until his death. He carried on a large and successful business as auctioneer and real estate and insurance agent. He was for many years a director of the Norfolk Mutual Fire Insurance Company. He was tax-collector of Roxbury for sixteen years, and was for many years one of the Selectmen and Highway Surveyors of the town. He was Special Commissioner of Norfolk County from 1847 to 1856, a period of nine years. He died Nov. 27, 1861, aged 78 years 6 months. His residence was the estate at the junction of Roxbury and Centre streets, the well-known " Parting Stone" belonging to it.

TIMOTHY P. WHITNEY, of Wrentham, was a native of Douglass, but early removed to Wrentham. He was for many years a Deputy Sheriff of the county, and for eighteen years Keeper of the Jail and House of Correction in Dedham. He was Special Commissione of the County from 1817 to 1853. He died at Wrentham, of paralysis, Nov. 30, 1853, aged 68 years and 10 months.

JOHN A. GOULD, of Walpole, was born in Milton, October 4, 1785. He was Selectman, Assessor and Overseer of the Poor, in Walpole, from 1830 to 1833, inclusive, and again from 1819 to 1854, inclusive, and was Special Commissioner of Norfolk County from 1853 to 1856. He died July 9, 1860, aged 74 years and 9 months.

NATHANIEL FOSTER SAFFORD was born in Salem in 1815, and was graduated at Dartmouth College in 1835. He studied law with Hon. Asahel Huntington, of Salem, and commenced practice at Dorchester in 1839, where he acted as a magistrate and also as a Master in Chancery, in the period of jurisdiction under the operation of the insolvent laws, and was Representative to the General Court in 1850 and 1851. In 1853 Hon. Samuel P. Loud having declined further service on the Board of County Commissioners for Norfolk County, Mr. Safford was nominated for the office by the Whig party, and there having been no choice by the people after two trials, Governor Clifford appointed Mr. Safford to fill the vacancy, and at the first meeting of the Board, he was elected Chairman, a position which he continued to fill by successive re-elections until January 1, 1868. January 1, 1873, Mr. Safford (who, after the annexation of Dorchester to Boston, had removed to Milton), having been elected Commissioner at the previous November election, was chosen Chairman of the Board, which position he now holds.

BRADFORD SUMNER FARRINGTON was born in Wrentham May 12, 1812. He was Town Clerk for several years, and for twenty-three years a Deputy Sheriff of Norfolk County, and during a portion of the time Keeper of the Jail and House of Correction at Dedham. He was County Commissioner for three years from 1854 to 1857. He removed to Roxbury in January, 1857, and after the annexation of that city to Boston, was appointed Deputy Sheriff, which office he held at the time of his death, which occurred suddenly, of heart disease, July 31, 1869, at the age of 57 years.

SETH MANN, 2d, was born in Randolph, February 28, 1817, and was graduated at Brown University in 1839. He was a member of the School Committee for four years, Selectman and Assessor twelve years, and Deputy Collector of Internal Revenue from 1862 to 1875. He was County Commissioner from 1856 to 1859, and Representative to the General Court in 1861, 1876 and 1877.

SAMUEL BRADLEY NOYES was born in Dedham, April 9, 1817. Fitted for college at Phillips Academy, Andover, and was a member of the class of 1844 in Harvard College. Studied law with Isaac Davis, at Worcester, and Ezra Wilkinson, Dedham; was admitted to the bar in 1847, and the same year commenced the practice of law at Canton. He was for several years Trial Justice and Commissioner of Insolvency, and was a Special Commissioner for the County of Norfolk from 1856 to 1859. In 1864 he was appointed Special Agent of the United States Treasury, and Acting Collector of Customs for the district of Nassau, Florida, which office he held until he resigned in 1866. On the passage of the U. S. Bankrupt Law, in 1867, he was appointed Register of Bankruptcy for the second district of Massachusetts, a position which he still holds.

GEORGE W. GAY was born in Roxbury, April 30, 1817, but has for many years been a resident of Sharon, which was the native place of his parents. He has been Selectman, Assessor, Overseer of the Poor, and was Representative to the General Court in 1856. He was Special Commissioner for nine years, from 1856 to 1865.

LUCAS POND was born in Wrentham, October 3, 1797. His calling in life was that of a farmer, in which he achieved decided success. He was much in public life, filling nearly every office in his native town; being a Representative to the General Court in 1831, and Senator from Norfolk County in 1840. Eight days after he was eighteen years of age he was commissioned as corporal of an independent company of militia, and became captain in 1825. He was promoted in 1828 to be lieutenant-colonel, in 1830, colonel, and in 1831, brigadier-general. At his own request he was discharged from service in 1833. He was County Commissioner from 1857 to 1863. During his whole life he has resided in that portion of Wrentham called Pondville, and which is now included in the town of Norfolk.

CHARLES ENDICOTT was born in Canton, October 28, 1822. He was for several years Town Clerk, Selectman, and held many other town offices. He was Deputy Sheriff for the county from 1816 to 1853, and Commissioner of Insolvency from 1855 to 1857. He was admitted to the bar in 1857, and commenced the practice of law in his native town. He was Representative to the General Court in 1851, '57 and '58, Senator from Norfolk County in 1866 and '67, and a member of the Executive Council in 1868 and '69. He was County Commissioner for six years, from 1859 to 1865. He was State Auditor for six years, from 1870 to 1875, inclusive, and in the fall of the latter year was chosen State Treasurer, which office he now holds.

Asa B. Wales, of Weymouth, was born in Lyme, N. H., Feb. 22, 1801, and was the son of Atherton Wales, a native of Randolph. He worked on his father's farm until he was 20 years old, when, after passing two years at school, he went to Boston, where, for the five following years, he was clerk in hotels in Boston and Charlestown. In April, 1830, he removed to Weymouth, and bought the hotel at the "Landing," which he kept for forty-two years. In April, 1843, he voluntarily abandoned the sale of intoxicating liquors. In 1872 he sold his hotel property and removed to North Andover, where he now resides. Mr. Wales was Special Commissioner of Norfolk County from 1859 to 1865.

Milton M. Fisher was born in Franklin, January 30, 1811, and in 1832 entered Amherst College, but was compelled by ill-health to leave in 1833. After teaching school for several years, in 1835 he began business as a trader, in Franklin, and in 1836 removed to Westborough, where he served for several years on the School Committee, and was also Postmaster. In 1840, after a brief residence in Upton, he removed to Medway, where he engaged in the manufacturing of straw goods, in which he continued until 1865. He was for several years one of the Selectmen of the town, of which board he was chairman, and was Senator from Norfolk County in 1859 and 1860. He was County Commissioner from 1863 to 1869, a period of six years, and was Chairman of the Board for three years. He is President of the Medway Savings Bank and the Dean Library Association, and Manager of the Medway Insurance Agency.

David H. Bates was born in Weymouth, June 3, 1815. When three years old he removed to Braintree, where he has since resided. During the early part of his life he was a bootmaker, but for the past twenty years has been most of the time occupied with public business. He was Selectman from 1854 to 1867, and from 1868 to 1871, and re-chosen in 1876-77. He was County Commissioner from 1865 to 1874, a period of nine years.

Otis Cary was born in Bridgewater, June 14, 1804, and removed to Foxborough in 1834, where he has since lived, and for the greater portion of the time carried on business as an iron-founder. He has for many years been prominent in town affairs, serving as Selectman for ten years, and also in other offices. He was Representative to the General Court in 1860 and '61, and a Senator from Norfolk County in 1863 and '64. He was Special Commissioner from 1865 to 1868; has been President of the Foxborough Savings Bank since its organization in 1855, and has occupied many other positions of trust and honor.

Amos H. Holbrook was born in Bellingham, November 23, 1818, and now lives on the same land which has belonged to the family for six generations. His life has been passed in farming pursuits, and in the performance of town and county business. He was Town Clerk ten years, Selectman ten years, Assessor seventeen years, and was a Special Commissioner of Norfolk County from 1865 to 1871.

Joseph McKean Churchill was born in Milton, April 29, 1821. He was graduated at Harvard College in 1840, and at the Harvard Law School in 1845, and soon after commenced the practice of law in Boston. He was Representative to the General Court from Milton in 1858, and a member of the Executive Council in 1859 and 1860. He was also a delegate to the Constitutional Convention in 1853, and for twelve years was an Overseer of Harvard College. During the war he was captain in the Cadet Regiment of Mass. Volunteers. He was County Commissioner from January 1, 1868, until April, 1871 (being Chairman of the Board for the last two years, when he was appointed Judge of the Municipal Court of Boston, which office he now holds.

Galen Orr was born in Shirley, December 9, 1815, but removed to Needham in early childhood. He learned the blacksmith's trade, and subsequently carried on business as a nailer and machinist. For many years he has been successfully engaged in the manufacture of blind-hinges and fasts. He was a member of the Board of Selectmen, and Overseer of the Poor in Needham, for the years 1855, '58, '59, '60, '61, '62, '63, '64, '65 and '72, during a portion of the time being Chairman. He represented the district of Dover, Medfield and Needham in the Legislature of 1864. He was a Special Commissioner from Jan. 1, 1869, to 1872, and County Commissioner from 1872 to the present time, and has just entered upon another term of three years.

John Q. A. Field was born in Quincy, January 3, 1825, and has followed the business of farming and stone contracting. Has filled the offices of Selectman, Assessor for three years, and Surveyor of Highways five years. Was Chairman of the Board of Selectmen in 1870, and in 1871 was elected Special Commissioner for three years, and re-elected in 1874 for another term of the same length.

George P. Morey was born in Walpole, April 25, 1826. He has been Chairman of the Board of Selectmen, Assessors and Overseers of the Poor, and for the past thirteen years Town Clerk. He was storekeeper in the Boston Custom House from 1861 to 1868, and was elected Special Commissioner for three years in 1871, and re-elected for three years in 1874.

JAMES HUMPHREY was born in Weymouth, January 20, 1819. He received an academic education, and was graduated at Phillips Academy, Andover, in 1839, with the first honors of his class. He was a teacher until 1852, when he entered the office of Hon. D. W. Gooch as a student at law, and was admitted to the Suffolk bar in 1855. He held the office of Selectman of Weymouth for twenty years, and during a large part of the time was the Chairman of the Board. He was Representative to the General Court in 1852 and 1869, and was a Senator from the Norfolk and Plymouth District in 1872. In 1874 he was elected County Commissioner for Norfolk County, which position he now holds.

COUNTY OFFICERS.

JUDGES OF PROBATE.

WILLIAM HEATH was born in Roxbury, March 2, 1737, on the estate settled by his ancestor in 1636, and was bred a farmer. His fondness for military exercises led him, in 1754, to join the Ancient and Honorable Artillery Company, which he commanded in 1770, having previously been made a captain in the Suffolk regiment, of which he became colonel in 1774. In 1770 he wrote sundry essays in a Boston newspaper, signed "A Military Countryman," on the importance of military discipline and skill in the use of arms. He was a member of the General Court in 1761, and in 1771–74; engaged with zeal in the Revolutionary contest; was a delegate to the Provincial Congresses of 1774–75; and was a member of the Committees of Correspondence and of Safety. Appointed a Mass. brigadier-general Dec. 8, 1774; major-general, June 20, 1775; brigadier-general (Continental Army), June 22, 1775; major-general, Aug. 9, 1776. He rendered great service in the pursuit of the British troops from Concord, April 19, 1775, and in organizing the rude and undisciplined army around Boston; and with his brigade was stationed at Roxbury during the siege of Boston. After its evacuation, he accompanied the army to New York; opposed the evacuation of that city, and near the close of the year 1776 was ordered to take command of the posts in the Highlands.

In 1777 he was intrusted with the command of the eastern department, and had charge of the Saratoga (convention) prisoners. In June, 1779, he was ordered to the command on the Hudson, where he was stationed till the close of the war. Returning to his farm, he became a delegate to the convention that adopted the Federal Constitution in 1788; State Senator in 1791–92; and in 1806 was chosen Lieut.-Governor of Massachusetts, but declined the office. July 2, 1793, he was appointed Judge of the Court of Common Pleas for the new County of Norfolk, and the same day was appointed First Judge of Probate for the County. He died January 24, 1814, aged 77 years.

EDWARD HUTCHINSON ROBBINS was born in Milton, February 19, 1758, and was graduated at Harvard College in 1775. He studied law with Oakes Angier, of Bridgewater, and commenced practice in his native town. He was chosen a Representative from Milton in 1781, and Speaker of the House of Representatives in 1793, which office he held for nine successive years. In 1802 he was chosen Lieut.-Governor, and held the office until 1807. In 1793 he was appointed Special Justice of the Court of Common Pleas for Norfolk County, and in 1799 was appointed Chief Justice of the same Court. In 1808 and 1809 he was a member of the Executive Council. He also held many other positions of trust and responsibility. On the decease of Gen. Heath, in 1814, he was appointed Judge of Probate for the County of Norfolk, which office he held until his death, which occurred December 29, 1829.*

SHERMAN LELAND was born in Grafton, March 29, 1783, and remained on his father's farm until he was more than 20 years of age. During the two or three years following he

---

* Judge Robbins was a man of fine personal presence, of genial manners and great kindness of heart. He was emphatically the friend of the widow and orphan, and his death was regarded as a great public loss. He lived and died on the fine estate on Brush Hill, now the residence of his son, Hon. James Murray Robbins.

attended school most of the time, and in October, 1805, commenced the study of the law, employing the winter months of that and the three succeeding years in teaching. He was admitted to the Bar at Worcester in December, 1809, and commenced practice at Eastport, Mo., January, 1810. October 11, 1811, he was appointed Prosecuting Attorney for the County of Washington. He represented Eastport in the Massachusetts Legislature of 1812, and in December of that year was appointed first lieutenant, and served under that appointment in the army of the United States upon the eastern frontier until April, 1813, when he received the appointment of captain in the 34th Regiment of Infantry in the U. S. Army and served until June 5, 1814, when he resigned his commission and resumed the practice of his profession. In July he removed to Roxbury, Mass., and in the year 1815 opened an office in Boston, and commenced practice in both the counties of Suffolk and Norfolk. He was a Representative from Roxbury in the Massachusetts Legislature for the years 1818, '19, '20 and '21. He was also a delegate from Roxbury in the Constitutional Convention of 1820. He was a member of the Senate of Massachusetts from the County of Norfolk for the years 1823 and 1824, and, during the temporary absence of the President, was elected President *pro tem*. He was again a member of the House of Representatives in the year 1825, and was Chairman of the Committee on the Judiciary. In 1824 he was a candidate for Representative in Congress for the Norfolk District, but, after several trials, his competitor, Hon. John Bailey, was elected by a small majority. He was again elected a member of the Senate from Norfolk County for the years 1828 and 1829, and was President of the Senate for the year 1828, and Chairman of the Committee on the Judiciary for 1829. On the 26th of January, 1830, he was appointed Judge of Probate for the County of Norfolk, in place of Judge Robbins, deceased, and immediately entered upon the discharge of the duties of the office, which he continued to perform until his death, which occurred November 19, 1853, at the age of 70 years.

WILLIAM SHERMAN LELAND was born in Roxbury, October 12, 1824. After leaving the public schools in his native town, he entered the law office of his father, Hon. Sherman Leland, then Judge of Probate of the County of Norfolk. On the death of his father in November, 1853, he was appointed to fill the vacancy, which position he continued to occupy until 1858, when, under the administration of Governor Banks, the law concerning Courts of Probate and Insolvency was changed, and he failed to receive the appointment as Judge of the new court. He resumed the general practice of law, and soon acquired a large and lucrative practice. He was for many years one of the Directors of the People's Bank of Roxbury, and was at one time its active President. He was one of the projectors of the Elliot Five Cent Savings Bank, and was chosen its President, which office he continued to hold until his death, which took place July 26, 1869, at the age of 44 years.

GEORGE WHITE was born in Quincy. Fitted for college with William M. Cornell, LL.D., and at Exeter Academy, N. H. Was graduated from Yale College in 1848, and from Harvard Law School in 1850. Studied law with Hon. Robert Rantoul, Jr., Boston. Admitted to the Suffolk bar, and became partner with Mr. Rantoul in 1851. Member of Constitutional Convention from Quincy in 1853. Appointed Judge of Probate and Insolvency in 1858, which office he still holds.

JUDGE OF INSOLVENCY.

In 1856 the Legislature passed an act (chap. 284) establishing a Court of Insolvency, of which Francis Hilliard, of Roxbury, was, July 24th, appointed the Judge for Norfolk County. This Court lasted until 1858, when an act (chap. 93) was passed which abolished the Court, and established the present Court of Probate and Insolvency.

FRANCIS HILLIARD was born in Cambridge, November 1, 1806, and was graduated at Harvard College in 1823. He was admitted to the bar in Middlesex County, and soon after removed to Roxbury, where he continued for many years in the practice of law. He was Representative in 1848, Judge of the Roxbury Police Court, and Commissioner and Judge of Insolvency for Norfolk County. He afterwards removed to Worcester, where he still resides.

REGISTERS OF PROBATE.

SAMUEL HAVEN, first Register of Probate for the County of Norfolk, was born in Dedham, April 5, 1771. He was graduated at Harvard College in 1789, and studied law with Hon. Fisher Ames, in Dedham, and with his cousin, Hon. Samuel Dexter, of Boston. On the formation of Norfolk County, in 1793, he was appointed Register of Probate. In 1802 he was commissioned as a Justice of the Court of Common Pleas; and in 1804 was appointed Chief Justice. When Elbridge Gerry came into office as Democratic Governor in 1810–11, the old Court of Common Pleas was abolished, and a new tribunal called Circuit Courts of Common Pleas was established with Democratic judges. Mr. Haven continued in the office of Register of Deeds until 1833, a period of forty years, but retired almost wholly from legal practice, when he resigned, and not long after removed to Roxbury, where he continued to reside with his daughter, the wife of Hon. Francis Hilliard, until his death, which occurred September 4, 1847, at the age of 76 years.*

JONATHAN HOLMES COBB was born in Sharon, July 8, 1799, and received his academic education at various schools. He fitted for college at Milton Academy, and was graduated at Harvard College in 1817. After leaving college he entered the law office of William Dunbar, Esq., of Canton, where he remained until October 9, 1818, when he sailed for Charleston, S. C., where he entered the office of Benjamin F. Dunkin, then a celebrated lawyer in that city. At the same time he opened a classical and English school; but on the appearance of the yellow fever in 1819 he returned to Massachusetts, and entered the office of Jabez Chickering, Esq., of Dedham, where he remained until admitted to the Bar in Sept., 1820, when, at the age of 21, he opened a law office in Dedham. Subsequently, for a year or two, he was editor of the "Village Register," and also had a law office in Boston. In 1831 he was actively instrumental in establishing the Dedham Institution for Savings, of which he was the first Secretary and Treasurer. About this time he engaged in the manufacture of silk, and published a work on the subject. In February, 1831, the Legislature of Massachusetts requested Gov. Lincoln to procure the compilation of a Manual on the Mulberry-tree and the Manufacture of Silk; and Mr. Cobb prepared the work, of which several editions were printed, and which was afterwards republished by Congress and distributed throughout the country. In 1837 he established a manufactory of sewing-silk, of which he was superintendent and principal proprietor, but which was burned down in 1845, involving the proprietor in great loss. On the retirement of Judge Haven in 1833, Mr. Cobb was appointed Register of Probate for Norfolk County, which position he now holds. He was for thirty consecutive years Town Clerk of Dedham, declining re-election in 1875. He has been deacon of the First Church for more than forty years, and for the same period of time an active magistrate of the county.

JONATHAN COBB, eldest son of Jonathan H. Cobb, was born in Dedham, March 2, 1829. In 1844 he entered a store in Boston as clerk, where he remained until January, 1849, when he went, overland, to California, by way of Mexico. Returned to Dedham in 1851, and soon after went into business in Nashville, Tenn., where he remained until March, 1859, when he returned home and entered the Probate office. He was appointed Assistant Register of Probate and Insolvency in January, 1862, which office he now holds.

CLERKS OF THE COURTS.

NATHANIEL AMES, first Clerk of the Courts of Norfolk County, was the son of Dr. Nathaniel Ames and brother of Fisher Ames. He was born in Dedham, October 9, 1741, and was graduated at Harvard College in 1761. He was a physician, and an active and violent partisan of the Jefferson school, and was a warm political opponent of his brother Fisher. On the organization of the county, in 1793, he was appointed one of the Justices of the Court of Common Pleas, and also as Clerk of the Court of Sessions. The records show that he acted as Clerk of both of those Courts. For two years following the organization of

---

* Judge Haven was the son of Rev. Jason Haven and Catherine Dexter Haven, daughter of Rev. Samuel Dexter and sister of Hon Samuel Dexter, Sen., of Dedham. Rev. Jason Haven was the son of Deacon Moses Haven, of Framingham, and was graduated at Harvard College in 1754. He was settled over the First Church in Dedham, February 5, 1756, and married the daughter of his predecessor.

Judge Haven's tastes were rather for theology than law, and the chief occupations of practical interest to him were horticulture and architecture. His attention to the last had reference only to personal enjoyment; but he was well versed in the principles of the science and their application to practical purposes, and often made useful suggestions to friends and public bodies engaged in building. He was one of the earliest in New England to accept the doctrines of Swedenborg, whose numerous works constituted his favorite reading, and in regard to which he sometimes wrote anonymously for the press. Yet he did not, till he removed from Dedham, a few years before his death, connect himself with any other church than that of which his father and grandfather had been pastors.

Mr. Haven built the fine house, and set out the English elms, on the estate now owned by Mr. John R. Bullard.

the county, the records of the Supreme Judicial Court were kept in Boston by John Tucker, Clerk of the Courts of that County. The record of the Court of Common Pleas has the following entry: —
" At a Court of Common Pleas, 26th day of September, 1797, Nathaniel Ames having, since the last session of the Court of Common Pleas, been removed from the office of Clerk by the Honorable the Justices of the Supreme Judicial Court, and John Lathrop, Jr., Esq., by them appointed to said office in his stead, as well as to the office of Clerk of the Supreme Judicial Court, agreeably to the Act of March 11, 1797."

Dr. Ames died July 21, 1822, aged 81 years.

JOHN LATHROP, JR., son of Rev. John Lathrop, D.D., was born in Boston in January, 1772, and was graduated at Harvard College in 1789. He studied law with Gov. Gore, and after opening an office in Boston, in 1797, removed to Dedham, where he was soon after appointed Clerk of the Courts of the County, which position he held but a short time, and soon after removed to Boston. In 1799 he embarked for India, where he remained for ten years engaged in commercial and literary pursuits. Returning to this country in 1809, he passed the remainder of his life in Washington and Georgetown as an instructor, lecturer and writer in the papers of the day. He died in Washington, January 30, 1820, aged 48 years.

HORATIO TOWNSEND was born in Medfield, March 29, 1763, and was graduated at Harvard College in 1783; studied law with Theophilus Parsons, at Newburyport, and settled in practice in his native town. In 1799 he was appointed Special Justice of the Court of Common Pleas, and about the same time received the appointment of Clerk of the Courts of the County, which office he continued to hold until 1811, when he was removed by Gov. Gerry. He was reappointed the following year, and continued in office until his death, which occurred at Dedham, July 9, 1826, aged 63 years.*

JOHN SHIRLEY WILLIAMS was born in Roxbury, May 3, 1772, and was graduated at Harvard College in 1797. He was for many years a lawyer in Roxbury and Dedham. In 1811 he was appointed Clerk of the Courts by Gov. Gerry, but was removed the next year by Gov. Strong. He was at one time County Attorney for Norfolk County. He died at Ware, Mass., while on a journey for his health, in May, 1843, aged 71 years.

JAIRUS WARE was born in Wrentham, January 22, 1772, and was graduated at Brown University in 1797. He was for many years a leading lawyer in his native town. He was a Representative to the General Court from 1809 to 1816, inclusive, and also in 1818, '19 and '23. He was a member of the Executive Council in 1825 and '26. In 1811 he was appointed an Associate Justice of the Southern Circuit Court of Common Pleas, and in 1819 Chief Justice of the new Court of Sessions, and again in April, 1822. September 1, 1826, having been appointed Clerk of the Courts of Norfolk County, he resigned the office of Judge. He continued in office as Clerk until his death, which occurred at Dedham, January 18, 1836, at the age of 64 years.

EZRA WESTON SAMPSON was born in Duxbury, December 1, 1797, and was graduated at Harvard College in 1816. He commenced the practice of law in Braintree, where he remained about twelve years, and on the death of Judge Ware, in 1826, he was appointed Clerk of the Courts of the County, and removed to Dedham. He continued in office until a few days before his death, which took place January 15, 1867, at the age of 69 years.

ERASTUS WORTHINGTON was the son of Erastus Worthington (W. C. 1804), and was born in Dedham, November 25, 1828. He was graduated at Brown University in the class of 1850. After residing nearly a year in Wisconsin he entered the Dane Law School at Cambridge, where he received the degree of LL.B. He completed his professional studies in the office of Hon. Ezra Wilkinson, at Dedham, and was admitted to the Bar at the February Term of the Supreme Court in 1854 at Dedham. He began practice in Boston, and was for some time a partner of the late Hon. David A. Simmons, of Roxbury. In 1856 he was elected Register of Insolvency for Norfolk County, which office he held until July, 1858, when he resumed practice in Dedham. He was also Trial Justice from 1857 to 1867. He was elected Clerk of the Courts of Norfolk County in 1866, and entered upon its duties in January, 1867. He has been twice re-elected to this office, the last time in 1876 for a term of five years, and continues to reside in Dedham.

EDGAR H. KINGSBURY was born in Canandaigua, N. Y., June 22, 1817. He lived in Brockport, N. Y., from 1825 to 1845, removing the latter year to Dedham. In April, 1846,

---

*Mr. Townsend owned and occupied the house afterwards owned by Ezra W. Sampson, and now owned and occupied by Hon. Tros. L. Wakefield. Lieut. Geo. H. Derby, U.S.A., well known as "John Phoenix," was his grandson, and was born in Dedham, April 2, 1823. He was a graduate of West Point, and a man of brilliant talents. He died in New York of softening of the brain, May 16, 1861, aged 38 years.

he entered the Registry of Deeds as a Clerk, and remained there until September, 1855, when he became clerk to Ezra W. Sampson, Clerk of the Courts of the County. At the February Term of the Supreme Judicial Court, in 1866, owing to the illness of Mr. Sampson, he was appointed by the Court as Clerk *pro tem*, in which position he remained until Mr. Worthington assumed the office, January 1, 1867. Mr. Kingsbury remained in the office as clerk to Mr. Worthington until the establishment of the office of Assistant Clerk; and June 25, 1867, he was appointed by the Supreme Judicial Court as Assistant Clerk of the Courts of Norfolk County, which position he still holds by successive reappointments.

SHERIFFS.

Hon. EBENEZER THAYER, of Braintree, the first Sheriff of Norfolk County, was the son of Hon. Ebenezer Thayer, also of Braintree, and was born Aug. 21, 1746. His father was for many years a prominent citizen of the town, having served in the office of Representative eighteen years, and was chosen Representative to the General Court seventeen years successively, and in 1776 was a member of the Executive Council. His mother was Susanna, daughter of Rev. Samuel Niles of Braintree. Mr. Thayer served the town many years as Selectman, Town Clerk and Treasurer; was Representative to the General Court in 1796, 1800 and 1801, a member of the Senate in 1795, '96, '97, '98, '99, and a member of the Executive Council in 1793 and '94. He was also a brigadier-general in the militia. On the organization of the county, in 1793, he was appointed Sheriff, but owing to ill-health resigned early in the following year. He died May 30, 1809, aged 63 years.

ATHERTON THAYER, half-brother to the preceding, was born in Braintree, February 9, 1766. His mother was Rebecca Miller, of Milton, who was the second wife of Hon. Ebenezer Thayer, Senior. On the resignation of the office of Sheriff by his brother, in 1794, he was appointed to fill the vacancy, and continued in the office until his death, July 4, 1798, aged 32 years.*

BENJAMIN CLARKE CUTLER, of Roxbury, was born in Boston, September 15, 1756, and was for many years a merchant, removing afterwards to Jamaica Plain. He was appointed Sheriff July 31, 1798, and held the office until his death. He died very suddenly at his residence on Centre street, Jamaica Plain, April, 1810, aged 54 years.

ELIJAH CRANE was born in Milton, August 29, 1754, and was the son of Thomas Crane, for many years a prominent citizen of that part of Stoughton now Canton. He early removed to Canton, where his regular business was that of a farmer, in which he met with marked success, although much of his time was devoted to public life. He was a man of large and erect stature, well developed form and graceful carriage, and was noted for his splendid horsemanship. He early took a deep interest in military matters, rising, by successive appointments, to the rank of Brigadier-General of the Second Brigade, First Division, M.V.M., to which he was promoted August 1, 1803, and promoted and commissioned Major-General of the First Division, June 16, 1809, which position he continued to hold until his discharge, June 8, 1827, a period of service in the highest military office of the State without a parallel in Massachusetts. He also attained high rank as a Mason, being successively Junior Grand Warden of the Grand Lodge of Massachusetts in 1820, '21, Senior Grand Warden in 1822, and Grand Master in 1832. On the death of Sheriff Cutler, in 1810, he was appointed Sheriff, and continued in office until 1811, when he was removed for political reasons by Gov. Gerry. The following year he was reappointed, and continued in office by successive reappointments until his death, the longest term of service as Sheriff ever held in the county. He died February 21, 1834, aged 80 years.†

WILLIAM BREWER, of Roxbury, was for many years a prominent citizen of the town, having been Chairman of the Board of Selectmen for several years, and was Represen-

---

* Atherton Thayer, like his father and brother, was a man of commanding appearance and of fine martial figure. It is related that at the funeral of Gen. Hancock, who died October 8, 1793, his appearance at the head of his troop of light horse (of which he was major) made such an impression that Sarah, daughter of Rev. Joseph Jackson, of Brookline, fell in love with him, sought him out, and married him against the wishes of her parents. He lived and died in the house which was for many years the residence of the late Hon. B. V. French. His brother, Hon. Ebenezer Thayer, Esq., lived and died in the house near the meeting-house, now owned by his grandson, Mr. Ebenezer C. Thayer.

† Gen. Crane was very fond of military life, and his long continuance in the office of major-general gave serious offence to many of the junior officers, whose promotion was thereby deferred. It is related that at a military supper given in the county, a false rumor of the general's death was circulated, when the following toast was offered, and drank with great gusto: "The late Major-General Crane: may he be eternally rewarded in Heaven for his everlasting services on earth."

tative to the General Court from 1801 to 1811, inclusive, and again from 1814 to 1817, inclusive. In 1811 he was appointed Sheriff of Norfolk County by Governor Gerry, which position he held for one year. He died August 2, 1817, aged 59 years.

JOHN BAKER, 2d, was born in Dorchester, February 27, 1780. He learned the trade of a wheelwright in Roxbury, and soon removed to Dedham, where for some time he carried on the same business. He was a Coroner, and for several years a Deputy Sheriff of the county. On the death of Gen. Crane, in 1834, Mr. Baker was appointed Sheriff, and held the office until his death, which occurred January 1, 1843, at the age of 63 years.

JERAULD NEWLAND EZRA MANN was born in Medfield, June 26, 1796. He learned the trade of a carriage-painter, serving his time with the Messrs. Bird of Walpole. In 1823 he went to Easton, where he remained but a short time, removing the year following to Taunton, where he remained five years, at the end of which time he went to Wrentham, and thence to Dedham, where he took the place of his brother-in-law, Major T. P. Whitney, as Deputy Sheriff and Jailer. On the death of Sheriff Baker, Mr. Mann was, Feb. 8, 1843, appointed Sheriff for the term of five years, at the expiration of which he declined a reappointment, but continued to act as Deputy Sheriff and Jailer until July, 1855, when failing health compelled his resignation. He soon after removed to Vernon, Conn., the residence of his youngest daughter, where he died, April 15, 1857, aged 60 years and 10 months.

THOMAS ADAMS was born in Quincy, April 20, 1804. In early life he was engaged in business with his father as a butcher, and afterwards was proprietor of different stage lines, and an extensive dealer in horses. He then went to Roxbury, where he continued to reside until his death. He was Deputy Sheriff under Sheriff Mann, and in 1848 succeeded that officer as Sheriff of the County. He was removed from office for political reasons in 1852, but was reappointed the following year, and continued in office until January 1, 1857. After Roxbury became a city, he was for two or three years City Marshal. He died suddenly, of apoplexy, January 2, 1869, aged 65 years.

JOHN W. THOMAS was born in Weymouth, April 1, 1815. Learned the trade of a shoemaker, and afterwards went into business as a manufacturer. Was a Representative to the General Court in 1852, a delegate to the Constitutional Convention in 1853, and a lieutenant-colonel in the militia. May 13, 1852, he was commissioned Sheriff of Norfolk County by Gov. Boutwell, but was removed the following year for political reasons. In 1856 he was elected Sheriff by the Republican and American parties, and assumed his position January 1, 1857. He soon after removed to Dedham, where he continues to reside. He was the first sheriff elected by the people in the county, and at each successive election was chosen by a large majority of the popular vote. He is now serving his seventh term, each of three years.

COUNTY TREASURERS.

ISAAC BULLARD, the first Treasurer of the County, was born in Dedham, July 10, 1744, and was a lineal descendant from William Bullard, one of the first settlers of the town. He was for many years in public life, having been Town Clerk for three years, Selectman five years and Representative to the General Court from 1794 to 1801, inclusive, and again in 1806 and 1807. He was chosen deacon of the First Church, May 28, 1780, which office he continued to hold until his death. On the organization of the county, in 1793, he was chosen County Treasurer, to which position he was annually elected until his decease, which occurred June 18, 1808, at the age of 64 years.

JOHN BULLARD, son of the preceding, was born in Dedham, January 9, 1773. He was also much in public life, having been twenty years a Selectman, and one year Town Clerk. On the death of his father, in 1808, he was chosen County Treasurer, which position he occupied by successive elections until his death, February 25, 1852, a period of forty-four years. He was 79 years of age.

GEORGE ELLIS was born in Medfield, September 2, 1793, and early removed to Dedham, where for several years he carried on business as a trader. He was captain of one of the Dedham militia companies; for several years a Deputy Sheriff of the County, and for fourteen years one of the Selectmen of the town. He was Secretary and Treasurer of the Dedham Institution for Savings from May, 1845, to June, 1855, when, owing to ill-health, he resigned. On the death of John Bullard, in 1852, he was appointed by the County Commissioners County Treasurer, and the two following years was elected by the people, failing of a re-election in 1855. He died June 24, 1855, aged 62 years and 10 months.

CHAUNCEY C. CHURCHILL was born in West Fairlee, Vermont, September 15, 1815. Received his early education in the district schools of his native town, and at Post Mills High

School. Removed to Amesbury, Mass., in March, 1837, and thence to Dedham, April 6, 1842. In April, 1855, he was elected County Treasurer by the American party, and on the change of the law concerning the office, was re-elected in November of the same year for a term of three years, and has since held the office, by repeated re-elections, until the present time, and January 1, 1877, entered upon another term of three years.

REGISTERS OF DEEDS.

ELIPHALET POND, the first Register of Deeds for the County of Norfolk, was born in Dedham, April 11, 1745. He was at one time colonel of a militia company, but during the latter portion of his life was known as Capt. Pond. He was Town Clerk for twenty-five years, and Selectman for sixteen years. On the organization of the county, in 1793, he was chosen Register of Deeds, and by successive elections held the office until his death, which occurred July 2, 1813, aged 68 years.*

JAMES FOORD was born in Milton, October 30, 1761. In early life he was a farmer, teaching school in the winter months. On the death of Mr. Pond, in 1813, through the influence of his friend and neighbor, Hon. Edward H. Robbins, afterwards Judge of Probate, he was elected Register, and the following year removed with his family to Dedham, where he continued in the office until his death, October 15, 1821. Aged 60 years.

ENOS FOORD, son of the preceding, was born in Milton, Oct. 21, 1796. In early life he was a teacher, and on the election of his father, as Register, assisted him in the work of the office, and on the death of Mr. Foord, Senior, in 1821, his son was chosen as his successor, and continued in office until his death, April 22, 1861, at the age of 64 years. For ten years, from 1834 to 1844, Mr. Foord was Secretary and Treasurer of the Dedham Institution for Savings.

JAMES, son of the preceding, was born in Dedham, in November, 1832, and on leaving school entered the office of his father, where he continued until his father's death, in 1861, when he was appointed Register by the County Commissioners, and chosen by the people at the ensuing November election. He declined re-election in 1873, and vacated the office January 1, 1874. He has for several years been a resident of California.

JOHN H. BURDAKIN was born in Cambridge, November 3, 1841. After writing for several years in the Middlesex Registry of Deeds he entered the Norfolk Registry office in January, 1863. On the declination of Mr. Foord, he was elected Register in 1873, assuming the office in January, 1874, and was re-elected for a further term of three years in 1876.

COUNCILLORS AND REPRESENTATIVES. 1776.

The following is a list of members of the Executive Council and House of Representatives in 1776, from those towns which afterwards constituted Norfolk County, with such brief sketch of the history of each as it was possible to obtain. Of course at this time the Senate was not in existence.

COUNCILLORS.

HON. JABEZ FISHER was born in Wrentham, November 19, 1717. He received only a common-school education, but from his early years was distinguished for that ready and strong common sense; that intuitive perception of the proper adaptation of means to any proposed ends; that discriminating acumen which at once and without any apparent effort

* He owned and lived on the estate on the Providence Turnpike about a mile south of the village and now known as the Asylum for Discharged Female Prisoners. His father, Col. Eliphalet Pond, was born in Dedham, May 17, 1704, and died January 19, 1795, aged 91 years. He represented the town in the General Court in 1761 and '63; was Town Clerk for twelve years, and Selectman for 10 years.

sovers the sound and practicable from the specious and visionary, which detects sophistry and baffles cunning; that inflexible adherence to principle; that courteousness of manners and that salient and unfaltering desire to be useful, — which, through the whole course of a protracted life, inspired the confidence, not only of his immediate neighborhood, but of the public, and raised him to those offices of power and trust, by the faithful and untiring discharge of which he became the pride — *decus et tutamen* — of his native town, and a benefactor of his country.

Mr. Fisher was a Representative from the town of Wrentham for several years, we believe, under the Provincial charter. He was certainly a member of that very full house of delegates that assembled at Salem on the 7th of October, 1774, and formed themselves into a provincial congress, and then adjourned to Concord and chose John Hancock President, and Benjamin Lincoln Secretary; of the second provincial congress, that first met at Cambridge, in February, 1775; and of the third, which convened on the last Wednesday of May, in the same year, and of which Dr. Joseph Warren was elected President. This last congress remained in session until July 19th, when the representatives assembled, who had been elected, agreeably to the advice of the continental congress and the provisions of the charter of William and Mary, to constitute a house of assembly. Of this house, also, Mr. Fisher was returned a member; and was one of the renowned twenty-eight who were then elected councillors, to act as a distinct branch of the legislature, and likewise to exercise the executive powers of the Government. Among the councillors elected at this time were all the delegates from Massachusetts to the continental congress, and who were then attending that body at Philadelphia, viz.: John Adams, Samuel Adams, Thomas Cushing, Robert Treat Paine and John Hancock. But on the adjournment of the congress at Philadelphia, on the first of August, these gentlemen returned to Massachusetts, and some, if not all of them, took their seats in the executive council. They returned to Philadelphia on the reassembling of the continental congress, on the 5th of September.

To be elected in such times for an office of so great responsibility, and to be associated with the members of the continental congress, with James Bowdoin, Benjamin Lincoln and other ardent patriots and wise men, forms in itself an enviable and lasting distinction. But the fidelity, zeal and ability with which Mr. Fisher discharged the duties of the office, during several successive years of darkness and peril that "tried men's souls," are the true measure of his merit, if not of his fame. No member of that honorable board was "in labors more abundant" than he. No one's judgment was more highly estimated, no one's firmness less distrusted. He was regarded as the special watchman of the country part of Suffolk (which, at that time, included the present County of Norfolk), and was always relied upon to arrange and bring into efficient action all the force, moral and physical, of that important section of the province. Much as was expected and demanded of him, he never disappointed any expectation which he had voluntarily excited, nor failed to effect any practicable purpose which he deliberately formed. No man better knew what was practicable, and no man deliberated more thoroughly.

When the Constitution of the United States was submitted to the several States for ratification and adoption, Mr. Fisher was the delegate returned from Franklin to the convention of this State, which assembled on this important subject in 1788. Though the delegates from the towns contiguous to that which he represented, opposed, and finally voted against the Constitution, he, in conformity with the will of his constituents — a will which he had greatly contributed to form — and the dictates of his own judgment, not only recorded his vote in favor of adopting that instrument, but by his efforts among a certain class of men in the convention, who went there with views utterly hostile to the proposed frame of government, but with patriotic hearts and minds fair and open, and to whom he had ready access, he is known to have been instrumental, by laboring in season and out of season, and by urging his sound, lucid, and enlarged views, in effecting a change in their ultimate opinion.

The time which Mr. Fisher was not called to devote to the public service, he employed in agricultural pursuits, which were the choice of his youth, and the amusement of his old age. He died on the 15th of October, 1806, aged 80 years.[*]

Hon. BENJAMIN WHITE was born in Brookline, October 5, 1724, and was graduated at

---

[*] See article in "Boston Monthly Magazine" for June, 1826, contributed by the late Judge Theron Metcalf.

Dr. Emmons preached a sermon on the Sunday following the death of Mr. Fisher, in which he bore strong testimony to his eminent worth and ability.

Mr. Fisher was a member of the Council in 1776, '67, '68, '69, '70, '71, '72, '76, '77, '78 and '79; of the House of Representatives in 1773, '74, '75, '86, '98 and '99, and of the Senate in 1780, '81, '82, '83 and '84.

Harvard College in 1744. He was a farmer, but very conspicuous for many years in public affairs. He was Selectman for eighteen years, and Town Treasurer seven years. He was Representative for several years, and a member of the Council from 1770 to 1779, inclusive. He died May 8, 1790, aged 66 years.

HON. EBENEZER THAYER was born in Braintree, July 31, 1721. He was Selectman eighteen years, and was chosen Representative to the General Court seventeen years successively, and was a member of the Executive Council in 1776. He died February 7, 1794, in the 73d year of his age, after a confinement of sixteen years. He was the father of Hon. Ebenezer Thayer and Major Atherton Thayer, the first two Sheriffs of Norfolk County.

REPRESENTATIVES.

Bellingham.

STEPHEN METCALF was born in Bellingham, December, 1731. He was for many years a Selectman of the town; Representative in the General Court in 1776, '77, '78, '79, '81, '82, '83; Senator from Suffolk County in 1785, '86, '87, '88, '89, '90, '91, '92, '93, and was in the Executive Council in 1794, '95, and '96. He was appointed Justice of the Court of Common Pleas for Norfolk County, July 2, 1793. He died July 26, 1800, aged 68 years and 7 months.

Braintree.

HON. JOSEPH PALMER, Esq., was born in England, but came to this country in 1746 with Richard Cranch, his brother-in-law, and purchased a large tract of land in Braintree (now Quincy), which he called Germantown, and where he expended much money in improvements. He was a man of good education and fine manners, and was soon called to positions of trust and honor. He was Moderator of the famous meeting of delegates held at the house of Richard Woodward, in Dedham, September 6, 1774, and member of the First Provincial Congress, October 7th, of the same year. He occupied a prominent position on the committees of that body, and was the only delegate from Braintree to the two following Congresses. He was also an active member of the Committee of Safety. He and his son were engaged at Lexington, the father acting as brigadier-general. He was afterwards stationed during the war at Hull, and in Rhode Island. He did not long survive the Revolution.

JONATHAN BASS, Esq.

Brookline.

MR. JOHN GODDARD was born in Brookline, May 28, 1730. He was Selectman and Assessor for twelve years, and Representative in 1776, '85, '87, '88, '89 and '92. He died April 13, 1816, aged 86 years.

Cohasset.

MR. JONATHAN BEAL.

Dedham.

MR. ABNER ELLIS was a native of Dedham, and lived and died at West Dedham. He represented the town in 1771, '72, '73, '74, '75, '76, '77, '78, '80 and '81.*

JONATHAN METCALF, Esq., was Representative in 1776, '78 and '79, and was conspicuous in town affairs.

Dorchester.

COL. LEMUEL ROBINSON was born in Dorchester, March 4, 1736. He was prominent in town affairs, having been Selectman and Assessor, and was Representative for the town in 1774 and '76. He died suddenly, July 29, 1776, aged 40 years.†

MR. JAMES ROBINSON.

---

* His son, Col. Abner Ellis, was Representative five years, and his grandson, Merrill D. Ellis, three years.

† Col. Robinson kept a famous tavern in Dorchester, which was a great place of resort for the patriots of that day. In the diary of John Adams there is an account of a meeting of the "Union and Association of the Sons of Liberty in this Province." August 14, 1769, the Sons met at Liberty Tree, in Boston, "where they drank fourteen toasts," and then adjourned to Liberty Tree Tavern, known as Robinson's Tavern, in Dorchester, where they dined at 2 o'clock. From three hundred to three hundred and fifty sat down to tables spread in the field under a tent. There were "three large pigs barbecued," and other provision in abundance. Forty-five toasts were given on the occasion, the last of which was, "Strong halters, firm blocks, and sharp axes to all such as deserve either." At 5 o'clock, P. M., the Boston people started for home, led off by Mr. Hancock

Medfield.

Mr. Daniel Perry, of Medfield, was born in Sherborn, November 24, 1724. Removed at at early age to Natick, where he remained until 1756, when he settled in Medfield. He was prominent in church and town affairs, and was for several years an Associate Justice of the Court of Common Pleas for the County of Norfolk. He was Representative in the General Court in 1776, '77, '78, '80, '84 and '85. He died July 6, 1804, aged 79 years and 7 months.

Medway.

Elijah Clark, Esq., was born in Medway, September 9, 1727. He was for many years Town Clerk and Selectman, and was Representative in 1776, '77, '78 and '79. He died October 7, 1801, in the 75th year of his age.

Milton.

Capt. Ebenezer Tucker was born in Milton in 1723, and was for several years a Selectman of the town. He was Representative in 1776, '77 and '78. He died in 1797, aged 74 years.

Mr. Joseph Clapp was born in Milton, June 7, 1726. He was deacon of the church, and removed to Sterling, where he died January 30, 1799, aged 73 years.*

Needham.

Col. William Mackintosh, of Needham, was born in Dedham, June 16, 1722. Married August 26, 1745. Ensign and first lieutenant in French war. Removed from Roxbury to Needham, May 23, 1764. In 1774 chosen first captain of one of the two militia companies in the town, and soon after was made lieutenant-colonel, and as such served at Lexington. On the 14th of February, 1776, by the Council of the State, he was appointed colonel of the first regiment of militia in Suffolk County, and served during the war with great credit. He was twelve years Selectman, and five years Representative. In 1779 he was a member of the convention which framed the Constitution; and in 1788 was a member of the convention appointed for the purpose of taking into consideration the National Constitution, and voted for its adoption. On the 19th of April, 1790, was appointed deacon in the church, which office he held until November 22, 1803, when, owing to infirmities, he resigned, and a unanimous vote of thanks was passed by the church. He died January 3, 1813, aged 90 years, 6 months, 18 days.†

Roxbury.

Dr. Jonathan Davis.
Col. Aaron Davis.

Mr. Increase Sumner was born in Roxbury, November 27, 1746, and was graduated at Harvard College in 1767. Studied law with Samuel Quincy; was admitted to the bar in 1770, and commenced the practice of the law in his native town. He was a Representative in the General Court from Roxbury in 1776, '77, '78 and '79. He was a Senator from Suffolk County in 1780, '81, '82. He was a member of the State Constitutional Conventions in 1777 and 1779. In June, 1782, he was chosen a member of Congress, in place of Timothy Danielson, resigned, but never took his seat in that body, having in August of the same year been made an Associate Justice of the Supreme Judicial Court. Judge Sumner was also a member of the Massachusetts Convention of 1789. In April, 1797, Samuel Adams having declined a re-election, Judge Sumner was elected Governor, receiving a large majority of votes. He was re-elected in 1798 and 1799, the last time by an almost unanimous vote, but was unable to enter upon the duties of the office. He was languishing on a bed of sickness at the time of the meeting of the General Court at the

in his chariot. Mr. Adams was present himself, and says, " To the honor of the Sons, I did not see one person intoxicated, or near it."

In 1775 Col. Robinson carted out some cannon from Boston which he kept concealed on his premises to prevent them falling into the hands of the British. The tavern of Colonel Robinson was afterwards owned and occupied by his grandson, the late John Mears, recently deceased, and was situated about half a mile south of the meeting-house of the late Dr. Codman. It was destroyed by fire a few years since.

* Mr. Clapp's daughter, Jerusha, married Andrew Putnam, of Sterling, and was the mother of Rev. Dr. George Putnam of Roxbury.

† From Rev. Stephen Palmer's sermon.

James Mackintosh, Representative from Needham, in 1876-77, is the great-grandson of Col. Mackintosh.

commencement of the political year; but the Legislature having some constitutional scruples about the right of the Lieut.-Governor to act as chief magistrate after the death of the Governor, without his acceptance of the office, this ceremony took place in the bed-chamber of the dying Governor. He died of angina pectoris, on the 7th of June, 1799, in the 53d year of his life, " mourned and lamented by the whole people."

Stoughtonham (now Sharon).

Capt. Ebenezer Tisdale was a Representative in 1776, '77 and '78.

Stoughton.

Col. Benjamin Gill was for many years prominent in town affairs.

Mr. Thomas Crane was for many years one of the most prominent citizens of the town, and lived in that portion now included in the limits of Canton. He was born January 6, 1727. He was Selectman for several years, and was Representative in 1776, '77, '78, '79 and '81. He afterwards removed to Milton, where he died, October 7, 1804, aged 78 years.*

Walpole.

Joshua Clapp, Esq., was born in Walpole in 1707. He was for many years one of the most prominent men in the town, being a captain in the militia, Justice of the Peace, for many years a deacon of the church, and Representative in 1768, '70, '71, '72 and '76. In 1745 he marched his company to Boston to help defend it from the attack of the French fleet, then daily expected. He died May 6, 1802, aged 95 years.

Weymouth.

Mr. Solomon Lovell was born in Weymouth in 1733. In the Revolutionary War he was actively engaged in the service of his country and rose from captain to general. In 1779 he had command of the land force in the Penobscot expedition, which was fitted out to attack the British troops at Penobscot, now Castine, Maine. He was a man of marked character, and possessed the entire confidence of the people of his native town. He was Representative in 1771, '76, '77, '78, '79, '81 and '83. On the organization of Norfolk County, in 1793, he was appointed Special Justice of the new Court of Common Pleas for the county. He died September 9, 1801, aged 68 years.

Mr. Nathaniel Bailey was born in Weymouth in 1731. He was a prominent citizen of the town. He was deacon in the church, Selectman, and Representative in 1772, '73, '74, '75, '76, '80, '82, '84, '88, '90, '92, '94 and '96. He died December 17, 1812, aged 82 years.

Wrentham.

Mr. Benjamin Guild was Representative in 1776, '77 and '78.
Mr. Joseph Hawes.
Dr. Ebenezer Daggett.

---

* Thomas Crane, Esq., was much relied upon by the General Court of Massachusetts during the Revolution, as appears by their resolves, in which they entrusted the charge of the State powder-mill, in Stoughton (now Canton, and on the spot where the Revere Copper Works are), and the manufacture of powder there, to his care and supervision. Mr. James Capen, of Stoughton, who died February 24, 1853, in the ninety-seventh year of his age, related not long before his death, that when the affairs of the Revolution wore a gloomy aspect, and the army was suffering for supplies, Thomas Crane, Esq., went around the town soliciting contributions for the relief of the army; and he well remembered that on producing his papers, Mr. Crane's tears fell on them like a shower, and that with great expression and emphasis he assured the by-standers that the child Liberty was about to be born, and that all that was needed was strength to enable it to be delivered. — Gen. Reg., July, 1853.

Mr. Crane, during the latter part of his life, owned and occupied the house in Milton now owned by John Oakes Shaw. He was the father of Sheriff and Major-General Crane.

COUNCILLORS, SENATORS AND REPRE-SENTATIVES, 1876.

[These sketches, with slight alterations, are taken from the " Boston Journal" of January 5, 1876. From 1866 to 1876, Roxbury, Dorchester and West Roxbury were, for purposes of repre-sentation, considered as a part of Norfolk County.]

COUNCILLORS.

District No. 2, which includes the whole of Norfolk County. — HON. HARRISON TWEED, of Taunton, Republican, was born in South Reading, February 17, 1806, and was educated in that town. He is agent and treasurer of the Taunton Locomotive Manufacturing Company, and was a member of the House in 1852 and '58, and of the Senate in 1868 and '69. Mr. Tweed was re-elected to the Council for 1877.

SENATORS.

First Norfolk District. — HON. ALBERT PALMER, Republican, of Roxbury, firm of Prescott and Palmer, ice dealers, was born in Candia, N. H., in 1831; studied at Phillips Academy, and was a member of the class of 1858 at Dartmouth College. He was a very active and useful member of the House in 1872, '73 and '74, and was in the Senate in 1875 and '76.

Second Norfolk District. — HON. JOSEPH E. FISKE, Republican, of Needham, was born in that town, October 23, 1839, and has held several local offices. He has been engaged in real-estate transactions, and was a member of the House in 1874. He distinguished himself during the war, and was successively orderly sergeant, Co. C, 43d Mass. Vols., 2d and 1st lieutenant and captain of the 2d Mass. Heavy Artillery, and aid-de camp on the staff of the late Major-General F. P. Blair, 17th Army Corps. He was a prisoner-of-war at Andersonville, Macon and Savannah. Mr. Fiske was educated at Harvard, graduating in 1861, and after the war entered the Andover Theological Seminary, graduating in 1867. He is at present Chairman of the Board of Selectmen and of the School Committee. He was also a member of the Senate in 1877.

Third Norfolk District. — HON. J. WHITE BELCHER, Republican, of Randolph, is a grain dealer and Clerk of the District Court of East Norfolk. He was born in the town in which he resides, November 14, 1823, and was educated at Randolph Academy. He was a Trial Justice for Norfolk County from 1866 to 1872; has been Chairman of the Selectmen, Assessors, and Overseers of the Poor for the past eighteen years; was an Inspector of the State Workhouse at Bridgewater in 1874, a member of the House in 1855, and of the Senate in 1875 and '76.

Norfolk and Plymouth District. — HON. E. ATHERTON HUNT, Republican, boot manufacturer of Weymouth, was born in that town, January 26, 1826. He was a member of the House in 1873, and of the Senate in 1875 and '76.

REPRESENTATIVES.

District No. 1, Dedham. — JOHN DOGGETT COBB, Republican, lawyer, was born in Dedham, April 28, 1840, and was graduated at Harvard in 1861, and at the Law School in 1866. He was clerk in the office of the Secretary of the Treasury, at Washington, in 1871 and '72. He was sergeant in the 35th Massachusetts Volunteer Infantry, and gradually rose to first lieutenant and adjutant, and finally captain. He was a member of the House in 1876, '77.

District No. 2, West Roxbury. — JOSEPH SAMUEL ROPES, Independent, merchant, was born in Boston, February 6, 1818, and educated in various New England schools, and the Gymnasium and University of St. Petersburg. Mr. Ropes has been President of the Boston Board of Trade, and was in the House in 1875, '76.

District No. 3, Roxbury. — WILLIAM STERLING KING, Republican, lawyer, was born in New York City, Oct. 6, 1818, and educated at Union College. He was colonel and brevet brig.-general of volunteers, U. S. Assessor of Internal Revenue, and Register of Probate for Suffolk County. He was a member of the House in 1855, '57, '75 and '76.

District No. 3, Roxbury. — HENRY W. FULLER, Republican, lawyer, was born in Hooksett, N. H., June 30, 1840, and educated at Dartmouth College, graduating in the class of 1857. He served five years in the army, entering as private and leaving as brigadier-general, by brevet. He was in the House in 1875, '76 and '77.

District No. 3, Roxbury. — EBENEZER ADAMS, Republican, mechanical engineer, was born in Norwich, Conn., Dec. 1, 1830, and educated in that place. He was a member of the Roxbury Common Council for two years, and was a member of the House in 1875 and '76.

District No. 4, Roxbury. — WILLIAM MORSE, Republican, builder and carpenter, was born in Wiscasset, Me., July 4, 1822. He was a member of the Roxbury Common Council for five years, Alderman one year, and in the Boston City Government three years.

District No. 5, Dorchester. — FREDERIC PIERCE MOSELEY, Republican, iron merchant, was born in Dorchester, September 20, 1820, and educated in that place. He was in the House in 1875, '76.

District No. 5, Dorchester. — GARDNER A. CHURCHILL, Republican, printer, firm of Rockwell & Churchill, of Boston. He was born in Dorchester, May 26, 1839, and educated in the public schools of that town. He left school at the age of fourteen, and went to sea, shipping in the merchant service as sailor, and rising to the rank of officer. During the war he was an officer in the United States Navy. He was Junior Vice-Commander, Department G. A. R. for Massachusetts in 1872, and was elected Commander of Post 68, Dorchester. He was a member of the House in 1875, '76.

District No. 6 Quincy. — JOHN D. WHICHER, Republican, manufacturer, was born in Quincy, December 25, 1825. He was a member of the House in 1876, and of the Senate in 1877.

District No. 7, Braintree. — JAMES T. STEVENS, Republican, tack and nail manufacturer, was born in Braintree, June 30, 1835, and during the war was first lieutenant and captain of Co. C, 4th Regiment, and captain of Co. I, 42d Regiment Massachusetts Volunteers. He was a member of the House in 1876.

District No. 8, Weymouth. — ELON SHERMAN, Republican, box-maker, was born in Marshfield. November 5, 1820, and educated in the public schools. He was a member of the House in 1876.

District No. 8, Weymouth. — WILLIAM SPRAGUE WALLACE, Republican, machine boot-fitter, of Weymouth, was born in East Braintree, October 11, 1838. He was a member of the House in 1876.

District No. 9, Holbrook and Randolph. — SETH MANN, 2d, Republican, of Randolph, was born in that town February 28, 1817, and was graduated at Brown University in 1839. He was County Commissioner three years, on the School Committee four years, Selectman and Assessor eleven years, and Deputy Collector of Internal Revenue from 1862 to '75. He was a member of the House in 1861, '76 and '77.

District No. 10, Stoughton. — WARREN P. BIRD, Democrat, mechanic, was born in Stoughton, October 18, 1843, and received a common-school education. He was a member of the House in 1876.

District No. 11, Canton, Milton, Sharon and Walpole. — EDWARD LILLIE PIERCE, Republican, lawyer, of Milton, was born in Stoughton, March 29, 1829, and was educated at Brown University and the Harvard Law School, graduating from the former in 1850, and the latter in 1852. At the breaking out of the war, he enlisted as a private in the 3d Regiment Massachusetts Militia, and was Special Agent of the United States Treasury Department in 1861, '62 in charge, of the freedmen and plantations in South Carolina. The following year he was Supervising Agent of the Treasury Department for the Department of the South. He was Collector of Internal Revenue for the Third Massachusetts District from 1863 to '66; District Attorney of Norfolk and Plymouth Counties from 1866 to 1869; and Secretary of the Board of State Charities from 1869 to 1874. He is the author of the well-known treatise on "American Railroad Law," and of the "Abstract of Special Railroad Laws of Massachusetts." He was a member of the House in 1875 and '76.

District No. 11, Canton, Milton, Sharon and Walpole. — ELIJAH A. MORSE, Republican, of Canton, is proprietor of "The Rising Sun Stove Polish Factory." He was born at South Bend, Ind., May 25, 1841, his father, Rev. Abner Morse, having removed from Holliston in this State, and he received a common-school education. He was a corporal in Co. A, 4th Regiment Massachusetts Volunteers, and served in Virginia and Louisiana. He was a member of the House in 1876.

District No. 12, Foxborough, Medway, Norfolk and Wrentham. — DAVID ALLEN PARTRIDGE, Republican, boot and shoe manufacturer, of Medway, was born in Milford, April 3,

1833, and educated in the public schools. During the war Mr. Partridge was first lieutenant in the 42d Massachusetts Regiment, adjutant and captain in the 51th Regiment, and was detailed while in service as A. A. G., and Assistant Provost Marshal. He has been Commander of "Wilder Dwight" Post 105, G. A. R., for four years. He was a member of the House in 1876.

District No. 12, Foxborough, Medway, Norfolk and Wrentham. — JOSEPH A. KINGSBURY, Democrat, grocer, of Foxborough, was born in that town Aug. 17, 1837, and educated in the public schools. He was a member of the House in 1876.

District No. 13, Bellingham and Franklin. — DAVIS THAYER, Jr., Republican, manufacturer, of Franklin, was born in that town, October 20, 1816. He was a member of the House in 1876.

District No. 14, Dover, Medfield and Needham. — JAMES MACKINTOSH, Republican, farmer and market gardener, of Needham, was born in that town, April 9, 1838, and is a member of the Board of Selectmen. He was a member of the House in 1876, '77.

District No. 15, Brookline. — MOSES WILLIAMS, Jr., Republican, is a lawyer, was born in West Roxbury, December 4, 1846, and educated at Harvard College. He was in the House in 1874, '75 and '76.

CENTENNIAL CELEBRATIONS, JULY 4TH.

[In nearly every town in the county the day was observed by processions, speeches, bonfires and illuminations, but those named below were *municipal* celebrations.]

BRAINTREE.

At the annual town meeting, in March, an appropriation was made and a Committee of Arrangements appointed, consisting of Elias Hayward, Elisha Thayer, N. E. Hollis, James T. Stevens, Josephus Shaw, S. A. Bates and A. T. Pratt, to arrange for a proper observance of the 4th of July by the town of Braintree.

The exercises of the day were as follows: Introductory Address, by Elias Hayward; Prayer, by Rev. T. A. Emerson; Address, by Asa French, Esq., President of the Day; Reading of the Declaration of Independence from the original records of the town, by Samuel A. Bates, Town Clerk; Oration, by Hon. Francis A. Hobart; Reading of Centennial Ode, by A. T. Pratt; Music, by Braintree Brass Band; Singing, by select choir under direction of M. A. Perkins. In the evening there were grand displays of fireworks and burning of tar-barrels at several prominent places in the town.

BROOKLINE.

The Committee of Arrangements having in charge the celebration of the 4th of July consisted of the following citizens : Edward I. Thomas, *Chairman; Murray M. Wing, Secretary;* Wm. I. Bowditch, Henry M. Whitney, Charles C. Cotting, Wm. H. Wilder, James M. Codman, Frank W. Lawrence, George P. Richardson, Moses Williams, Jr., William B. Sears, Alfred Kenrick, Jr., Benj. F. Baker, Philip Duffy, Michael Driscoll, Henry Mason, Francis Hunnewell, R. G. F. Candage, J. Emery Hoar, Wm. H. Lincoln, Charles H. Drew, Howard N. Brown, Warren Goddard, Jr., Charles H. Stearns, Alexander S. Arthur.

A national salute of thirty-eight guns was fired and the bells rang at sunrise, noon and sunset. At 6.30, A. M., two American elms were set out in front of the Town Hall with singing and a dance around the trees by the school-children. A procession consisting of Grand Army Post 143, the Fire Department and the several civic societies, with a military escort of the Boston Fusileers and the Brookline Cadets, marched at 3, A. M., through the principal streets of the town. At 11, A. M., there was a meeting of the citizens in the Town Hall, presided over by William I. Bowditch, Chairman of the Board of Selectmen, the exercises of which were as follows: Music, by the Orchestra; Prayer, by Rev. Henry C. Mabie; Centennial Hymn, written by John G. Whittier, and sung by the children's chorus; Introductory Remarks, by the Chairman; Music; Reading of the Declaration of Independence, by Francis Lewis Wellman; Song, by Myron W. Whitney; Address, by Wendell Phillips; *Keller's American Hymn*, by children's chorus; Address, by Edward Atkinson; Music, by Orchestra; *Star Spangled Banner*, sung by M. W. Whitney; *My Country, 'tis of Thee*, sung by children's chorus; Address, by Charles H. Drew, followed by the Benediction. In the evening, displays of old-fashioned bonfires of tar-barrels were made on Corey and other hills.

CANTON.

The day was celebrated under the direction of a Committee of Arrangements, consisting of Messrs. Thomas E. Grover, *Chairman;* J. Mason Everett, Elijah A. Morse, Ezra S. Brewster, Samuel H. Capen, Arthur C. Kollock, David T. Hagan, W. Henry Bense and Frank L. Gates. The exercises, which took place in the meeting-house of the First Congregational Parish, were as follows: Organ Voluntary, by Miss Clara B. Lopez; Reading from the Scriptures, by Rev. John W. Savage; Prayer, by Rev. W. H. Savery; *Paine's Centennial Hymn*, by chorus; Introductory Address, by Thomas E. Grover; Chorus; Reading of the Declaration of Independence, by Miss J. Annie Bense; *Keller's American Hymn*, by chorus; Historical Address, by Hon. Charles Endicott; *The Star Spangled Banner*, by chorus; Addresses, by citizens; Singing of *America*, by chorus and audience, followed by Benediction, by Rev. Clifton Fletcher. In the evening, displays of fireworks were made at several points.

FRANKLIN.

A large meeting of the citizens was held, which was presided over by Hon. Joseph G. Ray. After prayer, by Rev. St. John Chambré, *America* was sung by the audience, followed by the Reading of the Declaration of Independence, by Miss Mary A. Bryant. Waldo Daniels acted as Toastmaster, the first sentiment being "The Day we Celebrate," which was responded to by Rev. St. John Chambré. "The Spirit of the Hour" was responded to by Rev. Mr. Short; "Our Flag in 1776 and 1876," by Rev. W. M. Thayer; "Reminiscences of Franklin," by Stephen W. Richardson; "Our Fathers of the Past Century," by Rev. W. H. Daniels, of Illinois; "Our Public Schools," by Rev. S. W. Squire; "Then and Now," by James M. Stewart, of the Franklin "Register," "The Colleges of America," by A. Barclay Fletcher; and the closing sentiment, "The Church, Past and Present," by Rev. Geo. W. Ryan. After music by the band, an ample collation was served. The exercises of the day closed with a display of fireworks in the evening.

MEDWAY.

The day was celebrated by a meeting of the citizens in Shumway's Grove, at West Medway, at which Charles H. Deans, Esq., acted as President of the Day. A procession of citizens in carriages, preceded by a cavalcade and followed by those on foot, marched through the principal streets of West Medway to the grove, where the exercises were as follows: Prayer, by Rev. E. O. Jameson; Reading of the Declaration of Independence, by Hon. M. M. Fisher; Oration, by Rev. S. J. Axtell, Jr.; and Music by the West Medway Band. A fine collation was furnished by the citizens of West Medway. There was a display of fireworks in the evening.

HYDE PARK.

The day was celebrated with great enthusiasm, commencing with a procession in the morning, followed by a meeting of the citizens in the grove at the corner of Austin and West streets, which was presided over by Edwin R. Walker, Chairman of the Board of Selectmen. The exercises were in the following order: Singing by chorus; Prayer, by Rev. Perley B. Davis; Singing of *Keller's American Hymn*, by the chorus; Reading of the Declaration of Independence, by Mr. G. Fred. Gridley; Singing of *The Star Spangled Banner*, by Miss M. C. Pollard; Oration, by Hamilton A. Hill; closing with the singing of *America*, by the audience. At 4 o'clock, P. M., union religious services were held in the Orthodox Church, which were opened with prayer by Rev. Mr. Alderman, followed by remarks by Theodore D. Weld, Rev. P. B. Davis, and Rev. J. H. Gilbert, and closing with prayer by Rev. Mr. Gilbert. At 7 o'clock, P. M., an immense meeting was held in Everett square, for the purpose of dedicating the new pump presented to the town by the Women's Temperance Union of Hyde Park. Mr. Walker presided at the dedication; an address was made by Mr. Edward J. Humphrey, followed by a choice original poem by Mr. Charles F. Gerry. A flag, the gift of Mr. N. H. Tucker, was then presented by Miss Nettie B. Richardson, and accepted by Mr. Humphrey in a brief speech, after which the flag was run up to the mast-head amid the cheers of the assembled multitude. A regatta and an exhibition of athletic sports were among the other attractions, and at night a grand exhibition of fireworks closed the stirring observance of the day.

NORWOOD.

The celebration of the day was under the direction of a Committee of Arrangements consisting of Francis Tinker, Rev. George Hill, Geo. E. Draper, Francis O. Winslow and W. E. Locke. A procession was formed at 10 o'clock, which marched to Highland Grove, where the exercises took place in the following order: Address of welcome, by Rev. George Hill; Song of welcome, composed by Francis Tinker, and sung by the Alpine Quartetto; Introductory Remarks by W. E. Locke, President of the Day; Prayer, by Rev. J. P. Bixby; Reading of the Declaration of Independence, by Francis O. Winslow; Music by the band, and Singing by the quartette, after which Curtis Guild, of Boston, gave a patriotic address suited to the occasion. Mr. Sanford Mitchell sang the "Sword of Bunker Hill," and the audience joined in singing an original ode, written for the occasion by Rev. Theron Brown, after which addresses were made by Edwin Thompson and others. In the afternoon a picnic was held in the grove under the auspices of the Norwood Reform Club, and in the evening there was an excellent display of fireworks.

QUINCY.

At the annual town meeting, a committee was appointed, consisting of Messrs. Edward Whicher, Henry F. Barker, and James H. Slade, to make the necessary arrangements for a centennial celebration of the 4th of July. $600 was appropriated for the purpose, and $600 additional was raised by subscription. The day was celebrated by exercises in Yale's mammoth tent, erected on land of Mr. James Edwards, on Granite street. A procession was formed, under the direction of Edward Whicher, Chief Marshal, which marched to the tent, where James H. Slade presided. The exercises were as follows: Singing, under direction of Mr. John Farley; Reading of the Declaration of Independence, by six young ladies; Opening Address on the early history of Quincy, by Charles Francis Adams, Jr.; History of the First Church, by Elwin W. Marsh; History of Christ Church, by Rev. R. H. Howe; History of the Universalist Church, by Rev. G. W. Whitney; History of the Evangelical Church and Society, by Rev. Edward Norton; History of the Baptist Church, by Rev. C. H. Rowe; Sketches of Quincy, Hancock and Adams, by Professor W. R. Dimmock; of the Public Schools of Quincy, by Col. Parker; and of Quincy during the late war, by Charles H. Porter. There was also a regatta, entertainments for the children during the day, and fireworks in the evening.

RANDOLPH.

The town, at its annual meeting, appropriated $300 to defray the expense of celebrating the 4th of July, and chose the following Committee of Arrangements: J. White Belcher, Jonathan Wales, John F. Kilton, Seth Turner and James A. Tower, with the Selectmen. Subsequently, the committee organized by the choice of J. White Belcher, Chairman, and Jonathan Wales, Secretary. The sum appropriated by the town not being deemed sufficient for the purpose, a Centennial Tea-Party realized a further sum of $300, which was given in aid of the celebration.

On the 4th of July a procession was formed, under the direction of Capt. Hiram C. Alden, Chief Marshal, which marched through the principal streets, the houses and public buildings being finely decorated. At two o'clock a meeting of the citizens was held at the Town Hall, presided over by John T. Flood, Chairman of the Board of Selectmen, and an oration was delivered by Rev. John C. Labaree. A display of fireworks in the evening closed the celebration.

STOUGHTON.

In the morning a procession was formed, which marched to High-School Grove, were the exercises were as follows : Prayer, by Rev. J. Livsey; Music, by a select choir; Reading of the Declaration of Independence, by Francis Capen; Oration, by Halsey J. Boardman, of Boston. At twelve o'clock dinner was served, after which addresses were made by Rev. E. H. Capen, President of Tufts College, and a native of the town, A. M. Leonard, of Boston, and others. There was a fine display of fireworks in the evening.

SHARON.

A gathering of citizens was held at Massapoag-Lake Grove, at which William R. Mann acted as President of the Day. The Declaration of Independence was read by Rev. A. P. Chute; selections from the Scriptures were read by Rev. H. C. Weston; and prayer was offered by Rev. Lyman Partridge. George W. Gay gave the history of the churches, and William B. Wickes the early municipal history of the town. Music was furnished by the Citizens' Brass Band; and vocal music, under the direction of Sanford Waters Billings, was also given. In the evening a bonfire was kindled on Moose Hill, as in the olden time.

BURNING OF MEDFIELD.

The Bi-Centennial Anniversary of the Burning of the Town of Medfield, by the Indians, in 1676, was celebrated by the citizens of the town, February 21st, 1876, under the direction of a Committee of Arrangements, consisting of Rev. C. C. Sewall, Rev. J. M. R. Eaton, and Messrs. Jacob R. Cushman, Charles Hamant, and James Hewins. Bells were rung and salutes fired at morning, noon and evening. The literary exercises took place at the Town Hall, and consisted of an Opening Address by Rev. Charles C. Sewall, President of the Day; Prayer, by Rev. J. M. R. Eaton; Singing of St. Martin's by the audience; Historical Address by Robert R. Bishop, Esq., of Newton, a native of Medfield; and an appropriate poem by James Hewins, Esq. A recess was then taken for a collation in the vestry of the Unitarian Church. At 2, P. M., the exercises in the Town Hall were resumed by singing a hymn, written for the occasion by Rev. J. H. Allen, of Cambridge, followed by addresses from the President of the Day; Hon. J. B. D. Cogswell, of Yarmouth; Rev. Theron Brown, of Norwood; Henry D. Hyde, Esq., of Boston; Rev. Charles Hammond, of Monson; Mr. D. T. V. Huntoon, of Canton; Mr. Edward A. M. Allen, of Sherborn; Rev. S. W. Bush, of Boston, and others. The exercises closed with prayer by Rev. Mr. Crane. The proceedings of the day, including the admirable address of Mr. Bishop, have been published in an elegant pamphlet.

WINSLOW PARK, NORWOOD.

Winslow Park, a new park laid out on the corner of Walpole and Chapel streets, Norwood, by George Winslow, and his sons, was dedicated on Monday, November 6th. Mr. Francis O. Winslow made the opening address, followed by a patriotic address by Rev. J. P. Bixby. Mr. George Winslow, seventy-six years old, run up a beautiful flag from the elegant staff which adorns the enclosure, amidst music by the band and the shouts of the assembled multitude. The houses in the vicinity were finely illuminated.

TOWN OFFICERS, 1776.

BELLINGHAM.

Annual meeting, March 6th, 1776. *Moderator,* Stephen Metcalf, Esq.; *Town Clerk,* Aaron Holbrook; *Selectmen,* Stephen Metcalf, Eliphalet Holbrook, Jonathan Draper, Elias Thayer, Elisha Alden; *Assessors,* Stephen Metcalf, Samuel Scott, Jr., Aaron Holbrook; *Overseers of the Poor,* Benjamin Partridge, Samuel Scott, Joseph Chilson; *Treasurer,* Joseph Thompson; *Committee of Correspondence, Inspection and Safety,* Joseph Holbrook, Seth Hall, John Metcalf, Samuel Darling, Ezekiel Bates; *Constables,* Job Partridge, Joshua Darling; *Surveyors of Highways,* Melaciah Pond, Levi Rockwood, Ebenezer Thayer, Asahel Holbrook, Ezekiel Thayer, Ezekiel Cook, Benjamin Partridge, Jr., Israel Whitaker.

BRAINTREE.

Annual meeting, March 4, 1776. *Moderator,* Samuel Niles; *Town Clerk and Treasurer,* Elisha Niles. Mr. Niles dying in June, at meeting held July 5, Ebenezer Thayer was chosen to fill the vacancy. *Selectmen, Assessors, and Overseers of Poor,* Norton Quincy, Esq., Capt. Peter B. Adams, Dea. James Penniman, Maj. Edmund Soper, Col. Jonathan Bass, Thomas Penniman, Esq., Samuel Niles, Esq.; *Committee of Correspondence, Inspection and Safety,* Capt. Ebenezer Billings, Mr. James Clark, Dea. Daniel Arnold, Col. Ebenezer Thayer, Capt. Nathaniel Wales, Elisha Niles, Capt. Eliphalet Sawen, Mr. Nathaniel Belcher, Jr., Dr. Ephraim Wales; *Wardens,* Joseph Brackett, Elisha Niles, Samuel Jones; *Constables,* Capt. Peter B. Adams, Joshua Hayward, Hobart Clark; *Tythingmen,* Samuel Bass, Samuel Arnold, Capt. Joseph Hayward; *Fire Wardens,* Moses Adams, James Thayer, Seth Man, Jr.; *Surveyors of Highways,* Dea. Ebenezer Adams, James Clark, Capt. Peter B. Adams, Thompson Baxter, Josiah Veasey, Pearson Hayward, Jona. Thayer, Capt. Moses French, Samuel Holbrook, Thomas Hollis, Jr., Dea. Penniman, Jeremiah Thayer, Daniel White, Simeon Thayer, Samuel Belcher, Peter Thayer, Moses Spear, Capt. Eliphalet Sawing; *Committee to support petition to make Braintree the shire town of contemplated new county,* Norton Quincy, Elisha Niles, Jonathan Bass, Edmund Soper, Thomas Penniman, Capt. Peter B. Adams, Capt. Edmund Billings, Mr. Samuel Holbrook and Dr. Ephraim Wales.

BROOKLINE.

Annual meeting, March 11, 1776. *Moderator,* Hon. Benjamin White, Esq.; *Town Clerk,* Stephen Sharp; *Selectmen and Assessors,* Hon Benj. White, Esq.; *Messieurs* Isaac Child, John Goddard, Thomas Griggs and Col. Thomas Aspinwall; *Treasurer,* Hon. Benjamin

White, Esq.; *Committee of Correspondence, Inspection and Safety*, Lt. John Heath, Lt. Caleb Croft, Capt. Timothy Coroy; *School Committee*, Dr. William Aspinwall; *Constable and Collector*, Mr. Elnathan Winchester; *Wardens*, Samuel Croft, Moses White, Jr.; *Surveyors of Highways*, Mr. Samuel Croft, Mr. Samuel White, Mr. Joshua Woodward, Mr. Joshua Boylston.

COHASSET.

Annual meeting, March 4 and 11, 1776. *Moderator*, Abel Kent; *Town Clerk*, Thomas Lothrop; *Selectmen and Assessors*, Thomas Lothrop, Abel Kent, Ignatius Orcutt; *Treasurer*, Ignatius Orcutt; *Committee of Correspondence, Inspection and Safety*, Thomas Lincoln, Jonathan Beal, Jesse Stephenson, Lieut. Stephen Stodder, Jerom Stephenson, Lot Nichols, Thomas Brown, Daniel Tower, Daniel Nichols; *School Committee*, Aaron Pratt, Joseph Whitcomb, Hezekiah Hudson; *Collector of Taxes*, Aaron Pratt; *Constables*, Joseph Bates, Israel Whitcomb, Jr.; *Wardens*, Thomas Pratt, Lieut. Stodder; *Tythingman*, Ephraim Lincoln; *Culler of Fish and Packer of Mackerel and Culler of Hoops and Staves*, Micah Nichols; *Surveyor of Highways*, Job Turner, John Wilcutt, Obediah Lincoln, Isaac Burr.

DEDHAM.

Annual meeting, March 4, 1776. *Moderator*, Jonathan Metcalf; *Town Clerk*, Isaac Whiting; *Selectmen*, Isaac Whiting, George Gould, Mr. Samuel Damon, Nath'l Sumner, Esq., Mr. Eleazer Allen, Dr. Joseph Haven; *Treasurer*, Lieut. William Ellis; *Committee of Correspondence, Inspection and Safety*, Isaac Bullard, Joseph Whiting, Dr. Moses Barker, Capt. Daniel Gay, Mr. Lemuel Richards; *Wardens*, Moses Guild, Nathan Ellis, James Draper, Josiah Fisher; *Tythingmen*, Eleazer Everet, William Smith; *Constables*, Timothy Draper. Timothy Allen, Asa Everet, Ichabod Ellis, Benjamin Farrington (William Badlam, who was also chosen, refused to serve, and paid the sum of five pounds as a fine); *Surveyors of Ways*, Timothy Whiting, Jr., Lemuel Fales, Henry Wight, Abijah Draper, Nath'l Richards, Thomas Smith, Ebenezer Gay, Nath'l Kingsbury, Ebenezer Everet, Jr., Asa Everet, Joseph Turner, William Coney, Benjamin Weatherbee, John Richards, William Gay, Oliver Ellis, Asa Richards, David Cleaveland; *Grand Jurors for one year*, Col. Ebenezer Battle, Capt. John Eaton, Dr. Ralph Day.

DORCHESTER.

Annual meeting, March 4 and 11, 1776. *Moderator*, Dea. Samuel Topliff; *Town Clerk and Treasurer*, Noah Clap; *Selectmen and Assessors*, Noah Clap, Dea. Samuel Topliff, Mr. John Minott, Capt. Ebenezer Withington, Mr. Bernard Capen; *Constables*, Philip Withington, Samuel Holden; *Collector of Taxes*, Thomas Clap, Jr.; *Committee of Correspondence, Inspection and Safety*, John Minott, James Robinson, Abraham Wheeler; *Auditors*, Col. Samuel Pierce, Mr. Daniel Leeds; *Tythingmen*, Col. Ebenezer Clap, Joseph Clap; *Surveyors of the Ways*, John Humphrey, Thomas Moseley, Capt. Oliver Billings, Capt. John Robinson, Col. Samuel Pierce, John Capen, Jr., Seth Sumner, Joseph Clap.

DOVER (then Fourth Precinct of Dedham).

Annual meeting, March 18, 1776. *Precinct Clerk*, Joseph Haven; *Precinct Constables and Assessors*, Joseph Haven, Joseph Fisher, Jesse Ellis; *Precinct Treasurer*, William Whiting.

MEDFIELD.

Annual meeting, March 3, 1776. *Moderator*, Timothy Dwight; *Town Clerk and Treasurer*, John Baxter; *Selectmen*, John Baxter, Simon Plympton, Capt. Samuel Morse, John Fisher, Joseph Clark; *Assessors*, Daniel Perry, Eleazar Wheelock, Jacob Clark; *Committee of Correspondence, Inspection and Safety*, Mr. Daniel Perry, Mr. Barachius Mason, Mr. Moses Bulling, Capt. Ephraim Cheney; *Constable*, Seth Smith; *Wardens*, Joseph Baxter, David Lovell, Jr.; *Tythingmen*, David Plympton, Henry Harding; *Surveyors of Highways*, Nathan Adams, Jona. Smith, Jr., Abner Mason.

MEDWAY.

Annual meeting, March 4, 1776. *Moderator*, Moses Richardson; *Town Clerk*, Elijah Clarke; *Selectmen*, Capt. Jona. Adams, Lieut. Moses Adams; Joseph Partridge, Jr., Ens. Nathaniel Partridge, Ens. Joseph Lovell, Lieut. Asa Clark and Corl. James Penniman; *Assessors*, Samuel Hill, Jr., Henry Ellis, Stephen Adams; *Treasurer*, Henry Ellis; *Committee of Correspondence, Inspection and Safety*, Elijah Clarke, Major Josiah Fuller, Joshua Patredge, Simeon Cullen, James Boyden; *Constables*, John Wheeler, Amos Richardson, George Barber; *Wardens*, Stephen Clark, Nath'l Patredge; *Tythingmen*, Daniel Richardson, Lt. Moses Thompson; *Surveyors of Highways*, John Morse, Capt. Job Plimpton, Henry Daniels, Capt. Thomas Metcalf, Lt. Nathaniel Clark, Lt. Ab n. Harding.

MILTON.

Annual meeting, March 11, 1776. *Moderator*, David Rawson; *Town Clerk*, Amariah Blake; *Selectmen*, Capt. Ebenezer Tucker, Amariah Blake, Mr. Ralph Houghton, Dea. Joseph Clap, Mr. William Pierce; *Treasurer*, William Tucker; *Constables*, Mr. Samuel Henshaw, Mr. Arthur Adams; *Committee of Correspondence, Inspection and Safety*, Mr. William Badcock, Major Joseph Badcock, Mr. John Swift, Mr. Lemuel How, Mr. Stephen Badcock; *Surveyors of Highways*, Mr. William Badcock, Mr. Josiah Vose, Capt. Daniel Vose, Mr. William Pierce, Dea. Joseph Clap, Mr. Nathan Vose, Mr. Ebenezer Tucker, Jr., Capt. John Bradley, Mr. Josiah Marshall, Mr. Joseph Tucker, Mr. Moses Fairbanks, Mr. Nathan Ford; *Wardens*, Mr. Joseph Jones, Mr. John Crehoro; *Tythingmen*, Major Joseph Badcock, Mr. Cornelius Gulliver.

NEEDHAM.

Annual meeting, March 11, 1776. *Moderator*, Dea. John Fisher; *Town Clerk*, Lt. Robert Fuller; *Treasurer*, Mr. Amos Fuller; *Selectmen*, Lt. Robert Fuller, Mr. Timothy Nowell, Mr. William Fuller, Mr. Amos Fuller, Mr. Silas Alden; *Assessors*, Robert Fuller, Jr., Capt. Robert Smith, Jonathan Kingsbury, Jr.; *Constables*, Nathaniel Ware, Ephraim Stevens, Joseph Drury; *Committee of Correspondence, Inspection and Safety*, Mr. John Slack, Mr. Michael Metcalf, Mr. William Smith; *Surveyors of Highways*, Lt. Samuel Townsend, Thomas Fuller, Capt. Caleb King-berry, John Slack, Timothy Fisher, Ephraim Stevens, Moses Fisk, Lt. Moses Bullard; *Wardens*, Samuel Alden, Josiah Newell, Jr., Benjamin Ward, John Slack; *Tythingmen*, Ensign Eliakim Cook, Mr. Jonathan Dewing, Mr. Ebenezer Newell.

ROXBURY.

Annual meeting, March 4, 1776. *Moderator*, Mr. Noah Perrin; *Town Clerk*, William Gridley; *Treasurer*, Mr. Noah Perrin; *Selectmen*, Maj. Nath'l Ruggles, Dea. David Weld, Col. Eleazer Weld, Col. Aaron Davis, Mr. Increase Sumner; *Constables*, Mr. Joshua Bowen, Mr. John Davis, Mr. Ebenezer Weld; *Collectors*, Mr. Joshua Bowen, Capt. William Draper, Lieut. Lemuel May; *Committee of Correspondence, Inspection and Safety*, Robert Pierpont, Esq., Capt. Thomas Mayo, Capt. Ebenezer Wales, Dea. Joseph Brower, Capt. Joseph Williams; *Auditors*, Col. Aaron Davis, Maj. Nath'l Ruggles, Capt. Joseph Williams; *Tythingmen*, Capt. Jeremiah Parker, Mr. Peleg Heath, Mr. Abijah Seaver, Mr. Isaac Williams, Mr. Ezra Davis, Mr. John Davis, *tertius*; *Surveyors of Highways*, Mr. John Brewer, Mr. John Davis Williams, Robt. Pierpont, Esq., Capt. Samuel Heath, Capt. Lemuel Child, Mr. Samuel White, Dea. Nath'l Weld, Mr. Joseph Richards, Jr., Mr. Paul Draper, Mr. Henry Williams, Mr. William Dudley.

SHARON.

Annual meeting, March 11, 1776. *Moderator*, Edmund Quincy; *Town Clerk and Treasurer*, Benjamin Hewins; *Selectmen and Assessors*, Benjamin Hewins, Mr. Ebenezer Hill, Capt. Edward Bridge Savel; *Committee of Correspondence, Inspection and Safety*, Edmund Quincy, Job Swift, Ebenezer Capen, Nathaniel Kingsbury, Nathaniel Clark; *Constables*, Samuel Billings, 2d, Nehemiah Carpenter; *Surveyors of Ways*, Capt. Ebenezer Tisdale, Elijah Baker, Benjamin Savel, Solomon Gay, Samuel Gould, Ebenezer Pettee, Jacob Leonard, Levi Morse, John Comings, Josiah Robbins, Jonathan Billing, Jr., Supply Belcher, William Lowis; *Wardens*, Oliver Everet, Benjamin Randall; *Tythingman*, Joshua Whittemore.

STOUGHTON.

Annual meeting, March 4, 1776. *Moderator*, Mr. Joseph Billing; *Town Clerk*, George Crossman; *Selectmen*, Messrs. Benjamin Gill, Robert Swan, William Shaller, Jonathan Capen, Adam Blackman; *Treasurer*, Esq. Dunbar; *Committee of Correspondence, Inspection and Safety*, Elijah Dunbar, Peter Talbot, Josiah Pratt, Theophilus Curtis, John

Kenny, Christopher Wadsworth, David Lyon; *Wardens*, Henry Baily, John Holmes, 2d; *Tythingmen*, Elijah Crane, James Pope, Moses Waills; *Constables*, Nathaniel Fisher, David Vinton; *Surveyors of Highways*, John Spear, Samuel Blackman, James Endicott, Elijah Upham, William Wheeler, Elihu Crane, Samuel Tucker, Redman Spur, Thomas Moore, Hezekiah Gay, Samuel Shepard, Samuel Bisbee, Seth Morton, John Haward, Aliezer Packard, Nathaniel Lindfield, Simeon Leach, Peter Gay, Samuel Commine, Turrel Allen, Asa Morse, David Capen, John Wadsworth.

WALPOLE.

Annual meeting, March 4, 1776. *Moderator*, Enoch Ellis; *Town Clerk and Treasurer*, Benjamin Kingsbury; *Selectmen*, Col. Seth Kingsbury, Major Seth Bullard, Joseph Day, Capt. Jeremiah Smith, Benjamin Kingsbury, Jr.; *Committee of Correspondence, Inspection and Safety*, Capt. Joseph Hartshorne, Enoch Ellis, Lieut. John Boyden, Nicholas Harris, Nathan Kingsbury; *Constables*, Ezekiel Boyden, Daniel Fisher; *Surveyors of Highways*, Jacob Clap, Benjamin Boyden, Henry Smith, Jr., Jacob Gay, Isaac Lewis, Richard Hartshorne; *Tythingman*, Joshua Allen.

WEYMOUTH.

Annual meeting, March 11, 1776. *Moderator*, Hon. James Humphrey, Esq.; *Town Clerk and Treasurer*, Josiah Waterman; *Selectmen and Assessors*, Hon. James Humphrey, Esq., Cotton Tufts, Esq., Nathaniel Bayley, Esq.; *Committee of Correspondence, Inspection, and Safety*, Cotton Tufts, Esq., Capt. James White, Col. Solomon Lovell, Nathaniel Bayley, Esq., Mr. Daniel Blancher; *Wardens*, Mr. Daniel Torrey, Capt. Thomas Nash, Capt. John Holbrook, Jr., Mr. Abner Pratt; *Tythingmen*, Mr. Matthew Porter; Mr. John Jones; *Constables*, Ensign Noah Tirrell, Capt. Samuel Arnold, Mr. Jacob Joy, Ezra Tirrell, Mr. Ebenezer Agan; *Surveyors of Highways*, Lieut. Joshua Torrey, Capt. Asa White, Capt. Eliphaz Weston, Mr. Matthew Pratt, Lieut. Asa Dyer, Major John Vining, Deacon Samuel Blancher, Lieut. Hezekiah White, Major Thomas Hollise, Mr. John Reed, Jr.

WRENTHAM.

Annual meeting, March 4th, 1776. *Moderator*, Mr. Samuel Lethbridge; *Town Clerk*, John Messenger; *Treasurer*, Asa Whiting; *Selectmen*, David Fisher, Lemuel Kollock, John Hall, Nathan Man, Samuel Allen; *Assessors*, Nathan Comstock, Jacob Pond, Joseph Hawes; *Committee of Correspondence, Inspection, and Safety*, Samuel Fisher, Dr. Ebenezer Daggett, Deacon Thomas Man, Joseph Fairbanks, John Crago, Daniel Holbrook, Hezekiah Fisher, Joseph Hawes, Capt. Asa Fairbank, Capt. Perez Cushing, Mr. Joseph Whiting, Jr.; *Constables*, Daniel Pond, Jacob Shepard, Joshua Grant, Lieut. Joseph Woodward, Simeon Fisher, Joseph Pond, Jr.; *Wardens*, David Fisher, Jeremiah Hall, Samuel Hawes, Joseph Hill, John Richardson; *Surveyors of Ways*, James Holbrook, Nathan Blake, James Smith, John Everet, Samuel Thurston, John Chever, Benjamin Ray, Daniel Farrington, James Chever, Elisha Hawes, Timothy Fisher, Jabez Ware, John Clark, Solomon Blake, Jr., Elisha Richardson, Joseph Gould, Stephen Blake, John Robbins, Asa Aldrich; *Tythingmen*, Robert Blake, 3d, Aaron Kingsbury, Elijah Ware, Obadiah Harris, Joseph Grant.

ANNEXATIONS

AND CHANGES IN TOWN LINES IN THE COUNTY OF NORFOLK, FROM 1793 TO 1877.

June 20, 1793. County of Norfolk established. — Chap. 72, Acts 1792.
February 23, 1797. Town of Canton set off from Stoughton. — 2 Sp. Laws, 118.
June 22, 1797. Boundary line between Needham and Natick changed. — 2 Sp. Laws, 177.
February 8, 1798. Part of Stoughton annexed to Bridgewater. — Chap. 10, Acts 1798.
June 21, 1803. An island in Charles river, between Needham and Newton, annexed to Newton. — 3 Sp. Laws, 224.

February 28, 1804. Part of Sharon annexed to Walpole (Ebenezer Baker farm). — 3 Sp. Laws, 322.
March 6, 1804. Part of Dorchester annexed to Boston. — 3 Sp. Laws, 369.
June 21, 1811. Part of Sharon annexed to Walpole (12¾ acres, belonging to heirs of Jonathan Fales). — Chap. 14, Acts 1811.
June 21, 1811. Part of Dedham annexed to Walpole (Isaac Smith's and John Ellis, Jr.'s estates). — Chap. 25, Acts 1811.
February 10, 1814. Part of Dorchester annexed to Quincy (at Squantum and the Farms). — Chap. 105, Acts 1813.
February 3, 1819. Boundary line between Wrentham and Foxborough established. — Chap. 44, Acts 1818.
February 12, 1819. Part of Dorchester annexed to Quincy (Caleb Faxon's estate). — Chap 70, Acts 1818.
February 21, 1820. Boundary line between Dorchester and Quincy changed (at Squantum). — Chap 124, Acts 1819.
June 14, 1823. Part of Scituate annexed to Cohasset (homesteads of Amasa Bailey and Caleb Bailey, Jr., about 90 acres). — Chap. 28, Acts 1823.
February 22, 1825. Part of Brookline annexed to Boston, and boundary line established. — Chap. 90, Acts 1824.
March 3, 1829. Boundary line between Medway and Holliston changed. — Chap. 133, Acts of 1828.
February 18, 1830. Boundary line between Wrentham and Attleboro' established. — Chap. 48, Acts 1829.
February 7, 1831. Part of Wrentham annexed to Foxborough. — Chap. 36, Acts 1830.
June 17, 1831. Part of Dedham annexed to Dorchester (28 a., 1 q., 29 r., owned by Abel Kenney). — Chap. 36, Acts 1831.
February 23, 1832. Boundary lines between towns of Bellingham, Franklin and Medway straightened. — Chap. 48, Acts 1832.
January 30, 1833. Boundary line between Sharon and Foxborough established. — Chap. 15, Acts 1833.
March 27, 1833, and March 28, 1834. Part of Foxborough annexed to Walpole. — Chap. 198, Acts 1833, Chap. 138, Acts 1834.
March 25, 1834. Thompson's Island set off from Dorchester and annexed to Boston. — Chap. 102, Acts 1834.
March 19, 1836. Boundary line between Boston and Roxbury established. — Chap. 37, Acts 1836.
May 19, 1837. Boundary line between Boston and Roxbury changed. — Chap. 202, Acts 1837.
May 23, 1838. Part of Newton annexed to Roxbury. — Chap. 167, Acts 1838.
March 13, 1839. Boundary line between Franklin and Medway changed. — Chap. 48, Acts 1839.
April 19, 1840. Boundary line between Scituate and Cohasset changed. — Chap. 58, Acts 1840.
March 25, 1844. Part of Roxbury annexed to Brookline. — Chap. 38, Acts 1844.
April 30, 1847. Boundary line between Weymouth and Abington established. — Chap. 138, Acts 1847.
April 30, 1847. Part of Canton annexed to Stoughton. — Chap. 147, Acts 1847.
February 28, 1850. Part of Sharon annexed to Foxborough. — Chap. 47, Acts 1850.
June 2, 1850. Part of Roxbury annexed to Boston. — Chap. 281, Acts 1850.
May 24, 1851. Town of West Roxbury set off from City of Roxbury. — Chap. 250, Acts 1851.
April 21, 1852. Part of Dedham annexed to West Roxbury. — Chap. 136, Acts 1852.
April 30, 1852. Part of Dedham annexed to Walpole. — Chap. 166, Acts 1852.
June 1, 1855. Part of Dorchester annexed to Quincy (at Squantum). — Chap. 267, Acts 1855.
May 21, 1855. Part of Dorchester annexed to Boston (Washington Village). — Chap. 468, Acts 1855.
April 24, 1856. Part of Braintree annexed to Quincy. — Chap. 132, Acts 1856.
April 26, 1859. Boundary line between Boston and Roxbury changed and established. — Chap. 210, Acts 1859.
May 8, 1860. Boundary line between Boston and Roxbury changed. — Chap. 172, Acts 1860.
April 20, 1861. Boundary line between Abington and Randolph established. — Chap. 86, Acts 1861.

April 25, 1864.   Part of Stoughton annexed to Sharon. — Chap. 119, Acts 1864.
January 6, 1868.   Roxbury annexed to Boston. — Chap. 359, Acts 1867.
April 22, 1868.   Town of Hyde Park set off from Dorchester, Dedham and Milton. — Chaps. 139 and 167, Acts 1868.
January 3, 1870.   Dorchester annexed to Boston. — Chap. 349, Acts 1869.
February 23, 1870.   Town of Norfolk set off from Wrentham, Franklin, Medway and Walpole. — Chap. 35, Acts 1870.
April 2, 1870.   Boundary line between Boston and West Roxbury changed. — Chap. 146, Acts 1870.
November 4, 1870.   Part of Brookline annexed to Boston. — Chap. 374, Acts 1870.
April 19, 1871.   Boundary line between Norfolk and Wrentham established. — Chap. 201, Acts 1871.
February 23, 1872.   Town of Norwood set off from Dedham and Walpole. — Chap. 32, Acts 1872.
February 27, 1872.   Boundary line between Dover and Walpole established. — Chap. 47, Acts 1872.
February 29, 1872.   Town of Holbrook set off from Randolph. — Chap. 61, Acts 1872.
March 7, 1872.   Boundary line between Mendon and Bellingham established. — Chap. 69, Acts 1872.
April 27, 1872.   Boundary line between Brookline and Boston changed. — Chap. 267, Acts 1872.
January 5, 1874.   West Roxbury annexed to Boston. — Chap. 314, Acts 1873.

NECROLOGY OF 1876.

BRAINTREE.

CALEB HOLLIS, for several years a Selectman of the town, died February 9, aged 81 years, 1 month, 23 days.
JOSEPH R. FRAZIER, Chairman of the Board of Selectmen for 1876, died Sept. 15, aged 65 years.

BROOKLINE.

GEORGE F. HOMER, Esq., Counsellor-at-Law, died of heart disease, April 14, aged 60 years, 9 months, 20 days. He was born in Boston, was graduated at the Latin School, and at Amherst College in 1834. He early went to Brookline, where he was a member of the School Committee, Trustee of the Public Library from 1857 to 1875, and Representative to the General Court in 1867.
DR. WALTER CHANNING, for many years an eminent physician in Boston, died July 27, aged 90 years, 3 months, 12 days.
COL. THOMAS ASPINWALL, a native of Brookline, died in Boston, August 11, aged 90 years, 2 months, 19 days. He was a son of the distinguished Dr. William Aspinwall, and was born May 23, 1786. He was graduated at Harvard College in 1804. In the war of 1812 he rendered conspicuous services, and in the memorable sortie from Fort Erie lost his left arm and was otherwise severely wounded. In 1816 he was appointed, by President Monroe, Consul at London, where he remained until displaced by President Pierce, in 1854, when he removed to Boston, where he continued to reside until his death.
DEACON DAVID COOLIDGE, died Nov. 30, aged 87 years, 8 months, 7 days. He was born in Watertown, and was a grandson of Joseph Coolidge, who was one of the patriots who fell at the battle of Lexington, April 19, 1775. Dea. Coolidge was a resident of Brookline, at the same place on Harvard street, for more than 50 years, and was a deacon of the Allston Baptist Church. He leaves seven sons.

CANTON.

LYMAN KINSLEY, for many years a prominent citizen of Canton, died in Cambridge, March 15, aged 68 years. Mr. Kinsley was born in Canton, March 7th, 1808, and succeeded to the business of his father, Adam Kinsley, as a manufacturer of iron, in which he acquired great prominence. He represented the town in the Legislature of 1849. He was a generous and public-spirited man, and was highly esteemed.
HON. JOHN S. ELDRIDGE, for many years a well-known resident of Canton, died in New York, March 23, aged 56 years and 6 months. He was born in Yarmouth, Sept. 23d, 1819, and after finishing his course of studies passed through the Law School at Cambridge in 1842, and

commenced the practice of law in Boston. He soon after became connected with the railroad interests of New England, to which he devoted the remainder of his life. He was for several years Trustee of the Vermont Central Railroad, and subsequently President of the Erie Railroad in New York, and the Hartford and Erie Railroad in Massachusetts. He removed to Canton about 1853, where he purchased a very large estate and became an extensive breeder of Jersey stock. He represented the town in the Legislature of 1859 and '60, and in 1865 was a Senator from Norfolk County. He was President of the Norfolk Agricultural Society in 1869, '70 and '71.

HORACE GUILD, a prominent farmer in Canton, died April 22, aged 73 years and five months. He was a native of South Dedham, but went to Canton in 1827 and became the owner of a large farm, of which he was a highly successful cultivator. He was for many years a member of the Board of Selectmen, Assessors, and Overseers of the Poor.

LIEUT. WILLIAM MCKENDRY, Jr , of Canton, died at the Massachusetts General Hospital in Boston, August 9, aged 54 years. He was born in Canton, August 25th, 1825, and after receiving a school education enlisted as a sailor before the mast in an East Indiaman, and before many years became captain. In the war of the rebellion he enlisted in the naval service under Farragut, where he achieved distinction, and at its close was transferred to the revenue service. Exposure in the service brought on disease which assumed so serious a form that by the advice of his family physician he was carried to the hospital, where he seemed to be recovering, when, without warning, and whilst sitting in his chair, he suddenly expired.

HENRY FISHER, a native of Canton, died in that town, Sept. 11, aged 71 years and 5 months.

NATHANIEL WENTWORTH, a native of Canton, died in that town, Nov. 29, aged 81 years and 5 months.

CAPT. WILLIAM MCKENDRY, a native of Canton, died in that town. Dec. 30, aged 80 years and 10 months.

DEDHAM.

JOHN I. SCHERMERHORN, Captain of Marines, U. S. N., died of rheumatism of the heart, January 16, aged 52.

MRS. PATTY E. BAKER, widow of the late High Sheriff, John Baker, died of old age, February 14, aged 85 years, 3 months, 3 days.

COL. LUTHER EATON, died of pneumonia, May 17, aged 73 years, 10 months.

JEREMIAH CREHORE, died of old age, May 24, aged 80 years, 5 months, 4 days.

HEZEKIAH WHITING, died of Bright's disease of the kidneys, May 31, aged 71 years, 6 months.

MRS. AMANDA N., wife of Henry Hitchings, and daughter of the late Frederick Taft, died of consumption, August 21, aged 49 years, 11 days. Mrs. H. was for many years a much respected teacher in West Roxbury.

HENRY CORMERAIS, died September 3, aged 56 years, 4 months, 10 days.

MRS. MARIA M., widow of the late Rev. John Lathrop, Chaplain U. S. N., died October 16, aged 74 years, 5 months.

MRS. CARRIE E., wife of Alfred Hewins, died of typhoid fever, October 21, aged 30 years, 3 months. "A spirit pure and bright, with something of an angel light."

MRS. MARY K., widow of the late Thomas Sherwin, and daughter of the late Col. Daniel L. Gibbens of Boston, died of paralysis, October 27, aged 65 years, 10 months, 6 days.

JOHN SKILLEN HOUGHTON, a native of Dedham, died at Philadelphia, of apoplexy, December 11, in the 64th year of his age. He learned the trade of a printer of Herman Mann, Sen., and before his majority edited and published the "Dedham Patriot and Canton Gazette," which had a large circulation. In 1839 and '40 he was the Washington correspondent of the Boston "Atlas." He was also one of the publishers and editors of the Boston "Daily Mail." He afterwards removed to Philadelphia, where he acquired a handsome property, and became the President of the Pennsylvania Horticultural Society, in the operations of which he took great interest.

DORCHESTER.

JOHN MEARS, for many years a prominent citizen of Dorchester, died April 29, aged 80 years, 7 months, 8 days. He was born in Roxbury, September 21, 1795, but when a few months old his parents removed to Dorchester, where he ever after lived. When 25 years of age he was chosen treasurer of the town, and continued in the office for seventeen successive years, and filled various offices of trust and responsibility for many years afterward. In 1831 he became a partner with the late David and Lorenzo Prouty in the manufacture of ploughs, and it was by that firm that the celebrated "centre-draft plough" was invented, which obtained the bronze medal at the World's Fair in London, the great gold medal from Nicholas I., Emperor of all the Russias, and the first prize from the Massachusetts State Agricultural Society at Worcester. This centre-draft principle has since been adopted by nearly every plough manufacturer in the country. Mr. Mears first successfully used and brought into operation in Boston cooking stoves using anthracite coal as fuel, and many of his cooking and parlor stoves are yet in use. He was highly esteemed for his business capacity and strict integrity.

REV. A. R. BAKER, D.D., died April 30th, aged 72 years. He was a native of Franklin, and was graduated at Amherst College in 1835. He studied theology at Andover, and was settled over Evangelical churches in Medford, Lynn, Needham and South Boston, but had resided in Dorchester several years. He was a man of decided literary culture, but of very conservative views on religious and political topics.

DOVER.

LUTHER RICHARDS, for many years a prominent citizen of Dover, died of cancer, at the Massachusetts General Hospital, in Boston, July 1, aged 65 years. He was born in Dover, April

27th, 1809. He was for many years Town Clerk and Selectman, and was a member of the Constitutional Convention in 1853. He was for many years Superintendent of the Unitarian Sunday School in Dover. During the last years of his life he resided in Boston, where he was engaged in the leather business. He was an honest, kind-hearted, public-spirited man.

ABNER L. SMITH, died of heart disease, August 15, aged 53 years, 6 months, 23 days. Mr. Smith was Town Clerk of Dover for 17 years, resigning April 18th on account of sickness. He was Chairman of the Board of Selectmen nine years, Assessor two years, member of the School Committee two years, Constable twenty years, and in 1869 represented the towns of Dover, Medfield and Needham in the General Court. He was a most useful and respected citizen.

HOLBROOK.

HON. ZENAS FRENCH, died November 10, aged 78 years, 9 months, 3 days. Mr. French was one of the Selectmen of Randolph for seventeen years, and represented the town in the General Court in 1837 and 1839. In 1852 he was a Senator from Norfolk County.

MEDWAY.

DEACON PAUL DANIELS, born in Medway July 7, 1789, died February 15th, aged 86 years, 7 months. He was for many years prominent in town and church affairs, and represented the town in the General Court in 1833, '34, '35 and '40.

REV. SEWALL HARDING, a native of Medway, and for many years pastor of the church in the East parish, died in Auburndale, April 12, aged 83 years. He was a graduate of Union College in 1818.

HON. WARREN LOVERING, died August 21, aged 80 years. Mr. Lovering was born in Framingham, but early removed to Medway, where he passed his life. He was graduated at Brown University in 1817, and soon commenced the practice of law in Medway Village. He was for several years Chairman of the School Committee, and represented the town in the General Court in 1826, '27, '29, '30, '31, '32, '36, '47. He was a member of the Executive Council of Governor Everett in 1836, '37 and '38. He was appointed Bank Commissioner by Governor Everett in 1839, and held the office until it was abolished. The latter years of his life were passed in retirement.

MILTON.

PHILARMON RUGGLES, a native of Walpole, N. H., died April 15, of heart disease, aged 78 years.

MRS. MARY DUSTIN, a native and resident of Milton, died in the Isle of Wight, of consumption, Nov. 20, aged 37 years.

NORFOLK.

JOEL H. ROBINSON, a well-known farmer, died May 14, aged 69 years.

NORWOOD.

REV. HARRISON G. PARK, died June 26, aged 69 years, 11 months. Mr. Park was son of Rev. Dr. Calvin Park, of Stoughton, and brother of Prof. Edwards A. Park, of Andover. He was a graduate of Brown University in 1824, and for many years was a preacher of the Trinitarian faith. The latter years of his life were devoted to the temperance cause.

HON. JOSEPH DAY died of apoplexy, September 26th. Mr. Day was a native of Walpole, but removed to South Dedham at an early age, where for many years he carried on the currying business, in which he amassed a handsome property. He took an active interest in town affairs, and was a representative to the General Court in 1845 and '46. He represented the Second Norfolk District in the State Senate in 1861 and '62. He was elected a Director of the Dedham Bank in 1855 and continued in the office until his death. He was 69 years of age.

QUINCY.

JEFFREY R. BRACKETT, died October 26, aged 61 years.

FANNY C. ADAMS, aged 2 years and 8 months, died April 11th, and JOHN Q. ADAMS, JR., aged 14 years, died April 12th. They were children of John Quincy and Fanny C. Adams, and died of diphtheria.

RANDOLPH.

HON. JAMES MAGUIRE, a native of South Carolina, but for many years a prominent boot manufacturer in Randolph, died of paralysis, Feb. 18, aged 69 years, 3 months, 27 days. Mr. Maguire was a Senator for Norfolk County in 1846 and '47.

ATHERTON WALES died April 20, aged 69 years, 4 months, 8 days. Mr. Wales was President of the Randolph Savings Bank from April 1, 1858, until his death.

JOHN ALDEN, a prominent boot manufacturer, died of kidney disease, August 2d, aged 76 years, 7 months, 18 days.

WILLIAM H. WARREN, died August 3, aged 48 years, 7 months, 27 days. For the past eleven years he was a Deputy Sheriff for the County of Norfolk.

REV. BENJAMIN WHEELER, died of heart disease, Aug. 27, aged 69 years, 5 months, 11 days.

ROXBURY.

HON. GEORGE FROST, died March 23d, aged 63 years and 3 months. He was born in Dorchester, Dec. 11th, 1819, and for many years had been the proprietor of a large bakery in Roxbury. In 1859 and '60 he was a member of the Board of Aldermen of Roxbury, and in 1864 and '65 a Senator for Norfolk County. He was for eight years a Trustee of Forest Hills Cemetery, and long a prominent member of the Universalist denomination. He died, after a lingering illness, of consumption. He enjoyed in a marked degree the respect and confidence of the community.

SHARON.

MRS. MARY HEWINS, widow of the late Dea. Joel Hewins, died April 12th, aged 85 years.

DEACON DANIEL PETTEE, died Sept. 13, aged 70 years. He was a native of Sharon, and for 26 years had been deacon in the Orthodox Church. He was Selectman for two years, and a useful and honored citizen.

MRS. OLIVE HEWINS, widow of the late Elijah Hewins, Esq., died September 19th, aged 90 years.

WALPOLE.

CAPT. NATHANIEL Y. FRENCH, died of paralysis, March 9, aged 65 years, 9 months.

JOEL FISHER FALES, a well-known machinist and inventor, died April 2, aged 45 years, 6 months, 3 days.

JASON BOYDEN, died August 22, aged 77 years, 9 months.

LEWIS CLAP, died October 8, aged 87 years, 1 month.

DEACON JEREMIAH ALLEN, died Dec. 20, aged 60 years. He represented the town in the General Court in 1856 and '57.

WRENTHAM.

NANCY WARE HAWES, died August 28, aged 96 years, 8 months, 6 days. Mrs. Hawes was the daughter of Capt. Nathaniel Ware and sister of the late Hon. Jairus Ware, and was born in Wrentham, Dec. 22d, 1779. In 1807 she married George Hawes, who was for many years prominent both in town and county, serving as colonel in the war of 1812, as Representative to the General Court in 1828, and Senator from Norfolk County in 1834. She survived her husband nearly forty years. One who had known her long and well paid this fitting tribute to her character: "Even since the infirmities of age came on, the mind of this venerable woman retained its freshness and buoyancy of spirit. Her keen sense of humor, her quaint drollery, was full of sound, good sense and real wisdom, and her words have been stored in many hearts. Her memory, which scores of years did not seem to enfeeble, helped to make her mind one of unusual quality and power. In person she must have been beautiful in youth, and was ever of commanding presence." Her pastor, in years gone by, thus wrote of her: "She was one of the elect and grand persons of that grand old town; one of those few who constitute the charm and crown of our New England towns, whose loss we can ill-afford in these days. Let us consider what she has been and what she still is, a character so strong, so sincere, so royal, and yet so humble."

APPENDIX.

The following valuable statistical matter is taken from the admirable and exhaustive Census of the State of Massachusetts for 1875, prepared and arranged under the direction of Hon. Carroll D. Wright, Chief of the Bureau of Statistics for the State. A portion of the matter relating to the manufactures of the County was kindly furnished by him in advance of the publication of the volume of the Census devoted to manufactures, for which, and for other attentions, the compiler desires to return his acknowledgments.

NORFOLK COUNTY.

[Incorporated March 26, 1793. Loss of population since the Census of 1865, 27,985; owing to annexation to Boston of Dorchester, Roxbury and West Roxbury, with a population of 78,000. Otherwise Norfolk County would have shown a gain of 50,015.]

BELLINGHAM. — Nov. 27, 1719. From parts of Dedham, Wrentham and Mendon. Boundary between Bellingham, Franklin and Medway established Feb. 23, 1832.

BRAINTREE. — May 13, 1640. See *Quincy* and *Randolph*.

BROOKLINE. — Nov. 13, 1705. Part of Roxbury annexed to Brookline, Feb. 24, 1844. Part of Brookline annexed to Boston, May 8, 1874. Gain, 1,413 over 5,262; due to building enterprise.

CANTON. — Feb. 23, 1797. Northerly part of Stoughton. See *Stoughton*. Gain, 874; from manufactures.

COHASSET. — April 26, 1770. Second Precinct of Hingham.

DEDHAM. — Sept. 8, 1636. Boundary between Dedham and Dover defined March 7, 1791. Part of Dedham annexed to Dorchester, June 17, 1831. See *Bellingham, Dover, Needham, Medfield, Walpole, Hyde Park* and *Norwood*. Loss, 1,439; from loss of South Dedham, set off as town of Norwood, 1872, and territory set off to Hyde Park, 1868. Chief loss from South Dedham, now Norwood, the population of which is 1,749.

DOVER. — July 7, 1784. Part of Dedham incorporated as a district, July 7, 1784, and as a town, March 31, 1836. Boundary between Dover and Dedham defined March 7, 1791; between Dover and Walpole changed Feb. 27, 1872.

FOXBOROUGH. — June 10, 1778. From parts of Wrentham, Walpole, Stoughton and Stoughtonham (Sharon). Parts of Stoughton and Sharon annexed to Foxborough, March 12, 1796; part of Wrentham annexed Feb. 7, 1831; and part of Sharon, Feb. 28, 1850. See *Sharon, Walpole* and *Wrentham*.

FRANKLIN. — March 2, 1778. Westerly part of Wrentham. Part of Medway annexed to Franklin, June 27, 1792. Boundary between Franklin and Medway established Nov. 3, 1792, and Feb. 23, 1832. See *Bellingham* and *Norfolk*.

HOLBROOK. — Feb. 29, 1872. Part of Randolph. See *Randolph*.

HYDE PARK. — April 22, 1868. From parts of Dorchester, Dedham and Milton. Population, 6,316, which the towns named lose. Hyde Park has lost since 1873, by the burning of a large woollen mill, and the shutting down of a rolling mill and a machine shop.

MEDFIELD. — May 23, 1651. Dedham Village. See *Medway*.

MEDWAY. — Oct. 24, 1713. Part of Medfield. Boundary between Medway and Sherborn established March 3, 1792. See *Bellingham, Franklin* and *Norfolk* in this county, and *Holliston* in Middlesex. Gain, 1,023 over 3,219; due to establishment of several boot manufactories.

MILTON. — May 7, 1662. See *Hyde Park*. Small loss, from loss of territory to Hyde Park.

NEEDHAM. — Nov. 5, 1711. Part of Dedham. Boundary between Needham and Natick, changed June 22, 1797. See *Newton*. Gain, 1,755 over 2,793; from general development of the building and manufacturing interests of the town, and perhaps from the establishment of Wellesley College.

NORFOLK. — Feb. 23, 1870. From parts of Wrentham, Franklin, Medway and Walpole. Boundary between it and Wrentham changed in 1871. Population, 920, which the towns named lose.

NORWOOD. — Feb. 23, 1872. From that part of Dedham called South Dedham and small part of Walpole. Population, 1,749, taken chiefly from Dedham, which see.

QUINCY. — Feb. 23, 1792. North Precinct of Braintree. Parts of Dorchester annexed to Quincy, Feb. 12, 1819, and May 2, 1855, and a part of Braintree, April 24, 1856. Gain, 2,437 over 6,718; from building operations and the desirableness of Quincy as a residence.

RANDOLPH. — March 9, 1793. Part of Braintree. Portion of boundary defined June 22, 1811. Part set off into new town of Holbrook, which see. Loss, 1,679; from loss of territory as above.

SHARON. — June 20, 1765. Formerly Stoughtonham, Second Precinct of Stoughton. Part of Stoughton annexed to Sharon, Feb. 12, 1792; also, March 26, 1864. Boundary between Sharon

and Foxborough established Jan. 30, 1833. Part of Sharon annexed to Walpole, May 1, 1874. See *Foxborough* and *Walpole.* Small loss, from loss of territory in 1874 as above.
STOUGHTON. — Dec. 22, 1726. Part of Dorchester. Part of Canton annexed to Stoughton, March 31, 1847. See *Canton, Foxborough* and *Sharon.*
WALPOLE — Dec. 10, 1724. Part of Dedham. Parts of Sharon annexed to Walpole, Feb. 28, 1804, and June 21, 1811; part of Dedham, June 21, 1811; and parts of Foxborough, March 27, 1833, and March 28, 1834. Line between Dover and Walpole changed Feb. 27, 1872. See *Foxborough, Norfolk* and *Norwood.*
WEYMOUTH. — Sept. 2, 1635. Boundary between Weymouth and Abington established March 31, 1847.
WRENTHAM. — Oct. 15, 1673. Boundary between Wrentham and Foxborough established Feb. 5, 1819; between Wrentham and Norfolk changed in 1871. Part set off to Norfolk, Feb. 23, 1870. See *Attleborough, Bellingham, Foxborough, Franklin* and *Norfolk.* Loss, about 700; from loss of territory as above.

POLLS AND VOTERS.

TOWNS.	Ratable Polls.	Native Voters.	Naturalized Voters.	Total Voters.	TOWNS.	Ratable Polls.	Native Voters.	Naturalized Voters.	Total Voters.
Bellingham	360	271	24	295	Needham	1,252	698	217	915
Braintree	1,190	829	176	1,005	Norfolk	254	169	27	196
Brookline	1.720	815	432	1,247	Norwood	474	312	87	399
Canton	999	506	227	733	Quincy	2,569	1,548	428	1,976
Cohasset	611	462	35	497	Randolph	1,185	816	243	1,059
Dedham	1,375	824	291	1,115	Sharon	373	283	32	315
Dover	188	126	22	148	Stoughton	1,306	923	228	1,151
Foxborough	800	640	55	695	Walpole	629	435	86	521
Franklin	755	494	74	568	Weymouth	2,773	2,131	293	2,424
Holbrook	509	391	37	428	Wrentham	660	503	46	549
Hyde Park	1,569	967	270	1,237					
Medfield	326	287	8	295					
Medway	1,100	700	165	865					
Milton	734	491	88	579	Totals	23,741	15,621	3,591	19,212

FAMILIES AND DWELLING-HOUSES.

TOWNS.	Dwellings Occupied.	Dwellings Unoccupied.	Total Dwelling-houses.	Families.	TOWNS.	Dwellings Occupied.	Dwellings Unoccupied.	Total Dwelling-houses.	Families.
Bellingham	250	7	257	319	Needham	781	41	822	934
Braintree	728	20	748	929	Norfolk	170	11	181	219
Brookline	1.065	30	1,095	1,338	Norwood	364	4	368	392
Canton	632	13	645	859	Quincy	1,507	27	1,534	1,941
Cohasset	421	75	496	523	Randolph	724	28	752	893
Dedham	1,124	42	1,166	1,253	Sharon	291	6	297	335
Dover	132	7	139	151	Stoughton	917	10	927	1,148
Foxborough	582	12	594	759	Walpole	428	19	447	520
Franklin	479	15	494	636	Weymouth	1,730	29	1,759	2,188
Holbrook	327	2	329	411	Wrentham	510	35	546	582
Hyde Park	1,056	143	1,199	1,350					
Medfield	227	8	235	269					
Medway	726	12	738	956					
Milton	476	43	519	574	Totals	15,647	640	16,287	19,479

CENSUSES OF POPULATION.

Towns	Date of Incorporation	Colonial Census 1774	U.S. 1790	U.S. 1800	U.S. 1810	U.S. 1820	U.S. 1830	U.S. 1840	U.S. 1850	State Census 1855	U.S. Census 1860	State Census 1865	U.S. Census 1870	State Census 1875
Bellingham	1719	627	735	704	766	1,034	1,102	1,055	1,281	1,413	1,313	1,240	1,282	1,247
Braintree	1640	2,871	2,771	1,285	1,353	1,466	1,758	2,168	2,969	3,472	3,468	3,725	3,948	4,156
Brookline	1705	502	484	605	784	900	1,043	1,365	2,516	3,737	5,164	5,262	6,650	6,675
Canton	1797			1,110	1,351	1,268	1,515	1,995	2,598	3,115	3,242	3,318	3,879	4,192
Cohasset	1770	754	817	849	994	1,099	1,233	1,471	1,775	1,979	1,963	2,048	2,130	2,197
Dedham	1636	1,937	1,659	1,973	2,172	2,493	3,117	3,290	4,447	5,673	6,239	7,195	7,312	5,756
Dorchester	1630	1,513	1,722	2,347	2,930	3,684	4,074	4,875	7,969	8,340	9,769	10,717		
Dover	1784		485	511	548	548	497	520	631	745	679	616	645	650
Foxborough	1778		674	779	870	1,004	1,165	1,298	1,880	2,550	2,679	2,278	3,037	3,168
Franklin	1778		1,101	1,285	1,398	1,630	1,062	1,717	1,818	2,041	2,172	2,510	2,512	2,983
Holbrook	1872													1,720
Hyde Park	1868												4,136	6,316
Medfield	1651	775	731	745	786	892	817	883	966	981	1,082	1,012	1,142	1,163
Medway	1713	912	1,035	1,050	1,213	1,523	1,556	2,043	2,778	3,230	3,195	3,239	3,721	4,242
Milton	1662	1,213	1,039	1,143	1,264	1,502	1,576	1,822	2,241	2,656	2,660	2,770	2,683	2,738
Needham	1711	912	1,130	1,072	1,097	1,227	1,418	1,488	1,944	2,401	2,658	2,793	3,607	4,548
Norfolk	1870												1,081	920
Norwood	1872													1,740
Quincy	1792			1,081	1,281	1,623	2,201	3,486	5,017	5,921	6,778	6,718	7,442	9,155
Randolph	1793			1,041	1,170	1,546	2,200	3,213	4,741	5,558	5,760	5,734	5,642	4,064
Roxbury	1630	1,433	2,226	2,765	3,669	4,135	5,247	9,089	18,364	18,469	25,137	28,426		
Sharon	1765	1,261	1,034	1,018	1,090	1,010	1,023	1,076	1,128	1,331	1,377	1,293	1,508	1,330
Stoughton	1726	2,097	1,994	1,020	1,134	1,313	1,591	2,142	3,494	4,370	4,580	4,855	4,914	4,842
Walpole	1724	967	1,005	989	1,098	1,366	1,442	1,491	1,929	1,945	2,037	2,018	2,137	2,290
West Roxbury	1851									4,812	6,310	6,912	9,010	
Weymouth	1635	1,471	1,469	1,803	1,889	2,407	2,837	3,738	5,369	6,520	7,742	7,975		9,819
Wrentham	1673	2,879	1,767	2,061	2,478	2,801	2,698	2,915	3,037	3,242	3,406	3,072	2,292	2,395
Totals		22,124	23,878	27,216	31,245	36,471	41,972	53,140	78,892	94,367	103,950	116,306	80,443	83,321

POPULATION, VALUATION, PROPERTY AND PRODUCTS.

Towns.	1.—Population.	2.—Whole Number of Farms.	3.—Total Acreage in Farms.	4.—Total Acreage Cultivated Land.	5.—Value of Farms (Land and Buildings).	6.—Total Value of Farm Property.	7.—Number of Horses.	8.—Number of Cows.	9.—Number of Sheep.	10.—Total Number of Acres of Land taxed.	11.—Valuation of Personal Property.	12.—Valuation of Real Estate.	13.—Products of Manufactures and Fisheries.	14.—Products of Agriculture and Mining.	15.—Total Valuation.	16.—Total Products.
Bellingham	1,217	150	8,787	2,235	$367,396	$390,551	177	289	8	10,806	$109,160	$418,808	$644,530	$94,017	$527,968	$638,547
Braintree	4,156	118	4,041	1,516	642,735	713,897	354	342	55	8,101	732,554	2,036,350	1,643,306	104,963	2,769,360	1,756,289
Brookline	6,675	6	300	240	120,000	126,120	682	288	57	2,766	9,883,900	17,695,200	361,538	9,231	27,579,100	373,792
Canton	4,192	175	7,754	2,025	730,065	822,051	365	348	7	11,371	1,161,440	1,874,115	3,084,681	93,522	3,058,655	3,188,203
Cohasset	2,197	67	3,258	824	352,881	413,325	207	184	1	12,576	689,630	1,437,440	106,729	72,000	2,528,060	179,729
Dedham	5,736	195	6,130	2,367	525,843	605,085	556	684	9	8,859	2,140,389	3,949,496	1,012,448	143,452	5,581,865	1,156,900
Dover	650	89	4,421	1,253	331,588	398,426	143	274	21	12,073	65,139	577,040	69,650	70,797	742,170	140,347
Foxborough	3,168	96	2,199	1,770	173,060	170,640	352	314	3	15,317	351,977	1,379,897	1,270,915	142,581	1,731,574	1,705,580
Franklin	2,983	212	13,605	3,207	643,178	742,280	321	476	...	12,673	372,600	1,061,600	1,049,796	11,477	1,437,200	1,413,796
Holbrook	1,726	40	365	446	24,655	29,810	146	75	...	4,409	280,070	738,570	676,403	6,920	958,640	1,061,273
Hyde Park	6,316	103	5,573	70	191,000	194,668	262	366	3	2,800	633,083	6,151,394	676,403	82,502	6,844,477	683,721
Medfield	1,161	177	6,579	2,185	455,718	504,253	181	183	...	8,068	389,090	634,215	490,756	149,419	945,295	573,342
Medway	4,242	114	10,002	2,863	595,245	671,377	403	640	...	12,991	361,200	1,429,725	1,548,951	137,286	1,783,925	1,698,330
Milton	2,738	124	4,487	2,401	1,210,700	1,301,519	526	400	3	7,890	1,051,370	3,150,500	427,757	134,632	7,236,840	940,043
Needham	4,548	94	6,522	1,601	973,878	980,963	497	411	51	13,500	1,053,470	326,068	489,386	68,943	4,738,181	1,705,903
Norfolk	920	28	2,708	1,537	292,301	340,591	147	275	...	8,983	95,055	1,343,807	434,086	36,473	431,123	558,329
Norwood	1,749	46	4,577	901	153,983	180,990	198	362	...	6,255	448,635	5,577,550	2,087,072	127,143	1,192,500	520,439
Quincy	9,155	70	4,613	1,018	549,005	622,219	703	518	2	8,756	1,736,475	2,585,550	434,087	54,797	2,461,230	2,214,215
Randolph	4,064	133	7,291	1,301	445,505	494,632	213	244	...	5,853	619,300	800,337	289,950	91,033	1,055,563	1,557,182
Sharon	1,580	56	4,644	2,101	411,256	475,138	411	258	...	13,727	281,226	1,743,350	1,455,805	139,530	2,204,175	772,072
Stoughton	4,852	150	7,291	1,018	262,942	289,918	389	499	21	11,649	640,825	1,069,525	692,700	110,725	2,576,314	1,595,375
Walpole	2,290	121	4,644	1,050	565,863	641,980	430	460	...	11,981	306,738	3,863,523	4,869,152	88,654	5,971,234	801,423
Weymouth	9,819	150	7,291	1,063	566,542	654,581	830	440	...	9,620	2,107,711	960,717	4,869,152	88,034	4,897,206	4,807,206
Wrentham	2,395	98	6,849	1,902	274,436	339,806	570	401	43	19,144	199,296	...	421,455	79,115	1,100,115	540,550
Totals	**88,321**	**2,331**	**135,112**	**36,559**	**$10,746,735**	**$12,006,448**	**8,658**	**8,753**	**276**	**234,168**	**$28,713,307**	**$63,202,692**	**$26,966,620**	**$2,087,539**	**$91,915,809**	**$29,054,159**

PROPERTY VALUATION.

Towns.	Number of Farms.	Number of Buildings.	Value of Buildings.	Acres of Land.	Value of Land.	Value of Farms (Land and Buildings).	Value of Fruit Trees and Vines.	Value of Domestic Animals.	Value of Agricultural Implements in use.	Total Value Farm Property.
Bellingham	150	224	$123,290	8,757	$144,106	$267,396	$4,788	$29,778	$7,580	$309,551
Braintree	118	273	312,850	4,944	329,305	642,755	20,077	39,565	11,500	713,897
Brookline	6			390	120,000	120,000		6,120		126,120
Canton	175	416	361,430	7,754	388,655	750,065	11,392	51,934	8,600	822,051
Cohasset	57	167	147,800	3,238	226,081	373,881	8,004	24,190	5,160	413,325
Dedham	89	243	243,080	6,186	282,763	525,843		54,940	24,296	605,085
Dover	96	277	167,840	5,423	163,538	331,363	21,706	33,447	11,855	398,426
Foxborough	46	116	57,370	4,219	115,639	173,060	355	2,334	300	176,049
Franklin	212	551	319,200	13,605	323,978	643,178	31,777	50,564	17,171	742,390
Holbrook	4	8	5,750	683	19,205	24,055		1,605	250	26,810
Hyde Park	3	9	21,000	365	170,010	191,000		1,468	2,200	194,668
Medfield	103	267	227,900	6,579	230,818	458,718	7,672	21,024	13,250	504,253
Medway	117	470	283,005	10,002	305,340	395,245	8,329	57,558	15,245	671,377
Milton	114	261	416,900	4,457	763,360	1,230,700	18,392	55,327	17,100	1,301,519
Needham	124	213	283,400	11,493	630,278	913,878	1,201	43,681	22,195	980,963
Norfolk	94	269	133,340	6,522	158,861	292,201	8,967	30,950	8,473	340,591
Norwood	28	69	60,425	2,371	93,758	153,983	1,776	15,876	9,355	189,590
Quincy	46	144	103,150	4,977	446,755	549,905	6,930	48,508	16,876	622,219
Randolph	70	287	232,100	7,990	213,408	445,305	9,673	26,306	13,048	494,632
Sharon	133	232	197,125	4,613	216,111	413,236	14,212	34,713	12,977	475,138
Stoughton	96	211	92,100	7,256	170,842	262,942	5,227	18,530	2,719	289,918
Walpole	150	227	275,910	4,644	289,953	565,863	15,039	39,675	22,222	641,999
Weymouth	121	274	283,600		282,942	566,542	20,995	33,445	13,509	624,581
Wrentham	99	268	134,600	6,649	139,896	274,496	13,695	43,888	7,817	339,896
Totals	**2,331**	**5,571**	**$4,490,075**	**135,112**	**$6,256,660**	**$10,746,735**	**$230,797**	**765,100**	**$263,816**	**$12,006,448**

VALUE

OF MANUFACTURES OF BOOTS AND SHOES, IRON AND STRAW.

Towns.	Iron.	Straw.	Boots and Shoes.	Towns.	Iron.	Straw.	Boots and Shoes.
Bellingham ..	$1,400	.....	$180,000	Milton ...	$22,857	.....	$900
Braintree ...	54,800	.....	276,114	Needham .	41,700	.....	71,000
Brookline ...	37,000	.....	72,050	Norfolk ..	2,942	.....	300,300
Canton	292,864	.....	.....	Norwood .	2,662	.....	2,500
Cohasset ...	8.000	.....	.....	Quincy ..	99,069	.....	443,821
Dedham ...	5,600	.....	3,350	Randolph .	10,000	.....	1,074,236
Dover.....	2,000	.....	600	Sharon...	61,700	.....	93,190
Foxborough..	.....	$1,003,000	.....	Stoughton .	6,767	.....	1,157,632
Franklin ...	11,400	359,568	85,500	Walpole ..	3,032	.....	1,890
Holbrook ...	.....	.....	1,044,996	Weymouth .	298,003	.....	3,285,357
Hyde Park ..	104,749	.....	.....	Wrentham .	5,750	$150,000	675
Medfield ...	23,500	393,500	.....				
Medway ...	25,300	170,000	1,048,400		$1,121,095	$2,073,068	$9,143,111

MANUFACTURES OF NORFOLK COUNTY.

Towns.	No. of Establishments.	Capital Invested.	Value of Goods made and Work done.	Towns.	No. of Establishments.	Capital Invested.	Value of Goods made and Work done.
Bellingham ..	11	$178,900	$544,520	Needham ...	73	$689,987	$1,549,244
Braintree ...	41	648,383	1,640.306	Norfolk ...	12	381.150	459,386
Brookline ...	23	85,600	364,558	Norwood ...	15	163,250	484,086
Canton	31	1,158,550	3,094,681	Quincy	178	1,036,591	2,087,072
Cohasset ...	11	11,000	45,150	Randolph ..	143	207,631	1,302,286
Dedham ...	27	752,100	1,012.448	Sharon	13	65,625	280,979
Dover.....	6	14.400	60,550	Stoughton ..	40	379,800	1,455,805
Foxborough..	2	525,065	1,093,000	Walpole ...	33	177.630	692,760
Franklin ...	47	325,625	1,270,915	Weymouth ..	144	1,417,675	4,809,152
Holbrook ...	33	224,000	1,040,736	Wrentham ..	32	150,590	421,455
Hyde Park ..	44	670,140	676,403				
Medfield ...	19	211,725	490,750				
Medway ...	45	270,775	1,548.931	Totals ...	1,042	$10,056,442	$26,905,040
Milton	19	305,250	422,757				

OTHER MANUFACTURES.

The following is an approximate statement of the value of other branches of manufactures produced in the county:—

Arms and Amunition $50.000
Agricultural Implements 18,000
Artisans' Tools 31,500
Boxes............. 130.000
Carriages and Wagons 122,000
Clothing 876,000
Cotton Goods 984,000
Food Preparations 518,000
Furniture.............. 51,000

Leather $736,000
Lumber 28,000
Machines and Machinery ..... } not included under "Iron" } 1,605,000
Metals and Metallic Goods .....
Paper 776,000
Woollen Goods 1,428,000

DOMESTIC AND AGRICULTURAL PRODUCTS.

Towns.	Domestic Products, for sale.	Domestic Products, for use.	Total Domest. Products.	Agricultural Products.	Total Domest. and Agricult. ural Prod'ts.
Bellingham	$22.694	$6,457	$29,151	$64,866	$94,017
Braintree	4.170	4,130	8,300	96,813	105,113
Brookline	. . . .	1,920	1,920	7,314	9,234
Canton	7,523	4,050	11,573	77,949	89,522
Cohasset	10,045	4,206	14,251	58,758	73,009
Dedham	4.961	116	5,077	138,375	143,452
Dover	9,854	3,386	13,240	57,557	70,797
Foxborough	1,252	391	1,643	12,937	14,580
Franklin	21,797	3,234	25,031	117,850	142,881
Holbrook	2,738	186	2,924	8,553	11,477
Hyde Park	. . . .	10	10	6,910	6,920
Medfield	8,382	5,442	13,824	68,768	82,592
Medway	10,096	5,359	15,455	121,143	136,598
Milton	13,021	1,776	14,797	122,489	137,286
Needham	12,324	637	12,961	143,598	156,559
Norfolk	9,856	3,185	13,041	55,902	68,943
Norwood	2,386	480	2,866	33,507	36,373
Quincy	2,952	546	3,498	119,645	123,143
Randolph	11.138	4.108	15,246	39,218	54,464
Sharon	14,441	4,470	18,911	66,142	85,053
Stoughton	95,202	1,857	97,059	42,471	139,530
Walpole	11.192	7,561	18,753	91,970	110.723
Weymouth	5,834	2,608	8,442	79,612	88.054
Wrentham	15,061	63	15,124	63.991	79,115
Totals	$296,919	$66,178	$363,097	$1,696,338	$2,059,435

www.ingramcontent.com/pod-product-compliance
Lightning Source LLC
Chambersburg PA
CBHW020554270326
41927CB00006B/838